On Strike at
Hormel

■ ■ ■

LABOR AND SOCIAL CHANGE,
a series edited by
Paula Rayman and Carmen Sirianni

On Strike at Hormel

■ ■ ■

The
Struggle for a
Democratic Labor
Movement

Hardy Green

TEMPLE UNIVERSITY PRESS
Philadelphia

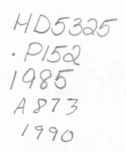

Temple University Press, Philadelphia 19122
Copyright © 1990 by Hardy Green. All rights reserved
Published 1990
Printed in the United States of America

The paper used in this publication meets the minimum
requirements of American National Standard for Information
Sciences—Permanence of Paper for Printed Library Materials,
ANSI Z39.48-1984

Library of Congress Cataloging-in-Publication Data
Green, Hardy.
On strike at Hormel : the struggle for a democratic labor
movement
/ Hardy Green.
p. cm. — (Labor and social change)
Bibliography: p.
Includes index.
ISBN 0-87722-635-0 (alk. paper)
1. Geo. A. Hormel & Company Strike, Austin, Minn., 1985–
1986.
2. Geo. A. Hormel & Company. 3. United Packinghouse, Food, and
Allied Workers, Local 9 (Austin, Minn.) I. Title. II. Series.
HD5325.P152   1985.A873   1990
331.89′28649′00977617—dc20   89-4991
                                                         CIP

CONTENTS

PREFACE

The 1985–86 strike at Geo. A. Hormel & Co. had enormous appeal for a wide range of writers, historians, and labor analysts. For the press, the Austin, Minnesota, strike offered a number of irresistible images: a group of white, small-town men, women, and children standing up in dramatic fashion to a Fortune 500 corporation. On the strikers' side was "labor's muscleman," the handsome, garrulous, and ever-optimistic labor strategist Ray Rogers. Opposing them, along with Hormel, was the country's second-largest International union, the United Food and Commercial Workers.

Industrial-relations academics and labor activists also turned to Austin, wondering whether Local P-9's energies would somehow be translated into a means of reviving the ranks of organized labor, down to under 18 percent of the country's work force. Historians rediscovered a living culture of Austin unionism dating back to the 1930s. Through all of this, quite a number of articles, television programs, and videotapes were generated.

Yet today the Hormel strike remains a blur. Many people who ordinarily follow labor events cannot say for sure whether the strikers won or lost: Did they get their jobs back? Is everything back to normal? What is more, there has been no overall record of the strikers' unusual accomplishments.

Hence this book. It is an insider's account. As a participant and witness, I was privy to on-the-scene and behind-
the-scenes developments. Knowing many of the participants
well, I feel that I can describe their motivations and experiences.

At the same time, the strike raised complicated cultural,
historical, legal, and strategic issues that require exploration.
Part of my account, therefore, is akin to a mystery story: Why
did one of the most significant fights against corporate demands for concessions of the 1980s take place at this place
and this time? Did the strikers choose the most appropriate
tools to achieve their aims? How did the strike change those
who took part in it?

I was not acquainted with the non-striker participants
during the events of 1985–86. But in the course of preparing
this book I have interviewed some of them and reviewed the
statements they all made at the time. Though I do not and
could not believably claim to be a neutral observer, I have
attempted to understand and present the UFCW's side of the
story, along with that of the Hormel company. Along the way,
I came to feel that there was real tragedy involved for both of
these parties. Lewie Anderson, chief International union opponent of the P-9 cause, has also become a victim of the institutions that made him. As this book went into production,
UFCW president William Wynn fired him from the position
of Meatpacking Division director, probably because of the
on-again, off-again militancy that led Anderson to privately
criticize the International's collusion with low-wage packers
such as IBP. Charles Nyberg, senior vice president at Hormel
and its chief spokesman, in many ways wanted to do right by
Hormel workers but could not see beyond our era's prevailing corporate truths.

The activities of other non-striker participants have not

been fully known before. Now, documents recently gained under the Minnesota Government Data Practices Act and the federal Freedom of Information Act show that Austin law enforcement officials came to regard all positive developments for the strike as setbacks for law and order. The sentiments and actions of state officials were more ambivalent. The Federal Bureau of Investigation, which has not yet turned over its files, admits to keeping tabs on several key participants.

The Austin strike was an exhilarating experience. But this is not an uncritical account. I gained a lot from the strikers and their supporters—and I felt, therefore, that I owed everyone the return favor of taking their efforts seriously. So I have tried to look back at the things we did together and say where I think we were right and where we were wrong.

Contrary to the wisdom of much of labor's leadership, P-9 members demonstrated that union workers are still willing to stand up to corporations that define them as just one of many means to the end of greater profitability. Austin's union members and the tens of thousands of workers across the country who came to their defense showed that there is a living culture that believes in mutual support among workers as a practical and ethical necessity.

This book could not have been written without the help of a great many people, particularly the official and unofficial P-9 archivists Lorraine Fossum, Millie Rios, and Dick Blin. P-9's former officers and members, United Support Group members, attorneys, and a variety of others, including Ray Rogers, UFCW International vice president Lewie Anderson, and Hormel senior vice president Charles Nyberg, made themselves available for many hours of interviews.

Emily Bass oversaw an ambitious freedom-of-information project, pursued under federal law and the laws of Minnesota and several surrounding states. The Austin Police Department regarded this project as undeserving of fee waivers and charged over $2,200 for releasing its voluminous files. Helping to defray these and other freedom-of-information-project costs were Communications Workers of America District 1, CWA Locals 1180, 1150, and 1034, International Brotherhood of Teamsters Local 111, the Fund for Open Information and Accountability, and Corporate Campaign Inc. Offering valuable ideas and criticism were Ted Lieverman and Philip Mattera. And countless hours were spent puzzling over what it all meant with Edward Allen.

FOREWORD

by DAVID MOBERG

Bucolic Austin, Minnesota, seemed an unlikely setting for one of the most dramatic labor battles of the 1980s. But during 1985 and 1986 around fifteen hundred meatpackers and their families tumultuously confronted the Hormel Company, a once-paternalistic business that has long dominated the small town. The intense conflict spilled over into the town, the national union, and the labor movement as a whole before turning back upon itself, dividing the workers as well.

These hard-working, normally undemonstrative midwesterners surprised everyone, including themselves, with their remarkable tenacity, creativity, and social awakening in the course of their long and ultimately losing effort. Whatever else it may prove, the saga of Local P-9 of the United Food and Commercial Workers reveals how much "ordinary" workers are capable of doing to fight for their interests, especially when given a little encouragement and guidance.

The Austin P-9 story is an emotionally charged tale of an uprising by workers who hadn't struck their employer in more than fifty years. They faced down the National Guard, fought a hostile union hierarchy, carried their message coast to coast, and roved around the packing plants of Iowa and Nebraska, attempting to spread their strike to sister plants. It was a conflict that pitted whole families, not just the workers, against the company. Hardy Green's strongly argued narrative of events benefits deeply from his insider role as a consultant to Local P-9.

But this story also raises fundamental questions about the American labor movement in the Reagan era and after—its tactics, strategies, internal democracy, and long-term perspective.

Meatpacking workers in the eighties faced a turbulent industry, with new anti-union firms undermining established companies, many of which were shuffled around in the paper chase of making and unmaking conglomerates. The marketplace mechanics were different but the effects similar to those felt by workers in industries wracked by foreign competition or deregulation. Wages fell dramatically; work injuries soared; the union floor of support, embodied in industry-wide pattern bargaining, collapsed.

Green focuses his attention on the union response. In theory Local P-9 and Lewie Anderson, the head of the UFCW's Packinghouse Division, agreed that wage concessions did not save jobs but simply pushed everybody's wages downward. Yet there were other leaders within the UFCW who were prepared to make concessions and did not relish fights with the companies. Also, Anderson was at best partially successful in persuading locals not to cut their wages in order to save their jobs, temporarily, at the expense of other workers. Eventually he urged a strategic retreat, attempting to set a pattern at a lower level.

Green's account takes the reader to the heart of this important debate about union strategy. Why fight concessions? Can unions still attempt to take wages out of competition? Was P-9 right in refusing the strategic retreat, especially given what its members regarded as a failed local history of earlier givebacks and the understandings they believed they had with the company? Could an inspirational, successful strike become the model for anti-concession battles and organizing efforts throughout the industry?

Each step in the P-9 conflict was a wager, a gamble on how much pressure either workers or management could generate and how much of a counterthreat could be mustered, a bet on public opinion and the support of other workers. For unions there are as many risks in doing nothing as in trying too much, and the sorry state of the labor movement is testimony to the cumulative effects of inaction. Success feeds success, failure feeds failure, and the depressing climate for labor in 1984 encouraged many labor leaders to hunker down and try little.

But Hormel workers felt they had just grievances. So if workers decide to fight, what tactics work? P-9's energetic, bluntly outspoken consultant Ray Rogers is famous within the labor movement for launching the "corporate campaign," which attempts to attack the corporation on all fronts, not just on the strike picket line. But in the P-9 case, the corporate campaign also became a way of preparing workers for a strike, of involving them and their families in an active struggle, not a desultory display of picket signs.

Never sympathetic to the P-9 strategy, the international union increasingly undercut the local, eventually imposing a questionable trusteeship and attempting to wipe out the memory of what had been a model strike (even destroying a mural the workers had created celebrating solidarity with other struggles as far away as South Africa).

Unions like the UFCW represent a strange hybrid of democratic, decentralist tendencies and strongly centralist, autocratic qualities. Good union leaders can draw creative energy from this tension, involving members from the bottom up, fashioning as much consensus as possible, but respecting local creativity. They are quite rare, but at the local level young president Jim Guyette had many of those qualities, and even his detractors admit that consultant Rogers had an exceptional talent for motivating people.

The vision union leaders and members have of themselves, their organization, their movement, deeply influences the balance leaders strike between central command and local autonomy and their willingness to risk a tough battle. For example, the UFCW president has powers to block local contracts that undermine conditions for other workers, a power that was not used as consistently as it should have been. But it is a distortion of the rationale for that power to interpret it—as UFCW leaders did in the P-9 case—as a license to interfere with locals that want to fight for something better, something that was likely to help, not hurt, fellow workers elsewhere. Leaders with a vision of workers' ability—and entitlement—to fight destructive trends in the industry would have embraced the P-9 campaign and used it toward their goal of a renewed wage floor.

Could P-9 have done better with different tactical decisions? Green intriguingly points to a critical moment when the local leadership was split and called off roving pickets that might have successfully shut down another key Hormel plant. Later they were unable to get the same support, in part because their international officers had organized against them. I still think that P-9 workers would have been better off moving their struggle inside the plant rather than letting Hormel bring in strikebreakers, but I understand how difficult it would have been for them to change strategies at that point. If the official labor movement had thrown its weight behind P-9 instead of trying to sabotage the strike, if the UFCW had supported the roving pickets at other plants, as strikers hoped, perhaps the strikers would have been proven right.

Even though Lewie Anderson opposed the Hormel local, he tried to adopt some of their tactics in later strikes. But Anderson was a man caught in the middle, too militant for many of his fellow officers, but unable to create elsewhere the spark that flared in Austin. Increasingly he complained about other union officials making local agreements that sabotaged the industry's limited wage recovery in the late eighties. In early 1989 he was fired, and the narrow business union philosophy of many UFCW leaders was further consolidated.

It is easy to dismiss the P-9 battle as misguided romanticism, a throwback to the Wobblies (and it was an ex-Wobbly who led an occupation of the plant in the 1930s to win union recognition). Of course, not all workers are likely to join such crusades, and not all face conditions that provoke drastic action. But then few people would have predicted that Republican-leaning air traffic controllers or pilots at Eastern and United could become militant strikers either.

Yet in the end the labor movement relies on a continued reinvigoration of emotional commitment. Its roots lie in the belief of average workers that they deserve just treatment and a voice in their lives at work. Its ultimate strength rests on concrete expressions of solidarity among workers. Without that fiery spirit, the life and strength drain out of the labor movement, and it becomes a bureaucratic house of cards, easy to topple. Even the highest labor official in Washington ultimately depends on that raw emotion, commitment, and willingness to challenge the status quo among workers in the packing plant, office, factory, hospital, or whatever workplace. The spirit of the P-9 strikers is not all it takes to make a labor movement, but without it, no labor movement of value will ever be made. Hardy Green's book captures much of that spirit.

On Strike at Hormel

I

"FAMILIES FIGHTING BACK"

Austin, Minnesota, is the all-American company town, located about a hundred miles south of Minneapolis, not far from the Iowa border. At first glance, the town's several thousand trim houses and manicured lawns, as well as its public schools and playing fields, seem immune to the passage of time. When men here talk about driving over to Green Bay for a Packers' game, it is easy to imagine that Vince Lombardi and Bart Starr are still playing.

You can travel most of the way to Austin from the Twin Cities via the Interstate, but just south of Owatonna you have to get off and continue down two-lane Highway 218 for the last 31 miles. When you pass Lansing Corners, the restaurant that is the only sign of life in the patch of ground known as Lansing, you are on the outskirts of Austin. In late 1986, there appeared another noteworthy signpost near Lansing: the words "Scab City" scrawled in three-foot-high letters on a dilapidated old barn near the roadside.

In December 1984 Austin became the site of a bitter union battle with the town's primary employer, Geo. A. Hormel & Co. Many observers say it turned into the strike of the decade, both because of the energy and imagination of the strikers and because of the nationwide response it aroused.

3

Before the strike began, the 1,500 workers began organizing support groups from various constituencies in Austin, then in other towns where Hormel had plants, such as Fremont, Nebraska, and Ottumwa, Iowa. Rank-and-file speakers took their anti-concessions message to picket lines and farmer, community, church, and political meetings—first in Minnesota, then across the Midwest, then from coast to coast. Once the strike was on, hundreds of workers joined car caravans for tours through the other Hormel towns, where they re-established the worker-to-worker ties that had first been forged in the 1930s, but that had atrophied since. Union literature was distributed door to door in dozens of towns and through the mails to thousands of American union members.

Over three thousand unions and other organizations from every state responded. Supporters from across the country came to Austin to attend mass demonstrations, marches, and rallies. Thousands sent letters of support, food, and funds and joined in the anti-Hormel protest activities that took place in virtually every U.S. city.

But in the end the strikers were defeated by the combined forces of the company, the state of Minnesota—which sent in National Guard troops to escort strikebreakers into the plant—and their own International union, the United Food and Commercial Workers.

Since the spring of 1986, the company has been smugly proclaiming victory and asserting that it foresees no need ever to rehire the replaced strikers. Even more outrageous from the strikers' point of view is the fact that after a period of trusteeship, or removal of local control, imposed by the UFCW to bring an end to the strike, union Local P-9 is being run by and for a membership composed of "scabs": those strikers who crossed their own picket line and the "replacement workers" who also crossed. During the trusteeship, the International signed a strike settlement with Hormel that gave the scabs priority job rights and severely limited the legally provided recall rights of those who stayed out, among other things cutting off all their claims to the jobs after September 1988. And the 1,000 loyal union people were issued withdrawal cards, forcing them out of the union altogether. There are many signs that suggest that the loyalists will never give up the fight. But they are aware that, for the moment at least, the bosses and their creatures, the scabs, have the upper hand.

The most direct way of coming into downtown Austin is to turn left off 218 at the Sunset Motel, and that road will take you right down to Main Street. Going this way, you pass many of the town's important institutions: On your left at the first stoplight is the graveyard where company founder George Hormel is buried, and in winter, when there are no leaves on the trees, you can catch a first glimpse of the company's plant off in the distance. Down the road on your right is the Austin shopping mall, a direct result of the good wages paid to the generations who worked for the meatpacker. On further, you pass the YMCA, St. Olaf's Hospital, and the A&W Root Beer drive-in before you get to Main Street's stores and the Austin Law Enforcement Center, which houses the sheriff's office and the jail.

I first came down these roads in 1985 in order to document the serious problem of on-the-job injuries sustained by the Austin meatpackers. I had recently gone to work for Ray Rogers' union consulting firm, Corporate Campaign Inc., which had been hired by local union members, after a lot of wrangling with UFCW, their international, to run a campaign to pressure Hormel into reversing a unilaterally imposed 23 percent wage cut. Having worked with a lot of union men and women before, I thought I knew what the people here would be like: folksy but not too articulate or thoughtful, pro-union because they wanted to live ordinary lives outside the shadow of poverty. The flat, wintry landscape didn't seem to promise anything exceptional—March was still the dead of winter, though on my first trip no snow covered the fields where the rich, black earth waited to be turned for another year's corn crop.

Meatpacking is the most dangerous occupation in the United States. In 1986 Hormel predicted that some 36 percent of the Austin workers would be disabled in the coming year through a workplace injury; that same year, workers say they saw company reports showing the total injury rate to be 202 percent.[1] Over a period of several days, I listened to a litany of horrors, as a steady stream of workers came forth to describe the tendonitis, shoulder, arm, back, and hand injuries, and nervous disorders brought on by the rapid and demanding work at Hormel's state-of-the-art plant.

As I listened, I discovered among the Austin meatpackers a particular difference from the New York union members I had known. When the effort to roll back concessions at Hormel first began, some Austin union members felt that they should not have to take a pay cut, even though other meatpacking workers might have to. Those people said that Austin workers should make more than the average wage, since they had to work harder and faster and their plant was the most productive of all the Hormel plants. What's more, it was said, the townspeople had always had a special relationship to the company and the Hormel family. A confused pride in working ability and hometown colored the thinking of many.

It may be that such responses were more characteristic of workers who had lived in Austin longer, or maybe they were simply expedient arguments that some people hoped would flatter the company into seeing things their way. But you heard such statements all the time.

This way of seeing things did not last, though. The great majority of the current work force had never experienced any special relationship with Hormel. They had been at the company for only two or three years; some had worked at other meatpackers or other Hormel plants and saw nothing special about work in the Austin plant, except possibly the high speed of the line.

So the "we-ought-to-get-more" argument quickly fell by the wayside, replaced by the argument that concessions, particularly from a profitable industry leader such as Hormel, do not serve the workers' long- or short-run interests and must be fought. At bottom, Austin meatpackers felt intensely that they had been swindled. On many occasions, they said, the company had promised never to pay them less than they were making when the new plant opened. "When I was hired on the 25th of October, 1982, they told me: 'You're going to be working for George A. Hormel. Go out and buy yourself a car . . . buy yourself a home,'" recalled Darrell Busker. "You established yourself at one level, then suddenly you were down to $8.25."[2]

The larger social vision of the local members, like that of most Americans, was contradictory. In one sense, it was conservative. As their ever-present "Families Fighting Back" signs indicated, the Austin workers wanted to hold on to what they had, to preserve a middle-income way of life that they saw being threatened by industrial change. Older workers in particular longed for the days of paternalistic management at the company, days when "Jay Hormel Cared," in the words of signs that they later posted around town. But out of such instincts grew a resolve to take a stand that would mean a better future for all American workers, to roll back "corporate greed," and to reform a labor movement that had grown bureaucratic, insensitive, and pro-corporate.

In time, the Austin campaign and strike would literally transform P-9ers' lives and ideals. Many of these Scandinavian midwesterners voted for Ronald Reagan; yet in May of 1986, as the workers' national union was attempting to bring an end to the strike and restore businesslike relations with the company, a thousand of these people turned out to dedicate a mural painted on the side of their union hall to the South African revolutionary Nelson Mandela.

The workers and their family members were helped toward this transformation by their unusual leaders—including hometown boy and local union president Jim Guyette and outside "consultant" Ray Rogers—and by a great many others who, once the crusade was underway, made their way to Austin as if to Mecca.

Rogers is a short, heavily muscled, dimple-faced man on the other side of 40 with few interests outside of work for social justice and vegetarianism. In the tradition of a long line of abstemious true believers such as Ralph Nader, he has few needs in the way of clothing or food. Gastronomic indulgence means popcorn or ice cream. For office furniture, nothing could be better than a card table. His idea of a blissful vacation, he once told me, would be to take two weeks off, go somewhere with nice weather, and just lift weights till he got in really good shape.

Self-confidence runs deep in Rogers' personality. In the darkest days of the strike, he would express weariness and some impatience to get it over with, but almost never allowed himself a discouraging word. He always had time to listen carefully to the ideas of every rank-and-filer—and there were some doozies: "I saw the National Guard driving the wrong way down a one-way street," I remember one worker saying. "Can't we do something like get them arrested for reckless driving?"

Over the years Rogers has developed a rousing speaking style to rival that of the most fervent hellfire preacher. Still, some have accused him of arrogance and called him a publicity addict. "Why does he have to go on TV all the time— why does he put himself forward in the newspapers like he does?" critics ask.

Such criticisms miss the point. Unlike many big-time union leaders, Rogers is not interested in notoriety per se, but only as a means of reaching a goal. He genuinely tried to put others, particularly the local union officers, forward as spokespeople. But in the end he was often fearful that unless he spoke up, something might get left out—the message might lack that one bit of information, backed by energy and enthusiasm, that would sway the audience to join the cause.

"You can create a moment in history where people will turn to Austin and say, 'That is where they turned back the onslaught against the labor movement.'" Thus did Rogers promise the Austin workers a place in the history books.

The unusual thing about it was not the rhetoric, but the fact that the workers took Rogers up on this offer, made before a January 1985 rally of 3,000 townspeople in the Austin High School auditorium. In the ordinary course of events, you expect JFK-inspired liberals, Marxists, or even New Rightists to respond to the tug of "history." But when average working people put down their tools and set aside family responsibilities for such an abstract proposition, something is happening.

Not that all of the rhetoric was abstract: Guyette, for example, was a master of particulars. On the surface, Guyette bears little resemblance to Rogers: Tall, blond, and soft-spoken, he is as cool and cautious as Rogers is hot. They are media opposites, Rogers playing well to live audiences, Guyette playing perfectly on television. Guyette was no Nader, but rather, with his three fair-haired and ridiculously polite children and his pretty, equally committed and outspoken wife, the picture of a family man. When he spoke in his soft, sometimes whispery voice, people sat up.

"Hormel is a very profitable company, Oscar Mayer is a very profitable company, and they ought to be paying the highest wages in the industry," he would tell an audience of meatpackers from another Hormel plant in Fremont, Nebraska.

> They ought to bring the bottom of the industry up, rather than what's been happening, with the top of the industry being brought down. But the industry really wants $5.00 or $6.00 wage rates. People ought to understand that we're going to have to defend something at some point. It may as well be 10.69 or $10.00, rather than let it slide to $8.00 or $6.00. How far it goes depends on us, because the companies are going to keep pushing until we tell them that we've had enough—we're not gonna give any more.

Neither argument moved the workers' International union, which opposed the campaign from the beginning—not, UFCW leaders insisted, because they were sellouts, but, they said, because their national strategy dictated that they do so.

International officers such as Lewie Anderson, director of the union's Packinghouse Division, held ideals that were every bit as contradictory as the P-9ers'. A hog-manure shoveler in the Sioux City, Iowa, stockyards at age 14, then a local union leader during several violent strikes at beef packer

IBP, Anderson was groomed for his position by Jessie Prosten and other "progressives" out of the tradition of one of the CIO's old "red" unions, the United Packinghouse Workers of America. He was on the left-liberal side of most current political and social issues. And for years he opposed concessions. In 1980 and 1981, just after he became Packinghouse Division director, he was faced with numerous locals that were adamantly in favor of giving wage concessions in order to save jobs. Anderson and others took a hard line, saying that giving concessions would not save anything.[3]

As a consequence, Anderson oversaw a number of plant closings, arguing that it was more important to hold on to a livable national wage rate for the majority of workers than to allow weak packers to continue operating at the expense of that rate. But by 1984 Anderson had signed on to a strategy that was dubbed "a controlled retreat" by International president William Wynn. In its most basic form, the idea was to allow wages to fall to a certain level among unionized packers, while simultaneously organizing nonunion packers and raising their wages, in order to get to a single "national" rate. In other words, the union wanted to reconstruct pattern bargaining. Once a national pattern was re-established, the strategy suggested, union locals would rally, and all would together push wages back up again.

Anderson was never a strong supporter of democratic procedure. Rather, he helped to promote a UFCW catchphrase that "leaders must lead"—they must make the tough choices that the members will not make. And this was his method during both the period in which he opposed concessions and the period in which he favored letting wages fall: As late as 1983, he put a Perry, Iowa, Oscar Mayer local into trusteeship for going too far in granting givebacks. Perhaps the repeated experience of opposing locals that wanted to

give in got him accustomed to opposing rank-and-file activity. Then, under the new strategy, he became allied with
the corporate drive to depress wages at long-organized packers such as Hormel.

Over time, the International worked hard on behalf of
Hormel, regularly and repeatedly declaring that P-9 had
chosen "the wrong target at the wrong time," attacking the
local officers as "inexperienced" leaders of a "suicide mission," falsely declaring the local "nearly bankrupt" on the
eve of the strike largely because of Corporate Campaign's
bills, delivering mass mailings to AFL-CIO affiliates across
the country to discourage them from sending money to the
local, sending a "special organizing team" of spies in to find
a pretext for putting the local into trusteeship, and finally
ending the strike, imposing a trusteeship, and agreeing to a
formal strike settlement with the company that virtually en-
sures that no striker will ever return.[4] It worked so hard, in
fact, that P-9 members inevitably speculated that some of the
national officers must be getting an extra payday.

But, as I have said, Anderson and other International officers also saw themselves as defending the best traditions of
American unionism. They resorted to extraordinary measures to undermine the local. But they felt themselves bitterly misunderstood: Why couldn't the workers and their
supporters see that there would be a better day if everybody
worked together under the direction of UFCW officers and
staff professionals? The UFCW must be allowed to coordi-
nate the struggle, to choose the time and place to confront
corporate greed.

In the eyes of many midwestern meatpackers, it came to
seem that that time and place might never come. It was always much easier, it seems, for Anderson to cut a deal behind the scenes—another pay cut, "the best we can do this

year," we have to "live to fight another day," etc., etc. As Fred Carson, a former local vice president at the Armour plant in Mason City, Iowa, told me: "Anderson is such a big shot, he don't ever want a strike. He'd rather shove a contract down your throat—make you vote over and over on it till you get it right."[5] All across the Midwest, there are workers who share Carson's bitter memories and low opinion of Anderson.

P-9 business agent Pete Winkels, a chubby, chain-smoking roadside philosopher, expressed a common rank-and-file sentiment during an August 1985 meeting with Hormel workers in Ottumwa, Iowa. Winkels said he had stopped at a farmer's house on the drive down from Austin and asked to use the facilities. While he was in the outhouse, he said, a UFCW representative also came in. Then, somehow, the UFCW man accidently dropped a dollar bill down the hole into the excrement below. As an astonished Winkels looked on, the rep proceeded to throw in his wallet, followed by his gold watch and his gold rings. "Why did you do that?" Winkels said he asked the representative. The rep replied: "You don't think I'm going down there just for a lousy dollar, do you?"

■ ■ ■

Between the fall of 1984 and the spring of 1985, P-9's members and supporters became a very organized and active bunch. Significantly, the first group to get organized was not the workers at all, but their spouses—primarily wives and a few husbands—who were outraged by the immediate effect the wage cut was having on their families.

The United Support Group was probably born when Jeannie Bambrick, a worker's wife, telephoned Guyette's wife, Vicky, to say that the women should do something. They decided to call a meeting of spouses on a late September evening in a local park. The turnout was tremendous: 300 women and men attended. Like Bambrick and Guyette, few had known each other beforehand. "Jim would tell me stories of the other men in the plant," explained Vicky Guyette, "but I never knew them, and I certainly didn't know their wives."[6]

As it got dark, the meeting continued, with no light except from the few flashlights some had brought along. The gathering was determined to do something to strike back at the company, and that something turned out to be demonstrating, or what they called "bannering," in front of the plant. As Bambrick recalled:

> We didn't expect there to be a strike—we thought if they saw we were united and determined, they'd give in. So we found people whose yards we could stand in nearby the corporate office and the plant. Though it was cold and raining, there were over a hundred women there. We got all charged up and held another meeting in the park that same night. And we decided to banner the plant every week—on Thursday, since that was payday. The bannering meant a lot to the guys—they'd get their reduced paychecks, but they'd also see us out there with signs and banners and feel like we were beginning to fight back.

That was the last meeting held in the park, though. P-9 executive board member Floyd Lenoch came out and told them that thenceforth they could meet in the union hall.[7]

The support group demonstrated P-9 members' and supporters' capacity for self-organization. But members of the group say they would never have attained the level they ultimately reached without Ray Rogers and Corporate Campaign.

When Rogers and his partner Ed Allen first came to town

in October 1984, they were amazed by what they saw. As they arrived at the site of a mass union meeting, they found several hundred women with signs and banners waiting outside to greet them. And rather than the anticipated fifty-odd union members, the hall was crammed with over three thousand P-9ers and family members.

At that meeting many members expressed two desires: to strike the company as soon as possible and to get out of the UFCW immediately. But Guyette and Rogers convinced them that a careful, strategic approach might be more effective. Ironically, Rogers argued that the problems between the local and the International could be ironed out, since he knew UFCW president Bill Wynn to be a reasonable man. Then Corporate Campaign's partners went back to New York to work out a plan. When Rogers returned to another mass meeting in December, it was with a proposal to set the members and supporters loose on a particular set of targets:

> We talked about tapping the power of ordinary people's skills, imagination, and energies. And we talked about taking the support group and making it an activist organization. We set up an office and called it the War Room. Then we began weekly demonstrations. We knew we had to take the struggle beyond Austin, to expand it throughout the Midwest and even nationwide if necessary. Before the strike we had a large group of activists ready to do that, and we knew we'd have an even larger group if a strike took place.[8]

Rogers' strong emphasis on mobilizing the membership has often been overlooked because of Corporate Campaign's other, and seemingly more innovative, aspect: finding a company's vulnerable "pressure point" and applying pressure to it. Rogers had been the author of the original corporate campaign when he worked for the Amalgamated Clothing and Textile Workers Union in the 1970s. He began looking at ways to bring pressure against an employer when working on that union's drive to organize the Farah company. But the full possibilities of what he (and soon everybody else who was interested in labor) called a corporate campaign were not revealed until Rogers applied his imagination to the target the union called "the country's worst labor law violator," J. P. Stevens & Co.

For 11 years, beginning in 1963, Stevens had responded to the union's organizing drive by viciously bullying its workers and taking advantage of southern state governments' hostility toward unions. In 1974 the Textile Workers Union won formal recognition through a National Labor Relations Board election. But that was only the beginning of a new phase of the struggle: The company continued its policy of intransigence, engaging in surface bargaining with the union (now the Amalgamated Clothing and Textile Workers Union, following a merger between the Textile Workers and the Amalgamated Clothing Workers) with no intention of ever reaching an agreement.

The union protested against the company's stalling tactics before the NLRB, and in 1977 an NLRB administrative law judge found that "the record as a whole indicates that [Stevens] approached these negotiations with all the tractability and openmindedness of Sherman at the outskirts of Atlanta." ACTWU kept after Stevens, continuing its high-profile boycott and legal campaign.[9] But it also decided—at first reluctantly; then, when nothing else was working, with more enthusiasm—to let Rogers try his ideas.

The corporate campaign built upon the union's attempt to paint J. P. Stevens as a pariah in the corporate world. The key to victory, it suggested, was to break corporate power down into manageable pieces, to identify the weak spots and pressure points where unions and other groups could focus their political and economic resources. Rogers, his co-workers, and allies forced an unprecedented number of resignations and dismissals of top officials at Stevens and at companies with which it shared board members, including Manufacturers Hanover Trust Co., Avon Products, and New York Life Insurance Co. Additional pressure was also brought to bear against top officials of the Seaman's Bank for Savings, Sperry Corporation, and Metropolitan Life Insurance Co. But, as Rogers still emphasizes, none of this involved mere embarrassment; rather, it was a test of strength, an exercise of union and coalition power versus corporate power.

In October 1979, under heavy pressure, Seaman's Bank chairman E. Virgil Conway, who was a Stevens director, met with ACTWU president Murray Finley and said that he would do everything in his power to get meaningful negotiations going between Stevens and the union. At the time, union activists were holding Conway and his bank to account for Stevens' actions: The bank had been prevented from opening a new branch for nearly a year because of a growing clamor over Seaman's "redlining" practices, raised at New York State Banking Department hearings. Within the savings bank industry, Conway's Stevens link was also becoming a hot issue, as politicians and consumer advocates pushed for legislation that would require election of mutual bank trustees by depositors. In addition, several hundred ministers had called for Conway's resignation from a church pension board.

In the spring and summer of 1980, criticism of Sperry Corporation's directorate interlock with Stevens had become so intense that Stevens finally began serious negotiations at the highest levels with ACTWU. When no settlement materialized, union members raised the Stevens issue on Sperry's home turf: Nearly 700 union supporters, including the "real Norma Rae," Crystal Lee Sutton, kept that company's stockholders' meeting tied up for five hours with a spirited dialogue, and 650,000 proxy votes were cast against the Stevens official who sought re-election to Sperry's board.

But the real crunch came when the union went after Metropolitan Life Insurance, Stevens' major creditor. The union challenged that insurer's board by invoking a little-known New York law that gives policyholders the right to elect an insurance company's board of directors. To bring such an election about, a small percentage of such policyholders must sign the petitions of an insurgent slate. When that happens, the enormous costs of the election must be paid by the company.

When Metropolitan chairman Richard Shinn heard that the union was organizing to make such an election a reality, he requested a meeting with union president Finley. At it he guaranteed an imminent Stevens settlement. Then, in the words of the *Wall Street Journal:*

> Mr. Shinn met with Whitney Stevens, the new chairman of Stevens. . . . Mr. Shinn says he applied "absolutely no pressure" on Mr. Stevens. . . . Without my ever having to say anything, [Stevens] realized that if in the course of good business dealings they could settle with the union, it would minimize our election problems.

Thereafter, there was a union and union contracts at 10 J. P. Stevens textile plants in the Carolinas and Alabama. (Seventy other plants remained unorganized, however.) Once they discovered the real story behind the settlement, union advocates and other observers heralded the corporate campaign as a new tool with incredible potential. *Newsweek* magazine announced, "The entire labor-management world was marvelling at Rogers' work. . . . his tactics could revolutionize the labor movement."[10]

But later campaigns had mixed results. Rogers left the Amalgamated and, along with his ACTWU co-worker Ed Allen, established a consulting firm, Corporate Campaign Inc. Initial clients included the Air Line Pilots Association, whose campaign against nonunion New York Air was cut short when the Professional Air Traffic Controllers went out on strike and reaped Reagan's anti-union whirlwind. The Paperworkers' union had CCI research and begin planning for a campaign against International Paper. It worked like gangbusters: The planning stage, during which the union packed the company's annual stockholders' meeting with angry members asking questions about company labor policies and began investigating the company's environmental record, was sufficient to cause IP to back down from a set of extreme demands and agree to establish a more positive bargaining framework for the future. But easy victories bring their own sort of problems, and this one was so easy that few people remember it today.

Campbell Soup Co. accepted unique, three-way collective bargaining and grievance procedures (involving the Farm Labor Organizing Committee and a group of midwestern growers who supply the company with tomatoes and other vegetables) after its financial ties with Philadelphia National Bank, Equitable Life Assurance, and Prudential Life were threatened.[11] But an effort on behalf of the Machinists' union's beleaguered seven-month-old strike at Brown & Sharpe Manufacturing Co. in Rhode Island was aborted by the national union amid acrimonious charges, brought on, Rogers claims, by the national union's fear of a mobilized membership. In that campaign, Rogers enlisted rank-and-file members to pressure the Rhode Island Hospital Trust National Bank, which served as a major lender to Brown & Sharpe and on whose board the B&S president served. He also got them to campaign against the re-election of U.S. Senator John Chafee, a relative of B&S chairman Henry D. Sharpe, Jr.[12]

Such was the experience and approach that Rogers and CCI brought with them to Austin. Rogers immediately got the members moving to publicize their issues. In January members braved below-zero temperatures to deliver 12,000 leaflets to Austin homes. That same month, a busload of spouses and members—actually made up overwhelmingly of support group members and retirees, rather than workers—accompanied Rogers and Allen to the Hormel stockholders' meeting in Atlanta, the first ever held outside Austin.

Such actions at stockholders' meetings, made possible by the purchase of small amounts of stock and the distribution of proxy votes among protesters, have been a common corporate campaign tactic. The tactic draws the attention of the media, and it demonstrates to the large investors that the company has a serious labor-relations problem on its hands. Moreover, and perhaps most importantly, it allows the protesters a rare opportunity to have a face-to-face confrontation with corporate executives and directors. "The board members were all wearing their suits and other stockholders were dressed very nice, while we were there in jeans and sweatshirts," recalled Jeannie Bambrick. "It made you feel so small." But, said Vicky Guyette:

> The meeting was the first time for me that I realized how rotten they treated us. It was the first time we'd experienced a confrontation with them, and they tried to prevent us from asking questions. No one wanted to be first—we held back until the first questions were asked.

Then everyone's hand went up, everybody had a question. Barbara Olsen got in a real back-and-forth with [Hormel CEO Richard] Knowlton. Afterwards, we were so happy we partied all the way home on the bus.[13]

The company, it should be pointed out, also made its points. Management demonstrated to the workers that it existed in a world that went far beyond the town of Austin, and that it was isolated from the problems that the workers experienced in the plant. And although the P-9ers raised serious questions about the conduct of the company, the directors showed that they could simply ignore such questions.

Over subsequent months, union members began speaking tours to meatpacking towns and major cities, explaining their cause. Workers would take a few days off from work, sometimes drive all day to speak or leaflet, then drive all night to get back home. They helped bring into being support committees in other towns, notably in Minneapolis–St. Paul and in Fremont. And they began a campaign of turning up the heat on the First Bank System.

First Bank was a key element in Corporate Campaign's analysis of Hormel's pressure points. A giant midwestern bank holding company with branches in five states, the bank shared three top policymakers with Hormel (including its own CEO, DeWalt Ankeny, and Hormel CEO Richard Knowlton) and in December 1984 held 16 percent of the meatpacker's common stock. As early as 1926, Hormel had helped bail out the Austin National Bank, which later developed into the First Bank System. Board interlocks were continuous from that decade. And, more recently, First Bank Minneapolis had been one of three banks that made the 1982 construction of Hormel's new Austin plant possible with $75 million in loan guarantees.[14]

Given such historic and current relations, Corporate

Campaign reasoned that First Bank had the power to get Hormel to make a settlement. But aside from the Hormel Foundation, which held voting control over 45.6 percent of company stock along with a mandate "to keep the best interests of Austin and the surrounding community as its prime purpose," there were few other pressure points.[15] So direct pressure on the company remained vital.

■ ■ ■

The tabloid on injuries at Hormel was completed early in the spring of 1985 and distributed by the thousands. Local members had been organized by Rogers to fan out across the Midwest, distributing literature about Hormel door to door, at union meetings and plant gates, and outside branches of First Bank. "Legacy of Pain: Hormel's Injured Workers in Austin" hit the company hard, and Hormel immediately responded with a series of public relations broadsides, alleging that the situation was really not that bad and blaming the lost time on "Minnesota's liberal workers' compensation laws [which] make it attractive to remain off work."[16]

But the situation really was as bad as the Austin workers claimed. And "Legacy of Pain" showed them to be both exceptionally articulate and aroused about the injustices they had been dealt.

"We had one kid get stabbed in the leg in the kill area," said 25-year veteran worker Ron Kraft, recounting one of the article's many stories. "The guy next to him fell off a stand while heading hogs. The cement stand got all full of blood and he just slipped off. When he fell, his arm came back, and he stuck a knife 4 or 5 inches into the kid's leg.

"The kid turned snow white. He was lying there on the ground—I never saw blood spurt out of anyone so fast. They wouldn't touch him at the Austin hospital, so they had to rush him to Rochester. He nearly died on the way over there."[17]

The workers themselves spoke of how knives, meat grinders, sausage stuffers, and other machines operated as efficiently on human limbs as on hog parts. Poor machine and plant design; speed enforced by the "chain," or disassembly line; repeated motions; work in cold environments; and heavy lifting—all played a part in creating the enormously high annual injury rate. Workers also described the inadequacies of Minnesota's workers' compensation plan and the bizarre Qualified Rehabilitation Counselor system that assigns each worker out on disability a counselor, paid by the insurance companies, whose job it is to find suitable work for these crippled people. In other words, rather than reform the jobs that caused the injuries in the first place, Minnesota created another group of professionals who make a living off the workers' injuries.

Among the most common injuries at the plant was "carpal tunnel syndrome," a swelling of tissues in the wrist that leads to damaged hand and wrist nerves. The condition comes about as a result of repeating the same wrist motions over and over. First there is pain in the hands and wrists, then numbness and loss of circulation, particularly when you are at rest. If the motions that lead to the condition are stopped soon enough, the problem may subside; if not, medication followed by surgery to relieve pressure on the nerve may be required.

Elizabeth Anderson described how she began work at the plant in December 1982, boning hams in the area known as the "hog cut." She worked up to speed, on a job that required her to cut off the shank meat, take out the bone, and trim excess fat from 92 hams per hour. Four months later, she began to experience pain and numbness in her wrists and arms. Unable to bid out of the department, she continued the repetitive work until she was forced to have surgery in November and December 1983. Afterward, she was assigned to as many as a dozen "rehabilitation jobs," on which a person is supposed to be allowed time to heal. But almost every one of these seemed to involve lifting or exposure to heat or cold, subjecting her to further injury.

Finally, in July 1984, the company said that it had no further work for her and that, given her injury, there would be nothing for her in the future. By year's end, she and her husband had decided to move to Wisconsin and look for work there: He went on ahead, and she stayed behind to allow her children to finish the school term. But in March, in spite of its earlier assurance that it had no further work for her, Hormel offered Anderson yet another job. Under Minnesota workers' comp rules, this meant that she faced the choice of moving to be with her husband and losing all benefits or staying on and going through another round of what was likely to be unsuitable and injurious work at Hormel. Feeling herself to be handicapped for life, with only minimal strength in her arms, and outraged that the company would put her in such a position, she decided to leave.[18]

Hormel's willingness to produce maimed workers and then discard them was another reason for Austin workers' anger and militancy. And in its zeal to break the workers' spirit, the company repeatedly demonstrated that all the workers' concerns were connected: Hormel followed the October 1984 wage cut with a drastic cut in medical benefits, retroactive for several months, so that members were actually left owing the company money for benefits paid out in the past. "A lot of people never got that paid off," said Carl Pontius, who would later join the local executive board.

"That really teed everyone off and made people anxious to fight."[19]

■ ■ ■

In April 1985, P-9 intensified its activities aimed at First Bank. Hundreds picketed bank branches, distributing leaflets that described the Hormel/First Bank connection and postcards to be sent to the bank urging that it either use its influence to restore the cut wages or sever ties with Hormel. (Such actions were referred to by the local as "bannering" rather than picketing, in order to avoid any suggestion of illegal secondary boycott activity.) The union encouraged supporters "not to put their money in places where it could be used against them," and millions of dollars were withdrawn. A hundred fifty P-9 members, along with activists from citizens' groups that had other complaints, attended the First Bank stockholders' meeting in St. Paul, while others demonstrated outside.

Hormel workers dominated the microphones and the agenda of that meeting, which was cut off early to avoid further questions from them. As in previous campaigns of this kind, bank spokesmen claimed that they had no influence over Hormel's corporate decisions, while Rogers and the union members claimed that the bank had the power to resolve the dispute. DeWalt Ankeny, bank president and a Hormel board member, said: "They attribute power to me that I don't have," adding that the bank was "monitoring what was going on" to determine if the union was engaged in an illegal secondary boycott.[20] And indeed, as would be demonstrated in time, there was a lot of "monitoring" going on.

Spring and early summer found the UFCW International

as resolute as Hormel and the bank. Between Rogers' two ini-
tial visits to Austin in October and December 1984, the local
and Corporate Campaign had attempted to persuade the
UFCW to support the Hormel campaign. Rogers, Allen, and
Guyette had gone to Washington to meet with Executive Vice
President Jay Foreman, Regional Director Wendell Olson,
Packinghouse Division director Anderson, and President
William Wynn. Not much was settled, and the UFCW officials agreed to have a further hearing of the issues at a meeting of officers from the several Hormel locals two months
later in Chicago.

But before that meeting, Anderson began openly denouncing the local and its proposed corporate campaign in
the press. And two Chicago sessions proved to be sham hearings: Though the local officers put Rogers and Allen through
a long grilling, they took no vote on the campaign; and less
than an hour after the second meeting, Anderson held a
press conference, complete with a large stack of printed materials, to announce that the UFCW had decided not to back a
campaign against Hormel, but instead to mount "a full-court
press" against ConAgra/Armour, which he referred to as the
worst corporate offender in meatpacking labor relations.[21] A
union press release announced the Packinghouse Committee's support for the Armour campaign and recommendation
that the UFCW "inform all local unions and the AFL-CIO
that the union does not 'endorse, support or authorize' a corporate campaign or boycott against the George Hormel company." It went on to say that P-9 had "chosen the wrong target at the wrong time," since "we cannot raise the roof unless
our foundation is solid."[22]

Anderson's and the UFCW's attacks on the local now
gained momentum. A January press release describing one of
the several arbitrator's rulings that allowed Hormel's wage
and benefit reductions added: "a lack of understanding of

the realities . . . can and often does bring about severe consequences for the membership."[23] In March, UFCW president Wynn sent out a letter notifying all UFCW meatpacking locals that they should offer neither moral nor financial support for P-9's "ill advised" campaign.[24] That same month Anderson publicly attacked the campaign as "bankrupt." And the International organized a petition from local presidents at Hormel and Wilson plants, criticizing the local for trying to raise wages at Austin above the level of other plants, for spreading "anti-union venom," and for pursuing "a suicide mission."[25]

Since October 1984, the local and Anderson had wrangled over when and under what conditions the Packinghouse Division director might come to Austin and address the members. In January, Anderson said that he was too busy to come and, as P-9 requested, clarify the UFCW's position on the corporate campaign. P-9 members then, on January 18, approved a three-dollar-per-week per-person assessment to finance that campaign. In late February, International representatives appeared at the plant to hand out unsigned letters that asked why the International officers were being denied the right to meet with the members "without the presence of officials from corporate campaign [sic]." Guyette told reporters that the UFCW officials had also demanded that their safety be guaranteed.[26]

On April 11 the UFCW announced that the local's mid-January two-to-one vote to fund the campaign was invalid, since not enough prior notice had been given to the membership.[27] Then, on April 14, Anderson, accompanied by his assistants Al Vincent and John Mancuso, UFCW Region 13 leaders Wendell Olson and Joe Hansen, and Jay Foreman, came to Austin for what turned into a five-hour meeting with the membership.

In that meeting, Anderson recounted his past efforts to

fight concessions, stating that he had seen 35 plants close and thousands of workers lose jobs in that fight. Members from such plants as Dubuque Packing and the "worker-owned" Rath Packing Co. in Waterloo, Iowa, had bitterly opposed the fight, wanting to allow pay cuts and thereby save their jobs. "We were called a no-good bunch of SOBs," he said. "The news media said, 'The UFCW just closes plants up.' It's a little too late to be worrying about not taking cuts: The horse is out of the barn now."

Spurred by plant closings, reorganization, and nonunion competition, the meatpacking industry as a whole had been very close to becoming nonunion, he said. To meet that challenge, the UFCW had taken up the strategy of trying to win a national rate at a lower level. He pointed out that after their wage cut, Austin workers were now earning less than the $9.00 rate established in "the chain settlement." Fighting to restore the $10.69 rate would only encourage Hormel to subcontract at lower rates and to acquire more low-wage subsidiaries, as it had in the Kansas-based Dold Foods and Iowa's FDL Foods.

P-9's officers and members were unconvinced by the presentation and the approach of "stabilizing the bottom." "You don't fix the basement when the roof is leaking," announced Guyette. "Workers at unorganized plants like Dold Foods want to know why they should join the union just to take a pay cut." He pressed Anderson to admit that no contract wage rates had been negotiated upward since 1981. Many members shouted from the floor questions about Anderson's and other officers' salaries—why wasn't Lewie taking a cut in his $70,000 annual wage?

Men and women came to floor microphones and asked earnestly why the International, if it wouldn't support them, couldn't at least leave them alone to fight with Hormel. "We believe in togetherness," said one speaker, "but the way you see it, Local 9 is out in the cold and all the other locals are all right."

"We can't understand an International trying to force us to take less," added Guyette. "In most places of the country you have to look for people willing to fight. You've got it here, and now you're trying to defuse it."

"We're not on your backs," Anderson responded. "You can proceed in your direction, but if you go outside of your local and try to drag others into it, that's another story."[28]

But in succeeding months, the International stayed on the local's back. In May, Wynn sent each member of the local a letter strongly critical of local leaders and the corporate campaign; large sections of it were reproduced in the Austin daily newspaper.[29] A group of local dissidents were given aid and legitimacy far beyond their numbers: In June these "P-10ers" somehow gathered 560 names on a petition to force a second vote on accepting the $9.00 and $10.00 "chain settlement." "It appears that a very large percentage of the membership is growing weary of the direction that has been taking place," Anderson told the *Rochester Post-Bulletin* on the eve of the vote.[30] But the vote to continue the campaign was overwhelming—722 to 178—as was the second vote on the three-dollar-per-member assessment to fund the corporate campaign.[31]

Anderson and the International were far from done. Nevertheless, as the days moved toward the expiration of the contract that had allowed the 23 percent wage cut, P-9 members seemed to long for a showdown.

The union and company met for the first negotiating session on June 25, 1985, though both sides knew that the contract would expire in August.[32] P-9 was usually represented by nine members of the local's executive board—Guyette,

Winkels, Lynn Huston, Skinny Weis, Floyd Lenoch, Jim Retterath, Keith Judd, Kenny Hagen, and Audrey Newman—plus bargaining committee chairman Dave Ring and attorney Ron Rollins; Hormel generally sent a 10-member team, led by Austin plant personnel manager Bill Swanson and including staff attorney James Cavanaugh.

P-9 presented its proposal at the second meeting, held on July 2. Most significantly, this attempted to reinstitute an incentive plan the local had given up in 1978; in grievance hearings, to again consider all past practices as binding—a right that had been limited under the expiring contract; to ensure that all transfers would be on the basis of seniority; to provide a means of expediting arbitration; to limit subcontracting of union work; to allow employees to honor any picket line at their plant; to conduct an ergonomic study of safety problems at the plant; and to raise the wage rate to $12.50, complimented by pay for overtime and lump-sum reimbursements for the previous wage and benefit cuts. The union also proposed a right to strike over safety, work standards, and unresolved grievances—three major irritants—during the life of the contract.[33]

"We'd had our experiment in trusting the company in 1978," Guyette told me. "Now we wanted a document that it didn't take a Philadelphia lawyer to understand."[34]

On July 17, Hormel presented its first offer. The company proposed to make seniority secondary to consideration of "ability to perform all the work operations" in case of vacancies or promotions, and it claimed the absolute right to assign all overtime, to abolish or alter jobs, and to transfer or subcontract work. It restricted the grievance and arbitrations system. It proposed abolition of the existing 52-week notice before any layoff, substituting a very limited three-month notice of plant closing. It allowed management to transfer workers throughout the plant on an involuntary basis. It gave the company the right to hire temporary workers without paying them benefits or allowing them to accumulate seniority. It eliminated consideration of any past practices in grievances and banned all "strikes, handbilling, boycotts or [attempts to] coerce or restrain the company, [or] any business affiliated with the company." And it restricted overtime and holiday pay. Initially, Hormel did not address the issue of wages.[35]

The company presented a second proposal on July 31. It altered the first proposal hardly at all, but an attached wage classification scheme began to suggest where Hormel wanted to go with wages.[36] Finally, on August 3, in the presence of federal mediator Hank Bell, Hormel negotiators announced that the company was seeking a $10.00 base rate, a freeze of current workers' wages at that rate, plus a two-tier wage scheme that would pay new hires $8.00 at the beginning and $9.00 by the end of the three-year agreement. Nowhere were safety issues addressed, nor was the company willing to consider a contract expiration date that would allow Austin to get in sync with contracts at the other plants.

Bell, who had been called in to help move negotiations along, observed at that meeting that "the parties are not settling on an approach." Indeed they weren't. And in spite of the mediator's urging on August 5 and 6 (and his frequent warnings to the local about the danger of striking), little agreement was ever achieved.

The 15th negotiating session was held on August 7, and immediately afterward Guyette called the company's employment manager, William Swanson, to give him the required 48-hour strike notice. Swanson said he was surprised and noted that the company had yet to give the union its final proposal. It finally did so on August 8—one day before the strike deadline.[37]

Hormel's final proposal improved the seniority clause but continued to limit seniority rights—language elsewhere allowed the company free reign to transfer workers and to assign regular and overtime work and restricted job-bidding rights. Most other provisions that the union had found objectionable remained, with only slight revision.[38]

Both sides treated the final session on August 10 as a post-mortem. Swanson again and again observed that the company "believes it has fulfilled the obligation to bargain in good faith" and that "negotiations are at an impasse." Former local president Floyd Lenoch announced, "This is the worst example of negotiating I've seen, and I've seen plenty."[39]

The negotiating committee unanimously recommended rejection of the Hormel proposal to the membership. And on August 14, 93 percent of P-9 members voted against it.

"Bargaining never really had a chance," union attorney Ron Rollins reflected several months later. Noting that in 1984 the company had replaced its old-line Minneapolis legal counsel with the Milwaukee firm of Krukowski, Chaet, Beck & Loomis, which was building a reputation as a union-buster, and that the local had retained Corporate Campaign Inc., he said that "the action just wasn't at the bargaining table."

"That was reinforced at the first bargaining meeting," he continued. "It appeared that the company had deliberately sent a bargaining committee made up of distinctly low-level officials from the Austin plant, though it was clear that important issues, like money, could not be decided by Austin plant officials. Although the words were neutral, it looked like a committee distinctly without authority." (Indeed, Hormel Vice President for Human Relations David Larson, the company's chief labor negotiator, absented himself early on from most meetings.) Rollins' opinion was that "the company's goal was to lay out a proposal that it would implement at impasse."[40]

Rollins was not alone in feeling pessimistic about negotiations. In a June 17 memo, Police Chief Don Hoffman advised the mayor that he had already contacted over seven big-city police chiefs and experts on "labor unrest" across the country, all of whom "are eager to provide us with their knowledge and experience." By July Hoffman was holding regular meetings with officials of the State Patrol, the union, and the Chamber of Commerce about the impending strike, and, according to another memo, police "continually meet with Corporate officers and also with [Hormel security chief] Ken Carlson and Gary Baker who is their security consultant."[41]

At midnight on August 16, a rowdy picket of 400 people lined the street across from the plant's main gate. Chants of "We're gonna win! We're gonna win! gave way to a countdown of the last 10 seconds before the contract's expiration, followed by cheers and shouts of exultation.

"Everybody's emotions were running very high that night," recalled support committee member Carole Apold.

> Some of the executive board members had gone into the plant to make sure that everybody was out: One of the main things I remember was Jim Guyette walking out and giving us the thumbs up as the security men closed the gate behind him.
>
> The next day, Danny Blazer told me that he heard horns honking and people chanting "P-9 Proud" all the

way over at his house, which is about a mile from the plant. In fact, we woke him up, and he got out of bed to see what was going on. Everybody who was out there just had a very strong feeling that we were doing what needed to be done.[42]

▐▌

THE WEIGHT OF THE PAST

We are in the battle in support of all unions and especially industrial unions. We will fight for farmers and workers and will aid representatives of them in times of trouble and strife. . . . We recognize that we are under a system which perpetuates wage slavery.

—*First edition of* The Unionist, *newspaper of the Independent Union of All Workers (forerunner of Local P-9), October 1935*

Gone are the dress rehearsals of civil war when workers moved into neighboring communities to help their fellow workers repulse tear-gas attacks. . . . From a fighting organization dedicated to remove 'wage slavery' the union has become an instrument administering the protective machinery established in the Working Agreement. . . . unless 'something radical happens,' workers are apathetic.

Fred H. Blum, Toward A Democratic Work Process (1953)[1]

When Fred Blum joined the Austin work force in the 1950s in order to conduct his study of what he called "the Hormel–Packinghouse Workers' Experiment," he was astonished by the mutual respect that existed between labor and management. After the 1930s—when workers shut down the plant, chasing foremen off the premises with clubs and roughly escorting company president Jay Hormel out in order to win a union contract—and until the 1970s, friendly relations persisted between Hormel and the Austin workers. How, then, did this relationship come apart?

According to Blum, a number of factors led members to expect labor peace and take Local 9 for granted in the early 1950s. Although the union had a militant past, growing as it did out of the radical Industrial Workers of the World (IWW) and winning union rights through a number of sitdown strikes, for years there had been no serious dispute between the workers and the company. Hormel worked hard at winning loyalty by giving workers the security of a guaranteed annual wage—originally a company idea, later codified in the union agreement—complemented by profit sharing and retirement benefits. Because the union had won "me too" contract language automatically awarding Austin workers whatever wage increase was won by workers at the "Big Four" companies that dominated the industry, Hormel avoided the strike wave of 1946 and the industry-wide strike of 1948. In fact, unlike other meatpackers and union locals, beginning in 1940 Hormel and P-9 had a perpetual Working Agreement of no fixed duration. It was occasionally modified, but for 38 years neither side ever terminated it.

"If I had to summarize workers' feelings about the company in one sentence," Blum reported, "I would repeat the words of a worker: 'If a man is going to work for anybody else, it is hard to beat Hormel.'. . . Disregarding minor variations in phrasing, it was the *single most often heard expression* in any conversation about the company."[2]

Thirty-one years later, an older worker reminisced to writer Stanley Aronowitz: "No kiddin', we actually looked forward to coming to work every day."[3]

Security and money was, in the main, the glue that made the workers and the union stick by the company. But there was more to it than that: From the late 1930s until 1978, the workers actually ran the plant.

The guaranteed annual wage—also referred to as "straight time" pay—ensured that every worker received a pre-set amount of wages each week and provided for a 52-week notice of layoff, guaranteeing that there would be no sudden interruptions in that pay. Blum described this combination as producing "a security unique in American industry."[4]

Additionally, in a scheme worked out by 1940, workers received incentive pay for work done over and above the standard that was set for a department or work gang. At first, a gang's only reward for finishing its allotted work early was the "sunshine bonus": the right to go home early. Later, it was agreed that if everyone in the gang consented, the group might work longer and receive additional pay (figured on a group, not an individual, basis) rather than leave early.

This setup had the effect of taking away most of a foreman's traditional authority. Beyond the team or departmental work standard, which was set in union negotiations, the gang set the pace of work. Union seniority took away a foreman's ability to give out assignments to whomever he chose.[5] And the union had a tradition of immediately resolving grievances right on the shop floor: "There wasn't any of this 'write up a grievance and have a hearing in three days' stuff,'" recalled one worker. "Instead, you could go to the 'bullpen,' an office downstairs, and have an immediate meeting with the foreman, a union steward, and the employment manager, who would very often insist that no one left until the thing was settled." All of this meant that Austin workers were much less easily threatened than other workers.[6]

As Blum perceived, the average worker understood this heritage partly as a gift from Hormel management—specifically, from Jay Hormel, who succeeded his father as president of the company between 1927 and 1946—and partly as something won by the union. But often they placed a greater emphasis upon the company's munificence.[7] In fact, Jay Hormel became quite a progressive employer, able to anticipate union grievances and committed to his "master plan" of welfare capitalism. (This inclination developed only after and as a result of the 1933 strike, during which he behaved like any tyrannical employer, threatening to move the company from Austin, organizing a force of 200 strikebreakers in Minneapolis, and, possibly, appealing for intervention by federal troops.)[8]

However, the tone of caring and generosity began to disappear as soon as Jay Hormel died. After 1954, company management took an increasingly severe attitude toward its workers and, despite its continuing support for local charities through the Hormel Foundation, became less and less committed to the Hormel family hometown of Austin.

As early as 1946, when H. H. Corey succeeded Jay Hormel as president, the company began buying and building facilities in other states: South Dakota, Nebraska, Iowa, California, Washington, Texas, Alabama, North Carolina, Georgia, and Hawaii. Both the U.S. Army and the civilian population of Britain had made it through the war on the company's most famous product, Spam. With peace at hand, Hormel looked to build upon this success and establish itself as an international force in the meatpacking and food industry.[9]

Geographic and industrial expansion continued during the following years, as did the ascension of corporate leaders from outside the Austin area. Among these was M. B. Thompson from South Dakota, who became company president in 1965 and later earned notoriety among generations of workers by reputedly remarking, "Before I'm through the workers will be living in tar-paper shacks."[10]

The union that faced this change of attitude remained formidable, in spite of the years of peaceful coexistence. More than a machine for dues collection or an insurance agency, the local retained the ideology and culture of an organization that had fought before and would fight again if the need arose. Just as Jay Hormel's liberality and Thompson's greed entered local legend, so too did tales of P-9 founder Frank Ellis' union leadership and of rank-and-file militancy dating from the 1933 strike.

In November of that year, neither Hormel nor the governor, Floyd B. Olsen, dared to declare full-scale war on the workers, though Olsen, himself a former IWW member, had mobilized 300 Minnesota National Guard troops. For one thing, the strikers were occupying the plant, where they had turned off the refrigeration system, endangering both $3,600,000 worth of meat and the $500,000 system itself, whose pipes would likely have frozen and burst within 24 hours of the shutoff.

Union zeal had swept Austin the previous summer. On one July evening, 600 Hormel workers signed union cards, responding to the company's high-handed attempt to impose a 20-cent-a-week deductible insurance plan (even though some workers were making as little as 40 cents an hour), to the tyranny of plant foremen, and to Frank Ellis' spadework. Ellis had started work in a packinghouse as a young man after his father's death in a Swift plant. He became an IWW organizer as a result of his experiences as a meatcutter. During his teens and twenties, he became a "boomer," riding the rails and working seasonal stints in packinghouses all over, agitating for the Wobblies all the while. He had been jailed from Texas to Minnesota, driven out of towns by gun thugs and sheriffs' deputies, beaten by vigilantes, and accused of disloyalty because of his opposition to World War I.

Then Ellis came to Austin, where, because of skills honed during almost 30 years in midwestern packinghouses, Hormel made him a foreman in the casing room. Ellis used his new position to hire other union men and get them transferred to departments throughout the plant. When the urge for a union and the strike came along, he was ready.

Jay Hormel insisted that the strike was the work of outside agitators. Mistrusting the governor's populist instincts, he attempted both to keep Olsen away from the scene and to pressure him to send in the militia against the strikers, among other things using major Minneapolis radio stations to create a sense of emergency. In the end, however, Olsen came to the town and personally worked out an agreement that provided for the rehiring of all strikers and ultimately for a two- to four-cent wage increase plus arbitration of all future disputes.

This victory was followed by several years of activism. Over the opposition of employer-backed anti-union groups such as the "Secret 500" and the "Citizens' Alliance," the Hormel packers organized city workers and all but four retail establishments in town into their Independent Union of All Workers, which, like its IWW predecessor, sought to represent every worker regardless of his or her craft. (Later the union became Local 183 of the CIO, and then Local 9 of the United Packinghouse Workers of America, or UPWA.) They engaged in further sitdown strikes in the plant, including the 1936 sausage department sitdown that won union shop status for the plant.

Austin militants helped organize packinghouse workers in plants across Iowa, Minnesota, and South Dakota: IUAW branches were built in Albert Lea, Faribault, and South St.

Paul, Minnesota, and in Mason City and Waterloo, Iowa. When the local newspaper, the *Austin Daily Herald,* proved to be a company organ, among other things attacking the union's candidate in the city elections, Local 9 began its own weekly, *The Unionist.* In 1936 the Austin local, along with another independent union from Cedar Rapids, Iowa, pushed the fledgling CIO to make a place for packinghouse workers. And the local continued to be a force once the Packinghouse Workers Organizing Committee was begun, its power reflected in the fact that Frank Ellis became one of four national officers chosen to lead the new United Packinghouse Workers of America in 1943.[11]

Such union experiences are seldom forgotten. Like many an organization, Local P-9 has a portrait of its founding father hanging in the entranceway of its headquarters; but unlike many successors, later generations of Austin union members know exactly who Frank Ellis was and what he and his contemporaries did. There remains, between a union that has known such experiences and one that has not, a tangible difference in the members' understanding of the "black line" that exists between management and worker.

■ ■ ■

Nevertheless, Local P-9 faced a period of dramatic structural change in the meatpacking industry with leaders who were very much of the belief that the members must rely upon the goodwill and generosity of the Hormel company. Frank Shultz, president from the 1940s till 1969, was of the generation that understood union-company relations as a test of strength; his successors—notably Ernie Jones, Barney Thompson, and John Hansen—were more inclined toward accommodation. All were inclined toward isolationism. As Hormel's Charles Nyberg told me in 1988:

> Frank Shultz wouldn't let the International representa-
> tives into town. The local helped out in other negotia-
> tions [elsewhere], but negotiations here were by P-9 and
> no one else. I remember the first time I saw the Interna-
> tional here in town, Jessie Prosten came in to help negoti-
> ate and I heard people say, "This is a switch—P-9 never
> needed help before."

Indeed, the first attempt to create a "chain," or structure for
pattern bargaining, occurred in 1973.[12]

The most influential of this accommodating breed of
leaders was the P-9 business agent for 15 years, Richard
Schaefer. It was Schaefer who really ran the union from 1969
to 1984—years that saw tremendous upheaval in the
industry.

For, beginning in the 1960s, a number of aggressive companies, particularly Iowa Beef Processors (now IBP Inc.) employed much larger facilities located out in the countryside
to challenge the hold of the "big four"—Armour, Cudahy,
Swift, and Wilson—on the industry and the market. Iowa
Beef drew upon a broadening pool of surplus rural labor and
broke down traditionally skilled work into less skilled tasks.
The company built massive, very modern, single-story
slaughtering and processing facilities and took advantage of
the new interstate highway system and refrigerated trucks,
rather than depending upon outmoded rail transport. And
Iowa Beef proved to be startlingly anti-labor, slashing wages
below the old packers' scales, then confronting strikes by
transforming its plants into walled fortresses, complete with
housing for strikebreakers so that they never had to leave the
area and face angry picket lines. Like California grape
growers in the 1960s, IBP found that it could use the Teamsters union against the meatpackers' union, and it signed

sweetheart deals with both the Teamsters and the National Maritime Union.

The old packers, which mostly operated vast, multi-product plants in large urban centers, felt the pressure of this competition. They closed old urban plants and began to look for ways to trim costs, particularly wages. Then Swift, Armour, Wilson, Morrell, Cudahy, and Hygrade were taken over by big conglomerates looking for short-term profits. In time, Armour's first conglomerate owner, Greyhound, would sell out to another, ConAgra, which laid off all union workers and reopened its plants with nonunion labor. Wilson would file for Chapter 11 reorganization in order to abrogate its labor contracts. Today, the industry is increasingly fragmented: Rather than operating huge plants that slaughter and process hogs, cattle, and sheep, companies tend to specialize in particular kinds of meat and to either slaughter or process. By 1984 the average slaughterhouse had only 500 workers and paid very low wages; the average processing plant employed only 100 workers. And the level of unionization fell from 80 to 70 percent.[13]

Neither Hormel nor Local P-9's leaders understood these coming changes well during the 1960s and 1970s. But Hormel, at least, understood that all meatpackers, regardless of the condition of their balance sheets, were going to drive wages downward, and it began demanding wage concessions as early as 1963, when higher production schedules began reducing workers' incentive pay.

The concessionary package that paved the way for a later labor explosion came in 1978. Since 1975 the company had been considering building an ultra-modern pork-slaughtering and processing plant, rather than spending millions to improve the old plant, and was looking at sites outside Austin, including Waverly, Iowa, and Mankato, Minnesota. (The fact that this was to be a slaughtering *and* processing plant shows that Hormel had not yet bought the logic that these functions should take place in different facilities with un-equally paid workers.) To make up for the building expense, Hormel executives said, the gang incentive system had to be eliminated and production increased. The union rejected this suggestion.

In early 1978 Hormel broke off negotiations over the in-centive and production-increase issues and announced that it would definitely not be building the new plant in Austin. It had already closed the beef slaughter, eliminating over two hundred jobs, and issued 52-week layoff notices to three-hundred-odd more workers. Faced with this familiar form of corporate blackmail and urged to give in by Schaefer, local members got the company to change its mind by agreeing to a package that included both a "transition agreement" and a "new plant agreement," the latter slated to go into effect once 750 people were working in the new plant. Thus the perpep-tual "Working Agreement," in place since 1940, was scrapped in favor of more conventional, fixed-term contracts.

These contracts temporarily froze wages, though, as in the Working Agreement, they provided for a pass-along of any change in wages negotiated with other companies as a "national pattern"; and they increased production schedules by another 20 percent. They allowed no strikes until three years after the "new plant agreement" took effect. As it worked out, this was a seven-year no-strike pledge.

And there would be no gang incentive in the new plant. Instead, once the new plant was on-line, old-plant workers would receive supplements to keep each one at an "average" of his or her former rate of pay. These supplements would come from an escrow account of around $20 million, made up of COLA (cost-of-living adjustment) payments that the workers would no longer receive. Until the new plant began operating, the escrow account functioned as a loan (which, workers say, averaged out at $12,000 per worker) to help the company build the new Austin plant. In exchange for these concessions, P-9 members received assurances from the company that wages in the new plant would be no lower than wages in the old one.[14]

However, the concessions did not usher in a period of stability in Austin. Adding to the confusion that resulted from working under three contracts, Local 9 was now a part of a new International union, the United Food and Commercial Workers. The UFCW had come into being in 1978 as a result of the merger of four unions, all troubled by the crisis in meatpacking and other basic industries. It was dominated by the leadership of the old Retail Clerks' union.[15] In 1980 the UFCW proposed that the Austin local, now known as P-9 to indicate its origins in the Packinghouse Workers union, agree to amalgamate with another Hormel union as a first step toward its incorporation into a large, amalgamated local. For a variety of reasons, including greater efficiency, the national union was promoting such reorganization across the country, but the resulting locals had a tendency to become distant from and unresponsive to rank-and-file workers. (The local representing the 900 workers at Hormel's Ottumwa, Iowa, slaughtering plant, for example, was Local 431, which represented 5,000 workers from 100 companies across Iowa and in Illinois. The officers of the local would represent the packinghouse workers at "chain meetings," Packinghouse Division conferences, and International conventions, even though most of them came out of another industry altogether, such as retailing.)

And in 1981, a year before the new plant was scheduled to open, the UFCW determined that there should be additional concessions from all Hormel locals, as well as from workers at the other old-line packers—Oscar Mayer, Armour, Swift, Morrell, and Wilson. The crisis in the industry was continuing, and national leaders insisted that existing contracts must be reopened, "to bring lower wage operators more in line with master agreement companies" and "minimize the wave of plant closings." The UFCW pressed members to accept contract language stipulating that "the cost-of-living adjustment which is now in effect will be incorporated into the rates, and there will be no increase or reduction in rates for the balance of the present term of the Agreement and for the 1982–1985 term of the Agreement." In exchange for this three-year wage freeze at $10.69 per hour and the reduction of COLA, Hormel agreed that there would be no plant closings in 1982 and that wage rates would be reopened for discussion in 1984.[16]

In each of these matters, the International had to win approval from the local membership. The proposal to merge Local P-9 with others was one of the first recommendations that Lewie Anderson made to the local, since at that time he had only recently been appointed Packinghouse Division director. It was not a good place to begin with such an independent-minded group. And it provided the occasion for the rise of another new leader, Jim Guyette.

■ ■ ■

"You have to understand that I really didn't get along with him all that well," recalled a retired P-9er who worked with Guyette in the loin cooler at the plant. "Nobody else wanted to think about how we were getting screwed by Hormel all the time. You just wanted to forget about it, to talk about something else. But not Guyette, he just wanted to talk about how the company was getting away with murder.

"In time we came to agree with him."[17]

In Jim Guyette were combined a number of attributes: In his middle thirties, he was young enough to speak to the new workers; yet, having begun work at the company in 1968, he had sufficient experience to speak to the older ones. Like his counterpart Pete Winkels, who became business agent in late 1984, he came from a long line of Hormel workers—Guyette's father and grandfather worked at the plant, while Winkels was a fourth-generation Hormel worker. A son of deaf-mute parents, Guyette demonstrated an unusual ability to articulate issues with precision, enforced by a steady gaze and calm manner, and to describe how and why things could and should be different. And he was a member of an increasingly unusual group: someone who had worked in both the old and the new plants, so that he was able to speak with authority about the changes that had come.

"I always wanted to be a farmer," Guyette once told me while describing his increasing involvement in union affairs:

> and I had no interest in becoming a bureaucrat or an institutional figure who'd be a union officeholder for 10 or 15 years. But I do enjoy getting those folks at times—you either control the situation or its controls you. It's kind of fun to match wits with them, like when the time-study people came around in the plant, I'd stand up to them and say that I didn't like people who made their living stealing from others.

Undoubtedly, Guyette's stubborn insistence upon "doing what's right" was also related to a sense of the injustice of his parents' handicap and society's treatment of them. But Guyette, who got along poorly with his father, was heavily influenced as well by his grandfather, a supervisor at the plant, who provided a positive feeling about unionism and a sense that a man cannot have dignity unless he stands up for justice.

At first, Guyette and the two or three others who agreed with him, mostly workers from the night shift, talked to other employees, denouncing what was becoming a regular practice of granting concessions to what they knew to be a very profitable company. They questioned the role that the International union was playing in urging workers to make such concessions. And they distributed leaflets, initially unsigned, among plant employees.

"We were concerned about the language that gave the company unlimited right to make time studies and the 'dual gain' wage structure—the practice of paying some workers the incentive and not others—which we saw as a two-tier system," said Guyette. "And we didn't like the escrow system—I felt that if the company needed money to build the plant they ought to go to a bank."

The "phantom leaflets" infuriated Schaefer and the executive board. Questions such as "why are P-9 officers talking about a 'chain concept' when we really have no chain?" and "why are we giving money to the company?" caused other rank-and-filers to ask questions and led local officers to say that outsiders were infiltrating the local's ranks. Finally, Guyette's night-shift fraction having become a committee, they put out a signed leaflet encouraging members to attend the next union meeting and ask questions.

Initially, local president John Hansen ruled that the dissidents could not put forth motions from the floor of the meetings. This shocked the membership and led to further support for their side from the day shift, who argued that their rights as dues payers must be respected. But the dissidents remained strangers to many workers: Guyette and the other night-shift workers found it difficult to attend union meetings because these were held on weekday evenings. Finally, after the controversy had members buzzing, Guyette took vacation time to attend a packed membership meeting where he argued for a motion "either to make *The Unionist* [the union newspaper] more than something to line trash cans with or to drop it." The meeting represented a "coming out" for the dissidents: At last, Guyette recalled one member saying, here is one of these night-shift radicals in the flesh.[18]

By the time Anderson came to Austin to promote the merger of P-9 and the other local, rank-and-filer Guyette was accustomed to speaking from the floor of union meetings. He spoke up again, opposing the merger, pointing out that the other local had different seniority rights from the Austin workers. Thus, he said, the merger would play into Hormel's desire to divide the work force and facilitate its drive for concessions. As chair of the meeting, Anderson ruled him out of order. Guyette then appealed to the membership, who first overruled the chair, allowing him to speak, and then voted down Anderson's merger proposal.

Thus the two men were pitted against each other from their first meeting. According to Guyette, Anderson chastised the local membership, telling them that they would live to regret the day they voted down the merger.

By year-end, the members had elected Guyette to the local's executive board. From this position he attended "Hormel chain" meetings, where he continued to speak out against the International's line that concessions—particularly as embodied in the 1981 wage-freeze and COLA-elimination proposals—were inevitable.

It is important to understand the UFCW structure through which communications between locals, the International, and the company took place. Unlike the old UPWA union practice of bringing as many as a hundred rank-and-file workers from all affected plants into meetings that hammered out negotiating strategy and master agreements, the UFCW allowed little participation by rank-and-filers, and its primary means of coordinating bargaining was through the participation of International officers. The decision to grant givebacks in 1981 was not the result of local discussions, but was announced to local leaders by way of a letter from UFCW president Wynn. The letter was read aloud by division director Lewie Anderson at a meeting of about thirty assembled officers from the company's 12 operating locations. The grouping of regional and local officials known as the "Hormel chain," had little formal standing: It never engaged in joint bargaining, never was able to negotiate a master agreement, had no by-laws or constitution, and, under the UFCW constitution, could not hold a chain-wide vote except under rare circumstances. But it was the UFCW's chief mechanism for coordinating pattern bargaining.[19]

According to Guyette, the UFCW and its loyalists saw him as an unstable element and tried to intimidate and later to discredit him, first with harassing phone calls, then, "time and again," by sending prostitutes to his room. (Ultimately, he says, the UFCW would offer him a position to shut him up, while both company Vice President David Larson and Schaefer would ask "what he really wanted" and urge him to "just let things happen.")[20]

Back home, with a majority of Austin's executive board urging local members to accept the concessions, Guyette gave a report urging rejection. The rank and file voted with Guyette. Then Anderson came again to Austin and forced a second vote on the proposed package, characterizing it as a vote on whether or not the local "wanted to remain in the Hormel chain" or go off on its own. Thus couched as a vote for or against solidarity, the 1981 concessionary proposal was approved. Members also believed that they had traded a wage giveback for the right to strike in 1984.[21]

It was neither the first nor the last instance of the International's using heavy-handed methods and appeals to unity to get members to vote its way. But it was the last time such methods would work in Austin—at least until the trusteeship was imposed in 1986. The 1981 vote may have led the UFCW to overestimate the utility of such tactics, for they would require serial votes and re-votes in the years to come. What they should have paid attention to, instead, was the growing unhappiness of the Austin work force.

The new $100-million plant opened in August 1982, and by the following year it was already clear that it was a disaster so far as the workers were concerned. To begin with, promises of security proved hollow. Most of the 3,000 old-plant workers were laid off (the first layoffs since the 1930s), retired, transferred to other plants, or otherwise gotten rid of before the new plant began operations. "The company wanted to get the older workers out of there and break with tradition," according to Guyette. "They didn't want a situation where, if the foreman treated people unfairly, these old veterans would come up and say, 'Look, Jack, this ain't the way it works here.' "[22]

The 20 percent higher production standards and elaborate automation enabled workers to churn out 440 cans of Spam a minute and 1,600 boned hams an hour with a much-reduced work force. *Meat Industry* magazine rhapsodized about the facility:

> The overall square footage . . . of 1,089,000 square feet is roughly the equivalent of 23 football fields. . . . Production volumes are beyond anything else in the industry. Over two million hogs are slaughtered and cut per year,

resulting in over 200 million pounds worth of over 400 products produced annually. . . . Each of the manufacturing divisions within the plant—hog kill and cut (including rendering), cured meats, canned meats, dry sausage, and prepared sausage—and the two huge warehouse systems are, in essence, plants unto themselves, housed, as one supervisor put it, in "a great big shell." . . . terminals feeding into the [IBM 8100 System 3] mainframe's memory give inventory managers access to the disposition of virtually every pound of meat inside the plant. . . . each of these warehouses features automatic stretch-wrapping of pallet-loads, automatic pallet size-checking, automatic slip-sheeting, and . . . automatic palletizing. . . . Throughout the plant are several pieces of equipment exhibiting new or state-of-the-art technologies for meat processing, including Protecon automatic ham deboners, Morrison Weighing Systems, automatic primal sorters, Langen and Challenge-Cook equipment for massaging and tumbling hams . . . and a Conco-Tellus forklift "robot" for shuttling unformed boxes from place to place.[23]

As a result of such technologies and the speedup, the 3,000 jobs at the old plant (there had been 4,000 in Blum's day) would become 1,500 jobs in the new plant. Approximately 1,100 of these workers were new hires.[24]

Moreover, in abolishing the incentive system, the 1978 agreement had eliminated a key ingredient of what Blum saw as a formula for labor harmony.[25] Even though the seniority system, the 52-week layoff notice, and the guaranteed annual wage remained, without the incentive system workers no longer controlled the pace of work. In the new plant, as in pre-union days, foremen determined the speed of the line. Production standards were no longer subject to negotiation, so the company's industrial engineers, who were more and more in evidence, cranked them up even beyond the agreed-upon 20 percent hike. And the foremen were clearly back in control, to the point of now demanding that workers raise their hands to go to the bathroom and harassing those who were out sick or injured with three to five phone calls a day.[26]

By their own admission, the new hires, some of whom later became the most diligent of strikers, were chosen by the company for their rural, nonunion backgrounds. But in time they were transformed—by the company's scornful attitude toward them, on-the-job injuries, wage and benefit cuts, and the message brought to them by those who had seen work in both the old and new plants and were able to describe the world they had lost.

Under such strains, factionalism was growing in the union local. Schaefer had his followers; there was the small group of radicals around Guyette; and an uncommitted middle was represented by Floyd Lenoch, who served as local president from 1981 to 1984. A devout Christian, Lenoch wanted strongly to get along with both the company, which he felt was honorable, and the International, in which he had faith.

As the union election at the end of 1983 loomed, Lenoch announced that he would run for executive board, but not for re-election as president. Increasingly, there were two distinct forces competing for union leadership—the dissidents and the old machine—and the center was not holding. Thus standing for election were Guyette, who had lost his executive board re-election bid in 1982 and a run for vice president in 1983, and Vice President John Anker, an ally of Schaefer's who argued that P-9 members' best hope lay in going along with the company.

Guyette won the election, 351 to 312. Since Schaefer remained local business agent, local leadership was seriously divided in its approach to matters of principle and practicality.

Immediately, the International tested Guyette's dedication to his principles. That spring, local officers met in Chicago, where they adopted a number of resolutions against concessions. They stated that in order to stand united, the union must secure and maintain common expiration dates in the various Hormel contracts. And they reiterated their support for the guiding principles adopted previously by the International: that there should be no mid-term contract concessions, no concessions whatsoever to profitable companies, and concessions to others only as a last resort and after bitter struggle. Nineteen eighty-five was declared a pivotal year in halting concessions, and, accordingly, locals agreed to stay in regular communication with each other and to back each other up if need be by refusing to cross each others' picket lines.

But no sooner was the meeting concluded than division director Anderson approved a meeting between Hormel and the Ottumwa local to discuss mid-term concessions without the participation of other locals.

Guyette wrote letters of protest to UFCW president Wynn, noting in one:

To say that our membership is upset with the actions of Local 431 would be an understatement, and I on behalf of our 1600 members at Hormel in Austin would ask you to intercede and stop such meetings which will not only violate Article 23 in any concessions which are made, but will destroy our chain and its entire concept which would not be in the best interests of the union movement.

> We have enough problems with employers today trying to destroy the union without each local striking out on their own and destroying ourselves.

The president of the Algona, Iowa, Hormel local joined him in protest.

It seems likely that Guyette enjoyed putting such a statement together, given Anderson's 1981 invocation of chain discipline to win further concessions from Austin. But Local P-9's objections were brushed aside by Wynn, and the International approved the Ottumwa mid-term concessions, though this put the local's expiration date out of sync with the rest of the chain and contradicted the Meatpacking Division's express policy positions.[27]

That June, Anderson wrote to all locals asking them to advise him whether they wished to remain in the "Hormel chain" and to enter as a group into wage reopener discussions with the company that fall. P-9 responded that it wished to do so, and its officers met with those of other chain locals in July. There, the division director again advanced the argument that it was futile to fight concessions. "I asked Anderson, once again, to tell us what his program was for fighting back," Guyette recalled.

> Anderson responded to me by stating that if I genuinely believed in fighting concessions, then I should "guarantee" that Local P-9 would go out on strike in September, "legal or illegal." He further stated, much to my surprise, that the Hormel company was going to take the position that a strike by P-9 in September would be illegal, despite the language in the 1982 agreement which Anderson had insisted we approve, providing for a wage re-opener and right to strike in September of 1984. I replied that, as Anderson well knew, I could hardly "guarantee" that P-9

would strike in September, when no strike vote had as yet been even proposed, let alone passed upon by the requisite two-thirds majority mandated by the UFCW Constitution. Second, I told Anderson that if, in fact, his claim that such a strike might be illegal was true, it was even more preposterous to expect me to "guarantee" on the spot that the membership of my local would vote to strike.[28]

Guyette's account of this exchange accords with his by-the-book personal style and insistence upon observing democratic process, and with Anderson's style of making decisions first and asking procedural questions later. It should be added, however, that the International offered a much different interpretation of these events in literature distributed in 1986 with the intention of discrediting P-9's leadership. According to that version:

All the locals except Local P-9 agreed in July to strike Hormel in September if the chain could not reach an agreement. Local P-9's president, Jim Guyette, expressed concern about the local's legal right to strike in light of the no-strike clause in their contract and questioned whether the local's members would support a strike by other Hormel workers. . . . the Austin facility represented 40 percent of Hormel's production, and hence was crucial to any successful strike by the chain. . . . In September 1984, Local P-9 broke ranks with the chain during negotiations, stating that it would negotiate separately with Hormel.[29]

This version suggests that P-9's leaders should have agreed to an illegal strike (which could quickly have been broken by a court injunction). It fails to discuss the confusing multi-contract situation in effect in Austin and the general lack of clarity about just how the 1981 wage reopener modified the "new plant agreement." Wage reductions seemed to have been ruled out by that 1981 agreement—P-9 members were told it provided for "no increase or reduction" in rates through 1985. But in addition to denying that the reopener had given P-9 the right to strike in 1984, Hormel was claiming that the "transition agreement's" language dealing with national pattern changes allowed reduction of Austin wages down to what had become the new prevailing rate.

To clarify matters and find out what their real rights were, P-9 agreed with the company to submit to arbitration the issue of its right both to strike and to have unreduced wages. According to Guyette, Anderson seized upon this decision to exile P-9 from chain meetings (with the exception of Schaefer, who was "chain chairman") after September 1984. P-9's opposition to the International's retrenchment program had begun to win adherents in the other locals, who were turning down all concessionary proposals. Subsequently, Anderson asked P-9 to "step aside" from the negotiating process, since Hormel had stated that it would only deal with P-9's wages through arbitration. P-9 did so, Guyette said, with the understanding that the local was not deserting the chain.

Two months later, in November 1984, UFCW representatives appeared at the Austin facility, passing out a letter ostensibly from the other chain locals that denounced P-9 for withdrawing from the chain. Guyette sent off letters of protest to the UFCW regional director and to Wynn's assistant. These were ignored. Then arbitrator George Fleischli ruled that the company did indeed have the right to reduce Austin workers' wages.[30]

Though "no reduction in rates" language had resulted in an arbitrator's reversal of wage cuts at the Oscar Mayer company, there was in fact no such language in the 1982 Hormel contract, though the Summary of Agreement distributed by

Anderson indicated that identical language existed in the Oscar Mayer and Hormel agreements. This "missing language" was to become the subject of heated exchanges between the local and Anderson. For a majority of P-9ers, it became the final, conclusive evidence of Anderson's treason.[31]

With the 23 percent wage and benefit cuts now put into effect, all of P-9's chickens had come home to roost: Company management had become so vindictive that it was now using language similar to that which guaranteed labor peace in the 1940s to cudgel its 1980s work force. Hormel was no longer interested in being a pathbreaker in industrial relations; rather, it had become a follower, combining a milder version of the IBP model with more automated work-place methods to win record profits. And the new ruthlessness in the industry had left P-9 part of a large, autocratic bureaucracy that defined unity as a by-product of obedience to national union authority.

None of this was acceptable to Guyette and his slim majority of backers. "The future is what happened today that you weren't expecting yesterday," Winkels wrote, explaining why his generation felt that it had to make history whether it wanted to or not. "When you corner an animal—even a timid animal—and you poke and prod and kick that animal long enough, the animal figures it'll have no alternative but to come after you and bite you," added Guyette.[32] P-9 had been poked enough—but it remained unclear how and when it would bite back. Then Guyette read about Ray Rogers' Corporate Campaign and its various successes in *Business Week* magazine. Within two months, Rogers had come to Austin to present a plan for fighting Hormel. Suddenly, the "cornered" union local had a sense of direction.

SPREADING THE WORD

ARE HORMEL WORKERS STRIKING FOR 69¢? NOTHING COULD
BE FURTHER FROM THE TRUTH! The package offered by the
company was nothing less than a UNION BUSTER'S DREAM COME
TRUE. Not only would it continue the 23% wage cut instituted
over a year ago, it would also FREEZE WAGES OVER THE NEXT THREE
YEARS and DESTROY VIRTUALLY ALL OF THE UNION PROTECTIONS
won since the 1930's. . . . THEY HAVE FORCED THIS STRIKE ON
US—that's why we are taking the fight to the doorsteps of
Hormel plants and to branches of the company's corporate
partner, First Bank, throughout the Midwest.

—*Local P-9 leaflet, September 1985*

What a sense of exhilaration most P-9 members felt during
the first weeks of their strike!

For years, they and their relatives had suffered bullying
threats from Hormel: Do this or we might have to close the
plant, do that or we might have to lay people off. They had
seen dramatic changes in the nature of work and control of
the shop floor between the old and new plants. They had
submitted to one giveback after another—including the loss
of the incentive system that made each worker feel that he
had a real stake in the enterprise—and found themselves
working harder and harder for less and less, supporting the

ever more extravagantly paid corporate leaders who didn't seem to regard the workers as human beings. Then, despite company promises that workers would never make less in the new plant, from out of the blue the company slashed their wages from $10.69 to $8.25 an hour.

In recent months, those indignities had been compounded when faceless arbitrators ruled that, yes, Hormel had the right to reduce their pay by 23 percent; and, yes, it could also reduce their benefits retroactively, and bill them for excess benefits already paid out; but, no, they could not strike in the spring of 1985. Then the company demanded even more in its only real contract proposal: a wage freeze for current workers at $10.00; a second, lower-wage tier for new workers ($8.00 per hour); an end to the 52-week notice of layoffs; no further consideration of "past practices" in grievance hearings; dramatically expanded management prerogatives; no change in procedures to make the plant more safe; and no adjustment in the out-of-sync contract expiration date.

The International union said that these disasters were largely P-9's own fault for "breaking with the chain," though it added that the company had gone too far in demanding a two-tier wage structure.[1] The Austin city council, the local Chamber of Commerce, and a "Committee for Positive Action" all demanded that P-9 drop its corporate campaign and just take the company's contract offer before the town's money tree withered away. The "committee" went so far as to post a full-sized billboard on Main Street reading "Ray Rogers Must Go," and took out newspaper advertisements offering similarly worded bumper stickers.

And always there were the slights and biases of the area press: Local television station KAAL and the *Austin Daily Herald* were unabashed in their favoritism toward the company; the *Minneapolis Star and Tribune* and the *Rochester Post-Bulletin* were not much better. "Hormel CEO 'cares and hurts' but not giving in" read the headline of one *Star and Tribune* article, in which a reporter who regularly covered the conflict sighed, "There are times when Dick Knowlton lies awake at night and wonders why it's happening."[2] In early June, dissidents who opposed the campaign brought before the members a proposal to accept the $9.00- and $10.00-per-hour package that existed in other Hormel plants. This became, in essence, a vote on whether to discontinue or go ahead with the campaign. On the day before that vote, the *Post-Bulletin* carried a lengthy story, "Local P-9 at a cross-roads," that allowed dissidents (quoted but for the most part unnamed in the story), the company, and Lewie Anderson to attack the local's campaign and misrepresent Corporate Campaign's fees. The article was accompanied by a cartoon "done by dissident members" that depicted Rogers as a cheerleader whose only goal was money and who would be pleased if the plant closed.[3] (Local members turned down the proposal—thus voting to continue the campaign—four to one.)

How fantastic, then, to do something more than vote: to take dramatic action and show all the know-it-alls that P-9 was not impressed with their knowledge. To show all who regarded them as merely means to Hormel's ends that they were human beings and they were calling some shots here too.

In 1968 striking Memphis sanitation workers carried signs reading "I Am A Man." It was a statement against the racism that had defined them as boys, but also a statement that they were human, no matter what the Memphis politicians said. Austin strikers' first buttons read "P-9 Proud"; picket signs read "Families Fighting For Dignity." They, too, felt the need to scream out their humanity to their employer. Carol Kough (whose husband, a striker, also served as Austin's mayor) repeated a common sentiment to the *Milwaukee Journal*:

> The workers have to raise their hands to go to the bathroom now. If they bring up any problem, they're told there's 5,000, 6,000 people waiting for their job. It's very degrading. I think if people had their dignity and could say hello to the foreman, this would have been settled a long time ago.[4]

■ ■ ■

Rogers had begun planning for a strike months earlier. As the summer months passed, and a strike looked more and more likely, he began gathering maps of the surrounding area and familiarizing himself with the other towns in which Hormel had operations. Once the strike began, he conducted four two-hour meetings with rank-and-filers in which he described "the whole operation."

The plan involved "canvassing" several hundred thousand homes across Minnesota, Iowa, and Nebraska, particularly those located in areas that were perceived to be liberal or sympathetic. Soon P-9 members were going door to door, distributing literature and discussing their issues in the Twin Cities and the small, outlying towns thereabouts; in the iron-ore region in and around Duluth; in Rochester; in Ottumwa, Iowa; and in Fremont, Nebraska. This literature included a special edition of *The Unionist*, "P-9 Fights Back," which described the issues; a leaflet entitled "Who's Behind Hormel's Cold Cuts," on the relations between the company and First Bank; and postcards that supporters could send to the bank's board and to Hormel questioning the wage cut and other bank activities and demanding a reply. Soon another leaflet was added, "Shakedown at Hormel," which showed a resolute P-9er with two guns pointing to his head, one held by a hand with a Hormel signet ring, the other by a hand with a First Bank ring. That leaflet repeated the strikers' case and announced that the strike was underway; an edition intended for Iowa distribution pointed out that "Iowa workers and farmers are under attack from a corporate combine made up of Hormel, FDL Foods [which Hormel was taking over], First Bank System, and the Banks of Iowa," of which First Bank owned 20 percent, intending to acquire the rest as soon as interstate banking laws allowed.

Following the initial literature distribution, the plan suggested that P-9ers should go out en masse to escalate pressure on the bank and to establish links with workers in other towns where Hormel had its key operations. According to Rogers, too often strikes lose power because workers remain isolated and inactive on picket lines in front of their plants while the company takes other steps to make up for the lost production. Rather than fall into this trap, P-9 would put a minimum number of pickets outside the Austin plant and send the rest out to build the fight across the country.[5]

Thus on August 23 a thousand strikers and supporters (including perhaps 200 from the Twin Cities) took their protest to First Bank headquarters in downtown Minneapolis. Their "bannering" line completely ringed the downtown block, and their loud chanting ("First Bank chooses, Austin loses") distracted office workers from their labors. One union member reported handing out 300 leaflets in an hour. This went on from 10 A.M. till mid-afternoon, followed by further bannering at the bank's suburban branches.

Perhaps the most dramatic instance of this approach came on August 26, when 300 P-9 members pulled out of

Austin in a caravan of cars and motorcycles for a five-day tour of Dubuque, Ottumwa, Sioux City, Algona, and Knoxville, Iowa; Rochelle, Illinois; Beloit, Wisconsin; and Fremont, Nebraska. Hormel had facilities in all but Sioux City. In towns with Hormel plants, the strategy included leafleting every home in the town, then lining up P-9ers in front of the plant, not to block entry, but to show their potential strength and to greet workers as they came off shift. In Iowa the strikers also "bannered" Banks of Iowa branches, questioning whether First Bank's intention to spread its empire across state lines truly benefited Iowans.

Rogers, Allen, and I traveled along with the caravan. Perhaps 25 men rode on big motorcycles, leading the way. The caravan that followed included cars, trucks, and recreational vehicles of every description. The three of us traveled in a rented Chevy Nova. It was tiny and slow compared with many of the other cars in the caravan, but nevertheless Rogers, who insisted on driving, pushed his way to the front of the pack whenever we fell behind.

With its rolling hills and pleasant, small-college campuses, Dubuque, the first stop on the tour, did not live up to my preconceptions of flat, characterless Iowa. But the FDL plant there was anything but pleasant: It was a long, run-down brick affair, situated down by the railroad tracks. Unlike more modern facilities that are surrounded by manicured grounds and set back from the road, the building stood right next to the sidewalk, so that any passerby could hear the final, all-too-human-sounding squeals of the pigs being slaughtered.

We spent a long, hot afternoon there. The 300 P-9ers stood along both sides of the road in front of the plant, waved and flashed their picket signs at the passing traffic, and attempted to engage FDL workers in conversation, over the objections of Business Agent Mel Moss and local executive board members, who handed out a counter-leaflet "provided by the national union." P-9 had made arrangements to camp about four miles outside town, and the strikers invited any FDL workers they could speak with to come by that evening to share a keg and some conversation.

The FDL workers were particularly underprivileged: Full-time workers earned only $7.75 per hour and part-timers, of whom the second shift was primarily composed, earned as little as $3.65 an hour. Few had ever seen their substandard union contract. Moss and other local officers attempted to play upon the disparity between the FDL and the Hormel wages, saying that the Austin people were greedy and presumptuous in asking the poorly paid FDL workers for "help."

For all of these reasons, and because my experience had been that few Americans would come out for a night union meeting when they could be home watching "Three's Company," I was dubious that any FDL workers would come out.

But I was wrong. As P-9 vice president Lynn Huston recalled:

> The local had about 15 to 20 older people who really knew something about unionism, and the rest were young people who were really scared and didn't question anything Moss told them. That evening people started rolling in to see us, mostly young part-timers from the second shift. They'd bring big droves of people over to talk to me, to ask how things should work. They had no idea about how to bring up resolutions, and they didn't know anything at all about the union's grievance procedure. I couldn't believe that they were ever in a union, because they knew absolutely nothing.
>
> It was just unbelievable. Well, we talked for about two

or three hours. Finally, one of them said, pointing to me: "This guy's really smart—you ought to run him for office." Some of our guys started smiling, and somebody finally said, "He's our vice president." These guys couldn't believe it: "Jesus Christ, what happened to the pinstripe suit?" they said.[6]

Though nobody said so, Huston's shoulder-length hair, earring, and hip manner probably made him seem an even less likely officeholder.

Many FDL workers had grievances similar to those of the Austin people, but it remained unclear whether they had the inclination to do anything about them. As one longtime worker recounted:

Seven years ago you'd work your ass off for the incentive, and then the company demanded that incentive pay be reduced by 15 percent. So, the people voted for it. Then they said we're taking half of it away, and the people went along with it. Then they said we're going to take the incentive pay altogether or move the plant. So, the people gave in to that too. Then the company bought plants in Rochelle and Milwaukee. They said, "Either you take a cut in wages or we'll shift everything there." Ultimately, they did shut the kill and cut, moving them to Rochelle.[7]

But in addition to those who expressed such grievances, there were among the FDL workers a number of "double dippers"—older workers who were looking forward to retirement, when they would collect pensions both from the plant's former owner, Dubuque Packing, and from FDL. "They weren't going to do anything that would risk their pensions, which could mean as much as $15.00 an hour," reported P-9 member Merrell Evans.[8]

The next day we moved on to Ottumwa, 160 miles south of Dubuque and 300 from Austin. And the mild success of Dubuque in no way prepared us for what we found there.

Ottumwa had been a strong union town: In 1937, the United Packinghouse Workers had established a beachhead at the Morrell & Co. plant there—the site of a number of walkouts and strikes—and the United Auto Workers also had a strong local at the town's John Deere facility. But Ottumwa had taken a real kicking when Morrell closed its plant, as the boarded-up windows of many small businesses showed. Earlier in the summer, when six carloads of P-9ers had come down to meet with supporters and to leaflet the town, there had been mixed reactions: Many people were fearful that P-9 would bring the problems of Austin to Ottumwa. But P-9 members in the late August caravan were greeted by their fellow Hormel workers like lost relations.

The strikers spent the morning leafleting neighborhoods and bannering at the Union Bank and Trust, one of the Banks of Iowa. Then we all went to the Hormel plant, which lies a good distance out from the center of town and sits back several hundred feet from the nearest road, safely behind a wire fence. There, along both sides of the road and extending 300 feet on each side of the plant, the Austin people threw up their most energetic informational picket of the trip during the hottest hours of the afternoon.

The reaction was electric. Truck drivers making deliveries to the plant and others who drove by showed enthusiastic agreement with the horn-shaped P-9 signs that urged them to "Honk For Labor." From the dock at the rear of the plant, workers raised clenched fists to show solidarity with the P-9 members, who were by this point screaming themselves hoarse to be heard, chanting, "We're gonna win, we're gonna win." And as each department came off work for the day, the workers walked to their cars, then drove past the fence and company security booth to the outside world, where P-9 leafleters greeted them and invited them to "come down to the campsite to roast the corporate weenie" that evening.

Hundreds of them did, assembling in an open-air pavilion. Again, Huston recalls the scene:

> About 80 percent of the local's membership came down to the city park where we were staying to hear what we had to say. After a while, since neither Guyette or Winkels was there, I got up to speak. I was sort of nervous, because there were maybe a thousand people there, and I wasn't used to speaking in front of such large groups. I said something about how it was obvious that we had the same enemy and that I was happy to see the response they were giving us. At first, nobody said anything. Then, I saw that there was a whole line of people standing at the left side of the stage, waiting to speak.
>
> One after another they got up and talked. They said they were so moved by what we were trying to do that they couldn't help themselves. A lot of them had tears in their eyes. They said we had to stick together, that it was the only way we'd get fair treatment. This went on for about an hour and a half. It was a little bit like a religious meeting: Guys would say, "I haven't always been a good union man, but I'm here to tell you now that I've changed." About seven or eight said that they'd never been able to say the word "Austin" before without following it with the word "assholes." They'd always wondered what Austin people looked like. Now, they said, "we know that you're just like us."

Thereafter, Huston said, Austin people, who'd frequently made Iowans the brunt of their jokes, "felt we couldn't tell any Ioweejan jokes any more."[9]

The next day, small groups went off to Algona, Knoxville, Rochelle, and Beloit, as the main body of the caravan set off for Fremont and a possible confrontation with the Nebraska state police. That state had a stiff—and probably unconstitutional—law that made it illegal to have more than two pickets within 50 feet of any entrance to the premises being picketed or any picket within 50 feet of any other picket. P-9's officers and Rogers were not sure what to expect. "We were warned that the state troopers were waiting to attack us," Rogers recalled. "I had visions of the sort of justice that the civil rights movement had faced in the South. And you know that the other side might send in professional troublemakers to start violence as a pretext for the police to smash you. As it turned out, though, we had the police eating out of our hands."[10]

The Nebraska state police had also been warned: The company had said to them that they should expect a violent scene as had occurred in past IBP strikes, with P-9ers attempting to beat up the Fremont workers. In fact, P-9ers intended just the opposite. Just as in Ottumwa, the strikers fanned out along the plant's perimeter road, immediately establishing an atmosphere much more like a celebration than a riot. Women and small children from Austin and Fremont were present. And, as ever, P-9 spokespeople and Rogers exuded courtesy and goodwill, following the instructions of the police—who were lined along the opposite side of the road—to the letter.

Several of the Fremont workers had worked in Austin, and others had family ties to the Austin workers. Thus, as they came out of the plant and crossed the road to the parking lot, there were greetings, shouted nicknames, and handshakes. The scene was only slightly less exuberant than in Ottumwa, to the puzzlement of the state police, who were left standing around idle, suffering through the sweltering afternoon heat with the rest of us. Before long, P-9 members were offering them water. At the end of the day, P-9 member Al McDowell, who had become a star performer via the union's bullhorn, effusively congratulated the State Patrol on their performance and thanked them for being there.

A meeting to discuss the crises facing Hormel workers was held at Fremont UFCW Local 22's hall that evening. The small auditorium was packed with several hundred workers, though only one local executive board member came, and local president "Skip" Niederdeppe announced that he had to be out of town.

The tone of the meeting was much more sober than that in Ottumwa. Guyette, who had rejoined the caravan after missing the Ottumwa activities, announced that P-9 had come to break down any barriers that existed and to answer any questions that the Local 22 members might have. He described the UFCW's retrenchment policy and the way that the spiral of concessions never seemed to stop. He told how during P-9's negotiations, "it became clear to us that the company was positioning for impasse," refusing to move from its final offer or to consider any contract expiration date that would put P-9 in sync with the expiration of any other Hormel contract. He described how the company–First Bank ties were reproduced in ties between the recent Hormel acquisition FDL and the Banks of Iowa, which shared board members. Finally, he turned to the topic that everyone understood as our real reason for being there, the possibility of Austin's extending its picket lines to Fremont:

The International has told us that we must get their sanction before we can have any roving picket lines. But
federal labor law says that we have the right to follow our
struck work [when it is farmed out to other plants]. We
intend to take advantage of that law. Right now we're only
doing informational stuff and putting our real pressure on
the bank. But if we get into a situation where people are
taking our jobs, we may not do a lot of asking [for sanc-
tion]. And if we get into a situation where everybody is
out in Ottumwa and Fremont, nobody in Austin will go
back until everybody in Ottumwa and Fremont goes
back.[11]

Many Fremont workers present took exception to
Guyette's comments, frequently raising questions about P-9's
past behavior. "We were told that there was a chain motion to
support whatever P-9 wanted and you turned down our help.
Is that true?" one worker asked. He was told that the motion
was instead to help P-9 "achieve the chain agreement" of
$10.00—in essence a resolution to cease its fight against con-
cessions. "Skip told us P-9 broke away from us and don't want
to have nothing to do with us because they feel they can do
better on their own. Yes or no, was that said?" another asked.
He was given a long account of Anderson's demand that the
P-9 board "guarantee" support for a 1984 chain-wide strike in
spite of its ongoing contract's no-strike pledge, and how P-9
was called a "noose around the neck of the chain" because it
could negotiate only on wages and not on benefits as well, as
the other locals wished. "We didn't remove ourselves from
the chain—obviously we walked because we didn't fly or hop
out—but we were congratulated by the others for stepping
aside and allowing them to go ahead with their negotiations
while we arbitrated ours," Guyette responded.

Rogers answered questions about how much Corporate Campaign was charging, countering accusations made in a recently released UFCW report that CCI was bankrupting the local.

A number of Fremont workers stood up for the Austin strikers. Said one: "We're increasing our production—up by 5 percent two weeks ago—to keep you guys out of work. And our bargaining committee people say we have to do it till we can arbitrate the issue. I say we ought to have a new election of officers and get these people the hell out of here." A woman said, "We're getting a little tired of being fooled. We've all got to get together."

Many wished to know how much money the local ought to send to help the strikers. Others said that Local 22 ought to be more like P-9, showing some pride by getting Local 22 hats and turning out in force for membership meetings. And a number expressed uncertainty about what was in their contract and wanted to know whether they had the right to honor a roving picket, since that contract remained unsigned.[12]

Like the one in Ottumwa, the Fremont meeting was a major step forward for rank-and-file unionism in that it allowed the average Hormel meatpacker to see and speak with counterparts from another local. But it also illustrated the heavy obstacles standing in the way of further such development— the distrust and uncertainty encouraged by the company and rival union officials over the years. Ottumwa had provided a heady draught of deeply felt commonality; but the Fremont meeting showed that more than deep feelings were needed if P-9 was to bring about a revival of democratic meatpacker unionism in the Midwest.

There were fundamental differences between the work forces of the two plants: Ottumwa, which had only opened in 1974, had almost all young workers. In Fremont—already an old plant when the company acquired it in 1947—the average worker was in his fifties, and perhaps half of the work force had 25 years seniority. "Fifty percent of these older workers just want to get their two more years in and retire," said one younger Fremont worker at the meeting. "They don't care what happens to the young guys, who are getting screwed." Whether as part of a conscious plan or not, those older workers also tended to "talk Austin down," in Huston's words.

In Ottumwa, there were more people who had been transferred from plant to plant, people who had experienced some abuse at the hands of the company. And as a group they had been coerced into taking the 1984 concessionary contract. Fremont workers, on the other hand, had often been favored by the company: Their contract was better than Ottumwa's, and they were allowed to keep the production system longer than any other plant.[13]

Still, the Fremont workers were, like the Ottumwans, impressed with the size of the caravan and the enthusiasm and confidence of the strikers. "You could look out of the plant lobby and see that there were 300 people out there lining the road," recalled Local 22 member Bob Langemeier, who became a key P-9 supporter. "Everyone had to be impressed that so many people came all that way—especially when we couldn't get 20 people to come to a union meeting across town."[14]

Though I was amazed at the response that the P-9 caravan elicited, Rogers was not. "The caravan, like everything else I've come up with, was just pure common sense," he told me. "You have to make a big impact in such times, to make a show of strength. We'd done the organization, we'd sent people on ahead of us, and we'd built the spirit. When people see something like that, they want a piece of it—they feel they've just got to see this, they've got to touch it."[15]

"It was a new and brilliant tactic thought up by Ray," Guyette said later. "Or, if he didn't think it up, it was a tactic that had been lost. I didn't know what kind of reaction we'd get, but I felt people were upset in all the plants, that they were hungry for information, and they felt that the UFCW was withholding important information from them. The caravan put a lot of local officers in a difficult position: They couldn't tell their people not to talk to us, yet they feared that we might wake up a sleeping giant."[16]

Sunburned and bone weary, we departed the next morning, winding our way back to Austin by way of Sioux City, Iowa. There, we threw up a brief informational picket in front of the First National Bank. It proved a good end to the trip, as local citizens waved and shouted their enthusiastic support for P-9. A Swift Independent meatpacking plant had closed on the very day of our arrival, so Sioux City residents felt a special identity with the strikers. Television crews and journalists of every description showed up to find out about the union campaign and to question the members about their caravan. And the hit-and-run picketing even drew a positive mention from the bank's chief officer, who told reporters that he had "no problem" with what the union members were doing.

Hormel Senior Vice President and General Counsel Charles Nyberg did have a problem, though. So did the UFCW.

Nyberg had followed the caravan on each step of its journey, to offer the company's side of the story to the press and "to observe firsthand what kind of picketing is taking place and what kind of messages they're spreading."[17] On the final day of the trip, signs of corporate nervousness showed through as Nyberg denounced the Nebraska state police for failing to enforce the state's anti-picketing law against P-9. The official in charge of the patrol, concealing his anger, responded that the pickets had presented no threat to public safety by appearing at the Fremont plant.[18]

From Ottumwa, Local 431 secretary-treasurer Louis De-Frieze spoke for UFCW officialdom in characterizing P-9's caravan. "Their whole program is to cause disunity, spread venom and make people dissatisfied with their union," he told the *Minneapolis Star and Tribune*.[19]

■ ■ ■

Back in Austin, rank-and-filers had begun to organize a plethora of committees: There were committees to encourage food donations and manage distribution, to staff an emergency hotline referring members with problems (ranging from stress to heat and utilities shutoffs) to helpful parties, to renovate the union hall, and to provide security and constant contact with the picket teams at the Hormel plant gates. A clothing committee set up a showroom in the basement of the hall that was filled with donated garments. A kitchen committee cooked up great vats of soup or stew and piles of sandwiches, available to anyone with an appetite at lunch- and dinnertime.

In the war room, the United Support Group, supervised by Guyette's mother-in-law, Lorraine Fossum, oversaw regular assembly-line mass mailings, with lists and materials provided by Corporate Campaign. The first 50,000-piece mailing (which became the prototype for the several others that would follow) encouraged readers to join the fight against Hormel's "concessions shakedown" by donating to P-9's Emergency and Hardship Fund.

The Communications Committee oversaw the small teams that went out to speak to union gatherings across the country. And a sign committee organized customized and mass production of hundreds of signs for picketing, erected a ten-foot-high fist emblazoned "Solidarity Growing" to stand outside the union hall, drew a huge map of the United States that pinpointed the sources of financial aid coming in to the local, and painted a six-panel wall mural depicting the struggles of American workers since the country's founding.

Committees' weekly meetings and daily activities led numerous observers to characterize the union hall as "a beehive of activity." But it also became a place where strikers came merely to hang out and gossip, to try out ideas for other activities on each other, the local officers, and Rogers—who regularly had a line of members standing outside the *Unionist* office that he had claimed as a base of operations. Striker Cecil Cain described the scene: "On the third day of the strike we met with Ray, each person describing what he'd do. I spent two days leafleting in Rochester. Then one Thursday I went by the hall and it was chaos. I realized that we needed somebody up front to direct traffic." Thus Cain became first a traffic cop, then custodian of a card file through which the local kept track of each striker's activity. In time he also made out weekly bar graphs that showed how many members had put in the required six hours work, and how many were above or below average, based on information received from the coordinators of each committee. When it was discovered that a striker was not doing enough, he or she was telephoned and encouraged to do more. (Cain's notes from December, one of the most intense periods of the strike, show that around five hundred were putting in an above-average number of hours, while nine-hundred-odd others were below average.)[20]

The traffic cop function became all the more important in early September, with the first of many big events that drew crowds of outside supporters to Austin. Back in March 1985, a Twin Cities Support Committee had been formed by Macalester College professor Peter Rachleff, UAW Local 879 president Tom Laney, Carleton College professor Paul Wellstone, steelworker Dave Foster, and many others. That committee and member unions, including Laney's Ford local in St. Paul and the Minnesota Education Association, became the first to sponsor a food caravan—composed of dozens of cars and vans and a semi truck filled with bread, potatoes, canned goods, and other staples.

"Hormel is not going to starve you out, we're going to see to that," Bud Schulte, a former meatpacker at the closed Iowa Pork plant in St. Paul, told the hundreds of P-9ers who rallied at a nearby baseball park after the delivery. The delivery was a big morale booster, encouraging P-9 to send out representatives to build support groups elsewhere, including, immediately, Youngstown, Cleveland, Pittsburgh, California, and New York.[21]

■ ■ ■

While the 300 P-9ers were touring through Iowa and Nebraska, there were two developments that boded ill for the union campaign. On August 20, Hormel announced that it had earned $9.5 million in its third quarter, an 83.6 percent increase over the level a year earlier.[22]

Whether or not this demonstrated that the company did not need wage concessions to stay competitive, it indicated that Hormel was in a strong position to withstand both a strike and a pressure campaign aimed at its financial backers.

Then, on August 28, the company announced that it was implementing its final contract offer—though it had no intention of opening the plant for "probably three months or longer"—and that it had filed a complaint of an unfair labor practice with the National Labor Relations Board, asking it to seek a federal court injunction to block further union activities at First Bank. "We feel Local P-9 and Corporate Campaign have been engaged in illegal secondary boycott activities almost from the day Corporate Campaign came to Austin," Nyberg said.[23] Hormel followed its complaints about Minnesota activity with complaints alleging similar secondary activity in Nebraska and Iowa (eventually, five such complaints were lodged).[24]

Guyette and Rogers responded positively to the secondary boycott charges when informed of them during P-9's five-day road trip. "We didn't threaten, coerce or restrain anybody," said Guyette. "It's obvious that the bank and the company are feeling the heat." "When Jim told me about the charges over the phone, I said, 'That's great news,'" Rogers announced to the gathering in Fremont. "Why? Because the company is feeling so much pressure that they have to take extreme measures to intimidate us. The campaign is working."[25] And Rogers carried on the bank campaign by taking a caravan of 80 union members to Duluth, where, after neighborhood canvassing, they joined with other unionists and members of Citizens Organizations Acting Together (COACT) to banner First Bank Duluth's downtown office.[26]

But on September 9 the NLRB's regional office ruled that picketing and distributing handbills outside First Bank branches did in fact constitute an illegal secondary boycott and moved to get a federal injunction that would give the ruling the force of law.[27]

P-9's leaders saw the ruling as an attack upon their basic rights. "This is something that could eventually go to the highest court in the land," Pete Winkels told a reporter. "We have rights that are guaranteed us under the Constitution, and we are talking about something that transcends this labor dispute. People have the right to demonstrate peacefully, and I don't think any company or bank can say that we can or can't do that."[28]

The very day after the NLRB ruling, 80 P-9ers were stretched out across three blocks in front of Des Moines' Valley National Bank (part of the Banks of Iowa system). "Keep 1st Bank Out of Iowa," their signs read, along with "Stop Hormel Greed." "Union members did not try to stop work on downtown construction projects and did not impede traffic into the bank," reported the Associated Press, "but their chants—and the horns of sympathizing truckers and other motorists—echoed off downtown buildings and could be heard for blocks."[29]

The next day 400 bannered First Bank St. Paul, competing in volume with the University of Minnesota cheerleaders' and band's "Salute to [Coach] Lew Holtz and the Golden Gophers," which was taking place in Federal Plaza across the street. "Lew Holtz has his fight and we have ours," said one P-9 member. Cheerleaders crossed the street to give Gopher buttons to the meatpackers, some of whom switched from union chants to "Win, Gophers, Win." However, the Gophers did not join P-9 as it went off to picket the NLRB's Minneapolis office.[30]

Thereafter, P-9 could be seen at First Bank branches or those of related banks in Rochester, Albert Lea, and Austin. A caravan of 200 also went to Sioux Falls, South Dakota, to extend the hand of solidarity to a group of Morrell workers who had gone on strike September 1 over company demands to reduce wages to $8.00 an hour—a 75-cent cut. Austin workers joined the Morrell strikers' picket line and invited them to visit the P-9 campsite, even though UFCW staff attempted to block their path. The strikers also bannered at First Bank of South Dakota.[31]

On September 23, U.S. District Court Judge Edward Devitt—who would in time become a P-9 nemesis—issued a temporary injunction prohibiting any further First Bank activities.

In front of two hundred strikers who had filed through metal detectors to get into the courtroom, Devitt listened to NLRB attorney James Fox argue that First Bank had no control over Hormel and that it was a distinct and separate entity. Attorneys representing P-9 and Corporate Campaign included Jim Youngdahl, a portly, bearded Little Rock native who had often dealt with the secondary boycott question, and Rick MacPherson. They argued that P-9's First Amendment rights should not be abridged, and that First Bank was far from neutral. But in a ruling prepared and typed before the oral arguments were even delivered, Devitt found for Fox, saying that there was reasonable cause to believe that the offense had been committed. He left the merits of the case to be heard by an administrative law judge the following week.[32]

The next Wednesday, though, instead of the drawn-out battle that was anticipated, Administrative Law Judge Harold Bernard, Jr., forced the NLRB to come to an immediate settlement with P-9. Five hours of caucusing took the place of courtroom wrangling, after the NLRB's Fox proved unable to explain how P-9 members' First Bank actions could be restricted without their free-speech rights' being abridged.

Under the settlement, the Hormel complaint against P-9 would be dropped. The union still faced the restrictions of Devitt's injunction that forbade "threatening, coercing or restraining" those engaged at commerce at First Bank; but since P-9 maintained that it had never "threatened, coerced or restrained" anyone, local leaders and attorneys said that the injunction allowed almost everything they had done before. (NLRB attorneys Fox and Ronald Sharp showed their confusion, stating that the injunction was still in effect and that "nothing had changed since yesterday," but adding, "We never alleged that Corporate Campaign as a whole was in violation.") The injunction would be dropped as soon as the NLRB's Washington office approved the settlement. And in the future, all such considerations would be taken up directly in federal court, not before the NLRB, because of the considerable First Amendment questions involved.[33]

These First Amendment issues were crucial. It seems likely that both Devitt and Hormel had overdone it: Devitt had issued a very broad injunction, ruling out virtually all activities involving First Bank and ignoring the National Labor Relations Act's "publicity proviso," which states that the rule against secondary boycotts cannot restrict free speech. Meanwhile, a Hormel lawyer had gone so far as to say that the workers' free-speech rights should be suspended until the issue was decided.[34] This drew the attention of the Minnesota Civil Liberties Union. It led Minneapolis attorney Margaret Winter, already supporting the union as an activist, Emily Bass, then a partner in the New York law firm of Rabinowitz, Boudin, Standard, Krinsky and Lieberman, and colleague Linda Backiel to begin working on an *amicus* brief, funded by the National Emergency Civil Liberties Committee, that would argue these constitutional issues. It also made the case a hot potato that Bernard was anxious to avoid.

Simultaneous with these developments, P-9 experienced another grudging affirmation—this one from the Minnesota AFL-CIO. After seeing Judge Devitt rule against them, the 200 P-9 members trooped over two blocks to the St. Paul Radisson Hotel, where the state federation was holding its convention. AFL-CIO officials had been ignoring the issue of the strike, as they thought the UFCW would prefer. But once the strikers arrived and lined up outside the doors of the convention hall to shake hands with delegates, the subject of the strike could no longer be avoided. Guyette and other local officers, official delegates to the convention, received a standing ovation as they filed in.

Guyette was not allowed to address the convention— there were too many groups on strike, the AFL officials said, and so, in the interest of fairness, no one could be allowed to talk. But the local passed around a letter from Winkels describing the reasons for the strike. In it he noted:

> There is now a letter circulating from UFCW President William Wynn to Lane Kirkland stating that P-9 "unilaterally withdrew from chain negotiation." Mr. Wynn has made a grievous error and did a great deal of damage from this false and misleading statement. P-9 was not even invited to these negotiations. . . . We see politics taking precedence over people. We read in the papers that the AFL-CIO has taken a "hands off" policy toward our strike. We hear of other unions denying support because of unfounded rumors. We are not allowed to address this convention for trade unionists in Minnesota because we did not get permission from someone in Washington, D.C. . . .
>
> Please feel free to ask us anything you want or need to know. The people of this state have had a tradition and history of being able to assess and make their own decisions. We have enough faith in you to do likewise. . . . As Edmund Burke said 200 years ago, "All that is necessary for the triumph of evil, is for good men to do nothing."[35]

Dan Gustafson, state federation president, ordered that a collection be taken on the floor for all strikers, and the gathering passed a resolution "in support of all unions engaged in properly sanctioned strikes and for a just and fair resolution of the issues of the workers of Local P-9."[36]

Note that, in this wording, the issues belonged to "the workers" of P-9, rather than to the local as a whole, including its officers. Such were the continuing concessions to the UFCW. But the resolution was an endorsement of the strike, nonetheless, which gave locals official sanction to send food and money and to come in person to Austin. And that would be very important in the weeks to come.

A COMMUNITY OF THEIR OWN

My mother got involved in January of 1985. She first came down to help with one of the mailings, then she got more and more involved. And she found out that she was somebody. Money couldn't buy what it's done for her—"Gol," she said, "somebody needs me."

—Vicky Guyette describing her mother's involvement in the United Support Group[1]

By October Austin residents were bitterly divided over the question of how best to preserve their community: Should one support the strike or should one side with the employer who provided one in four of the town's paychecks? For some—most union members or members of management families—the answer was a foregone conclusion. For others, it was a question of personal loyalty to friends and ideals. But it was difficult to avoid making a choice: It became no longer possible to be loyal to the Austin community as a whole. Ultimately, divisions surfaced in every social context, including the local schools, churches, and clubs. The stores in which one shopped, the restaurants or bars patronized— every social choice was shaped by the conflict.

Most area businessmen were unmoved by the local's argument that the pre-strike wage cut had brought serious economic harm—perhaps a $700,000 reduction in the local area's payroll. There were exceptions, made plain to all by "We Support Local P-9" signs posted in the windows of a few shops, such as Klagge's Ice Cream and Star Liquors. (A supermarket like the IGA, on the other hand, might be seen as signaling its hostility to P-9 with heavy promotions of Hormel products.) But when called upon to comment, most businesspeople focused upon the harm caused by the strike rather than the company's cutbacks. An early October *Rochester Post-Bulletin* article detailed their concerns: The owner of Ferris TV said that her business had dropped by 42 percent; the Cantonese Inn, Country Store Foods grocery, and Stephens In The Mall restaurant had closed for good; on their way out of business were such Main Street ventures as Gildner's men's store and a two-story Woolworth's.

Local police commented only that they had no reports of violence due to the strike, though P-9 members felt that the authorities had made clear which side they were on with the arrest of union member Bob Johnson for making "terroristic" bomb threats.[2] Local social-welfare agencies were also seen as supporting Hormel: The Victim Crisis Center, for example, was headed by a city councilman who had taken very public positions against the local's campaign, while the United Way, the YMCA, and the Salvation Army all depended upon Hormel Foundation money for their existence.

P-9 and United Support Group bannering at First Bank Austin brought out open hostility from passersby. "Nobody had more trouble bannering than Mom," recalled Jeannie Bambrick. "She'd get headaches and bawl afterwards, because all of a sudden people you didn't even know would curse you right on the street. We were brought up to turn the other cheek."[3]

And most area churches were hostile to the strikers. "They abandoned us," said Vicky Guyette some months later. "They stabbed us in the back—a lot of us are saying the churches don't seem the same as the ones we grew up with."[4]

Faced with such division and pressure from others in Austin, P-9 members came to depend upon institutions of their own invention and upon a few loyal established institutions. With these they created a new community.

The weekly United Support Group meetings ceased to be predominantly female gatherings made up of supporters rather than workers and became instead meetings open to all, including P-9 members, relatives, children, and anyone who had a word of encouragement. Most people took this change for granted, though some women felt that something had been given away. Vicky Guyette recalled: "After the strike started, we lost something. Women weren't getting together separately. We no longer had our own private space, a place we could cry and carry on. Our meetings just turned into union meetings; it was hard to keep the two separate. In a way something died."[5]

These meetings were a source of wonder to every outsider who viewed them. Unionists from big cities, accustomed to poor attendance at monthly meetings, saw hundreds of men and women file into P-9's hall (virtually every night of the week as the crisis became more acute) to share each other's company and find out the latest developments. Marxist students who came in from across the country saw the working class behaving as they had imagined it someday would. True believers from a hodgepodge of fringe callings saw in the gatherings a chance to reach the kind of audience they had always dreamed of.

"You got to the point where it was in your blood" is how Jeannie Bambrick described it. "One night you might think that you should just take it easy and relax. But after you'd eat and do the dishes, you'd look at the clock and say, 'Let's go down to the hall and find out what's going on.' My husband Mike and I began to take turns after a while."[6]

Just about anyone could and did speak before such meetings. Members of the Communications Committee reported on meetings they had had with other union locals or citizens' groups and how much money they had raised. There were reports from other committees, such as the food shelf and the stress-hotline team known as the "Tool Box." The local's executive board discussed the developments of negotiations (though when a particularly crucial vote loomed, an official union meeting would be held with only card-carrying members allowed) and communications with the International, other unions, and public figures. Speakers representing other unions and community groups were given a respectful hearing.

And the meetings were models of democratic procedure. It was over 20 years since the publication of Students for a Democratic Society's Port Huron statement, and not many of these meatpackers had ever attended college—instead, they had gone to Vietnam or into the National Guard. Nevertheless, their key leaders and many of the rank-and-filers were members of the sixties generation, and like those students of 20 years before, it was an article of faith with them that the experts had fouled everything up. They believed that there was no real choice but to have the group discuss and vote on almost everything.

The counterpart of the support group and union meetings at the Labor Center was the more relaxed community that could always be found at a local tavern, Lefty's Bar.

Lefty's sits smack in the middle of a row of bars that lines the western side of 10th Street, right across from the railroad tracks and a dilapidated freight station. It is, perhaps, the prototypical "east side" bar: one room with a pool table, a case filled with dusty bowling trophies, and a worn but always working popcorn dispenser. On the wall behind the bar are Minnesota Vikings and Twins banners, union bumper stickers, and a sign listing "Charges for phone call lying: Just left—25¢; Leaving now—50¢; Haven't seen—$1; Who?—$2; Not here—$3.75."

On a busy night at Lefty's, people might line the bar three deep, while a few would sit at the small number of tables and booths near the rear. But whatever time of day or night, there was usually at least a small crowd gathered at the front end of the bar, near the door and the television that was always tuned to news or sports. Customers drank Schmidts or Bud, and occasionally peppermint or peach schnapps. And conversation focused on the usual barroom topics—sports, local gossip, and of course the strike.

While union people went to other places as well, such as Red's Hiawatha Bar or even the Colonial, which was not on the east side but downtown, Lefty's was where P-9ers could be sure they would find each other, and where they knew they would not find company sympathizers. (No union people would go to Tolly's Time Out, a "company bar," and they had been raised to avoid shopping at a variety of nonunion stores—a cultural holdover from the strongly enforced consumer boycotts conducted by the IUAW.)[7] After a union meeting there might be a couple hundred people crammed into Lefty's, and out-of-towners who came for big rallies quickly learned that it was the place to hang out.

However, it was apparent to all that democratic participation and good feelings were not sufficient to support this community. Many weeks of striking had strained P-9ers' resources, and $40 a week in strike pay did not go far.

Food caravans organized and paid for by supporters provided one answer to the material hardships. The first of these, organized by the group of Twin Cities unionists and union supporters who constituted the Twin Cities Support Committee, came at the end of August. The idea may have come from Jake Cooper, a supermarket owner and a supporter of labor causes since his participation in the Minneapolis general strike of 1934, though several other committee members who were well versed in labor history were aware of earlier efforts of this sort. In Cooper's words:

In the 1934 strike there was a lot of food brought in to help the Teamsters union by farmers and other organizations. I was able to get food at cost, but there was also a lot of food that was just donated from other unions and individuals. A lot of the first caravan came from us, but from then on other caravans were primarily donations. Pastor Paul, a well-known Twin Cities figure who's helped poor people, got an awful lot of food for us. We approached farm organizations, but I don't think we got much from them. And we were in constant contact with UFCW Region 13, trying to pressure them to get involved, but they didn't want to be connected with us. They saw us as outsiders, as something like "unclean." They'd always say they would contribute on their own.[8]

Region 13 did contribute significantly to a fourth, mid-October caravan, as did the Twin Cities group. (Farmstead workers from nearby Albert Lea brought a second caravan in September, and on October 4, 60 Ottumwa members and supporters delivered $2,800 worth of food, paid for by local donations.)[9] Comprising over 125 trucks, vans, and autos carrying more than a hundred tons of food, the mid-October caravan was to be the largest of the deliveries. The food was unloaded and stored in the basement of the union hall, and given out over time by a union committee. On the day of the delivery, the UFCW put out a letter crediting the "large dollar" contributions of meatpacking locals in Iowa, southern Minnesota, and Nebraska, the Minnesota AFL-CIO, and the Iowa Federation of Labor, among others.[10] Following the food delivery, there was an outdoor rally from the local, featuring on the podium such uncomfortable allies as Region 13 director Hansen, Cooper, Twin Cities Support Committee chairman Pete Rachleff, and Duluth *Labor World* editor Dick Blin.

Another answer to the problem of material need came from the fundraising done directly by the members. Since August, small P-9 "communications teams" had gone out to leaflet and collect plant gate donations at factories across the Midwest. This effort provided firsthand information about the strike to thousands of other workers and produced needed funds. "These groups of three to seven people would drive somewhere and speak before church or school audiences," reported Cecil Cain. "Sometimes they'd bring back a hell of a check."[11]

But it was Rogers who conceived of and organized several 50,000-piece mass solicitation mailings for the two funds that produced the most strike support: the Emergency and Hardship Fund and the Adopt-A-Family Fund. The first of these depended upon irregular contributions of any size from a variety of sources; money was used for emergencies such as heat shutoffs or dire medical problems. Solicitations for the latter fund, though, specifically requested that individual union locals commit themselves to contribute $100 to $1,000 every month for a period of three months in support of one "adopted" family. P-9 families who wanted to be considered would submit statements of need, which were then reviewed by an anonymous United Support Group committee that received only an identification number, not the name of the P-9er concerned.

"I'm not sure where the idea came from," Rogers told me.

Certainly I've read advertisements with celebrities urging
people to adopt kids in Third World countries. I had been
thinking that this country contains more than 13 million
organized workers in unions all over the country, and
there had to be some way for them to help prevent the
company from starving out the Hormel strikers.[12]

Over the course of succeeding months, these funds raised
more than $1 million to aid the strikers. According to Cindy
Rudd, one of the administrators of the Adopt-A-Family Fund,
generally the goal was to make sure a family had about $600
a month. Among the unions that responded with heavy donations were the National Postal Workers, the Communications Workers, and flight attendants and machinists from
Northwest Airlines, who turned over 250 checks totaling
$10,000 to the fund. According to Rudd:

Some weeks we'd have 30 to 40 families adopted, each
receiving a different amount according to need. Some
people would come in crying, they were so happy to get
their checks. Everyone was supposed to send a thank you
letter, telling the funding local what their circumstances
were. R. J. Bergstrom sent a photo of his family holding
their check to the unions that adopted them, and Mike
and Jeannie Bambrick made posters that they sent.[13]

■ ■ ■

In early October Governor Rudy Perpich called upon the district director of the Federal Mediation and Conciliation Service to get both sides together for further negotiations. As a
result, mediator Hank Bell arranged for the parties to meet

on October 14. Virtually at the same time, the UFCW sent the local a mailgram urging it "to re-evaluate your entire program, reassess the terrible price paid by Austin members, to reappraise your objectives . . . and finally to objectively reconsider how best to secure an acceptable resolution."[14]

But nothing was accomplished in that bargaining session. The parties met for 90 minutes face to face, and then met separately with Bell and another mediator shuttling back and forth, for the remainder of the day. No progress was made; no further talks were scheduled. Hormel plant manager Deryl Arnold said that to his knowledge no new proposals were offered or compromises made. (He overlooked the local's proposal to tie wages to company profits in a way that would guarantee Hormel its highest profits ever; the company rejected the offer immediately.) Guyette said that the company refused to move away from the offer that the local had turned down in August.[15]

Two months of striking had brought no weakening of the will of either Hormel or P-9. For its part, the UFCW International continued to snipe openly at the local. And the bank campaign remained a hot issue: Hormel filed a further NLRB complaint against P-9, this time citing demonstrations at First Bank's Wisconsin branches. Before the NLRB's Washington office could rule on the September settlement worked out before Administrative Law Judge Bernard, the regional office again found for the company and ruled the Wisconsin demonstrations illegal. All these cases would now be brought before another administrative law judge.[16]

With things at this pass, P-9's leaders and Rogers felt that nothing remained but to turn up the heat: They began a serious discussion of extending P-9's pickets to Hormel's other plants, where struck work was being performed.

■ ■ ■

Other locals, of course, knew that it might be only a matter of time before P-9 extended its picket lines. That possibility had been mentioned over the summer prior to the strike on the several occasions when P-9 officers traveled to Fremont and Ottumwa to address union members there. Many of those union members thought that they might face P-9 pickets as early as August, when the large caravan traveled to Dubuque, Ottumwa, Fremont, and elsewhere. On that occasion, a memo from the law firm that represented several locals, Cotton, Watt, Jones & King, was distributed widely among the Ottumwa work force. This memo evenhandedly discussed the Ottumwa contract provisions that touched on the matter of "sympathy strikes," citing section 6.4, which stated:

> It is agreed that in the event an authorized picket line is in effect at the entrance to the plant, the Company shall not discipline employees who choose to honor such picket line. The Union agrees to use whatever influence they possess to remove such picket line from the plant.

The memo continued that it

> is not totally clear as to what is meant by an "authorized" picket line but the most reasonable interpretation would presumably be that it is a picket line which is authorized by the local union which placed the picket line there and, if the International Constitution requires, by whatever International Union authority is empowered to give such approval.

The memo added that the contract might be interpreted by

the Reagan-appointed NLRB as giving the individual protection, while leaving the union liable to penalties.[17]

After that caravan, P-9 members paid regular visits to the sites of other Hormel plants. In early October, P-9 members distributed literature to Hormel and FDL workers in Fremont, Ottumwa, Knoxville, Dubuque, Algona, Beloit, and Rochelle. Leaflets described P-9 activities, the details of the company's implemented contract, and the union's "preparations to deal with the struck work being performed by union members and with the possible re-opening of the Austin plant using strikebreakers." One leaflet read:

> DON'T ALLOW YOURSELF TO BE USED AS A STRIKEBREAKER Austin Local P-9 members are now in the 10th week of a strike. . . . Though there are indications that our strike is hurting them, the company claims to be unaffected. . . . THIS MEANS THAT YOUR LABOR IS BEING USED AGAINST US— AND IF THAT WORKS, THE COMPANY WILL USE OUR LABOR TO DEFEAT YOU WHEN YOUR CONTRACTS EXPIRE. . . . When we visit your plants next, we will have signs and literature that will make our intentions clear. At that point, ALL EYES WILL BE ON YOU: you will have the undivided attention of the meatpacking industry, the entire labor movement and the national media. . . .[18]

And on October 19, Austin members voted to pledge their support to any other union member who honored an extended P-9 picket line: No one would go back until everyone went back, they said.[19] Afterward, Rogers set up a phone bank to call other Hormel and FDL members, ask whether they would honor such a line, and reassure them of P-9's mutual support.

In Ottumwa, supporters circulated petitions encouraging the International to sanction an extension of P-9 pickets, and over 500 of approximately 750 workers signed. Similarly, in Fremont P-9 supporter Bob Langemeier got as many as 400 of his co-workers (in a plant employing around 850) to sign letters to Wynn urging him to grant the sanction. Unlike the Ottumwa contract, Fremont's did not specifically address the matter of extended pickets; neither did it contain the customary ban on striking during the life of the agreement, in effect giving Fremont members wide latitude.[20]

P-9 officers felt that they had won some allies in these two other Hormel locations at least. They also had an analysis of how the two locals differed from each other—and what those differences meant for P-9. As stated earlier, the Fremont workers were considerably older and therefore, one might reason, more conservative than the Ottumwa workers. Some also said that they were more privileged. "I always thought Ottumwa would be a stronger ally than Fremont," said P-9 board member Carl Pontius:

> I knew people who had gone there [Ottumwa] from Fort Dodge, where I worked before. I also felt the election of Dan Varner as steward—somebody who knew how they screw people around—was a big step for us. And I knew the history of the Fremont local—that they'd always been the first to give in. They made less money than others because they weren't willing to fight, they just leached off what Austin and Fort Dodge could win for them. But Guyette felt Fremont would be stronger for us, since a number of former Austin people worked there.[21]

Many months later, Guyette said that perhaps he had expected too much from Fremont. In hindsight, he said, one should have recognized that over the years Fremonters had been made to feel that "they were the cog that made the company run," and he observed that "Anderson always looked to

Fremont to start the vilification against P-9." But Guyette and Winkels had reason to expect support from Fremont, since it had been virtually promised them by Local 22 member and former Austinian Jerry Rosenthal.

Rosenthal, a hog-kill worker, emerged as the spokesman for the group that had been laid off from the old Austin plant and subsequently transferred to Fremont. His activism led to his election to the Local 22 bargaining committee. "He said he'd get everyone to honor any roving pickets and talked like this was something that had to be done," Guyette said. "'We're stuck down here,' he'd say, 'Let's make sure that the company doesn't divide us.' "[22]

Such grass-roots support led to what seemed for a while to be the biggest turnaround of the campaign: UFCW International president Wynn's statement of support for P-9's extended picketing in the absence of good-faith negotiating on the part of the company.

"We always thought that Wynn might be a reasonable man," reflected Winkels. "We thought that instead of dealing with Lewie or Jay Foreman, if we could talk to the top guy, maybe it would be better. Everyone was looking for some ray of hope."[23]

On October 4, Wynn had telegraphed Guyette that pickets were not to be extended beyond Austin. But later that same month Guyette sought out Wynn at an AFL-CIO meeting in California, where he encouraged him to consider the local's position and formally requested roving picket sanction. There followed a five-hour meeting in Chicago attended by the many Hormel chain representatives, including executive boards from Austin, Fremont, and Ottumwa. As many as thirty P-9 rank-and-filers stood outside the meeting. Guyette described the proceedings:

Not many people said anything. I remember that the president of the Beloit local attacked us as being selfish, and I said, "We're committed to all getting back to work or none of us will return." But the real turning point of the meeting came when Wynn found out that people were real ticked off. The Ottumwans delivered a strong message of support for P-9.[24]

At the end of the meeting, the local and the International issued a joint public declaration that, among other things, stated:

> The Local Union and the International are deeply concerned with the issues of health, safety, an effective grievance procedure, common contract expiration dates and worker dignity as well as economic matters. Local P-9 has pledged to negotiate in good faith and, in response to employer modifications in its final offer, is prepared to modify its proposals. If Hormel fails or delays in bargaining in good faith, the International union will sanction extension of P-9's picket lines to other Hormel operations.[25]

The announcement was heralded by banner headlines in Minnesota newspapers. "International union gives support to P-9" read the title of the *Rochester Post-Bulletin* account, which quoted Lewie Anderson as saying, "We are happy to report we are all of one mind." "It makes us feel good to have this kind of solidarity again," Guyette told the reporter. And UFCW press relations spokesman Allen Zack, who read the statement to reporters, told the *St. Paul Pioneer Press and Dispatch* that the decision to extend picketing "could come as early as tomorrow" and that it could affect one plant or "it could be all" of them.[26]

"I believed it was real—everybody did," said P-9 rank-and-filer Dan Allen several months later. "It sounded good," reflected Guyette, who had information that the company was running so low on inventory that it had sent 150 management personnel in to run bacon bits, bacon, and Spam lines in the idle Austin plant. At the other plants, orders were being shorted, while workers were being told that they would have to work Saturdays and Sundays at double-time pay. "We were ready to send the pickets at a time that would have really hurt Hormel, during the Christmas rush," he continued. "We thought at least it was a statement that Wynn would find it difficult to get out of."[27]

P-9's new leaflet describing the accord at FDL and the other Hormel plants was entitled "UNITED UFCW TO HORMEL: Bargain or We'll Shut All Your Plants Down."[28] Then, assisted by mediator Hank Bell, the company and the union scheduled a negotiating session for November 15. It would be only the second such meeting since the strike began.

■ ■ ■

Union negotiators met with attorney Rollins two days before their meeting with Hormel to examine their position. Rollins said P-9 should make a reasonable new offer and reviewed the local's chief concerns: maintaining the guaranteed annual wage and seniority; getting back to the pre-1984 package of escrow, insurance, and wages; on-the-job safety and the high production standards; frustration over the inert grievance and arbitration procedure; the term of the contract; and the union's desire to reinstate a past-practice clause.

Perhaps the most conservative member of the union board, Keith Judd, said that P-9 must "make their position clear on the guaranteed annual wage." The board as a whole

was adamantly opposed to Hormel's apparent desire to abolish this provision. Floyd Lenoch hoped that they could persuade the company simply to go back to the 1978 agreement.
And Jim Retterath, whom Rollins later characterized as a
moderate, John "Skinny" Weis, and Lynn Huston all agreed
that P-9 should narrow down its issues to the most important
and try to show Hormel that they were willing to compromise.[29]

On the day of the meeting with Hormel, UFCW regional
director Joe Hansen joined the union committee, along with
International representative Al Vincent. (Almost two and a
half years later, Lewie Anderson told me in an interview that
he had been edged aside, since he was perceived to have a
personality problem with P-9's members and leaders, and
other UFCW officers had been "slotted into the picture.")[30]
Hansen said that the joint Wynn-Guyette statement had
"caught the company short" and that he would be reporting
directly to Wynn as to whether or not Hormel was "stone-
walling."

At the meeting itself, Hormel spokesman David Larson's
opening remarks suggested little flexibility. He spoke as a
stern parent, describing the harsh facts of life to a group of
naive children.

The company was not greedy, he said: It had made $38
million in the previous year, but that was a pittance compared
with the sums drawn in by competitors like General Foods,
which earned $325 million, and Beatrice, which raked in
$888 million. The offer on the table, he continued, was com-
parable to that paid by the top 10 percent of the industry, and
he could not put company operations in jeopardy because of
the union's unwillingness to face reality. He also questioned
whether the union was truly prepared to bargain, given its

announced participation in the formation of a new, militant coalition that was having its founding convention in early December, the National Rank-and-File Against Concessions.

During the day, mediators Bell and Don Eaton shuttled back and forth between the company and the union, which only met face to face for a brief period. The mediators told the union that the company would not accept its proposals for expediting arbitrations or for using local ministers rather than professional arbitrators to settle some uncomplicated grievances. But the arbitrators did suggest a procedure for dealing more rapidly with the current backlog of grievances, dismissing some and submitting others for expedited, binding arbitration.

A subsequent meeting was arranged for November 21. On that day first Hansen, then Larson outlined the settlement reached at Morrell & Co., where a strike had also been in progress since late summer. That contract set wages at $9.00, and would raise them to $9.75 by September 1988. The rest of that day's session and the subsequent meeting held on the 23rd focused upon "problem" jobs—those held by the union to be excessively dangerous and demanding—and grievance difficulties. The company rejected the union's proposals for "baseball-style" arbitration, which P-9 felt would result in more reasonable opening positions by both sides, and for continuing the guaranteed annual wage. The mediators reported the company's position: "That boat has left the dock."[31]

Many months later Nyberg agreed to an interview with me. A short, powerfully built man who seems out of place in the expensive suits and Piaget watch he wears, he told me that P-9, not the company, was responsible for "gutting" the guaranteed annual wage, since the union's original proposals so altered the plan that it no longer contained benefits for both sides. "Livestock comes to market in gluts, and there are other times of scarcity when you don't need so many workers," he said. "The old tradeoff meant that the company didn't have to pay penalty pay for times when the raw material needed to get processed immediately," and also that workers would not be laid off in slack times.[32]

Such an interpretation seems opportunistic. P-9 negotiators had indeed proposed both time-and-a-half pay for overtime—the standard setup in most workplaces—and retention of 40 hours' pay even when the work week was shorter, along with a 52-week notice of layoffs. But they did not stand firm behind the overtime demand and repeatedly argued for retention of the guaranteed annual wage. Had it wanted to, Hormel could have insisted on keeping the traditional guaranteed wage setup; instead, it opted for the "flexible" use of workers found throughout its package.

Before the day was over, Hansen would announce that "the company is doing what they need to do to keep Bill Wynn off their back." Then Larson would tell the mediators that he was "recessing, not breaking off talks" and that in the future Hormel had to have not piecemeal proposals, but a complete package from the union, since the company already had an implemented contract.[33]

■ ■ ■

At this point negotiations were interrupted by the hearing called to deal with new illegal secondary boycott charges. Rogers had led a caravan of 50 P-9ers into Wisconsin, where they had bannered First Bank Milwaukee on October 3 and First Bank LaCrosse on October 7.[34] The new charges, backed by the NLRB on the 17th, meant, in effect, that the previous settlement was scuttled. Hormel asked that the local be found guilty of conducting a secondary boycott and be found in contempt of Judge Devitt's earlier cease-and-desist order.[35]

All charges—earlier as well as more recent ones—were consolidated and became the subject of a three-day hearing before federal Administrative Law Judge Thomas Johnston. This hearing was more dramatic than the previous one, as union attorneys now denied that First Bank represented a secondary party: The relationship between Hormel and First Bank, according to union attorney Jim Youngdahl, "far surpasses the normal manufacturer-banker relationship to a degree that the two entities are indistinguishable for purposes of economic pressure by the Union and the labor dispute." The union maintained further that its activity was not intended to sever Hormel's business relationship with First Bank and, moreover, that its "bannering" and leafleting were protected by both the publicity proviso of the National Labor Relations Act and by the First Amendment to the Constitution.[36]

To prove their case, they called two knowledgeable witnesses: Hormel chief executive Richard Knowlton and Corporate Campaign's researcher, Tina Simcich.

The administrative law judge refused, however, to allow the union to call former Hormel and First Bank director I. J. Holton, limited the time period that would be taken into consideration, and cut off all inquiry into the Hormel Foundation (which also had bank representatives on its board) and FDL Foods as irrelevant. Since the hearing officer's presumptions ran counter to the logic of "interlocking directorates" and shared corporate concerns, union attorneys were repeatedly required to narrow the scope of questioning and testimony.

Other witnesses, including Rogers, P-9 vice president Lynn Huston, and a number of investigators who had been paid by Hormel to observe and videotape First Bank demonstrations, preceded Knowlton and Simcich. In one case a videotape showed an investigator misrepresenting himself as a University of Wisconsin graduate student and attempting to get Guyette to say that P-9 wanted consumers to boycott the bank. Other investigators who testified included an off-duty deputy from the Dubuque County Sheriff's Department and an employee of an Ottumwa security firm. Several noted that "the pickets desired to have passersby conclude that the dispute was between P-9 and First Bank."[37]

Rogers testified that "Hormel and First Bank are so connected and intertwined, so intimate, that you have to view Hormel as an extension of First Bank." He described the union's mailings, the informational bannering, and door-to-door canvassing as "our own advertising program, our own billboards," and denied that any of this was intended to keep people from entering a bank, to get Hormel and the bank to sever their relationship, or to get customers to end their business with the bank. Instead, it was meant to get people to write letters, make phone calls, and "do everything that was lawful" to get the bank to use its influence and "stop being a rubber stamp" for Hormel's labor policy.

Huston seconded Rogers' testimony that the Wisconsin demonstrations were fundamentally different from the First Bank actions that had gone before: The union groups were smaller, and most were positioned much farther away from the banks—at least 300 feet. In each case, they said, only one person stood near the bank entrance handing out literature.[38]

On the following day, the union called Knowlton to the stand for an hour and a half of questions. Attorney MacPherson asked whether the personnel committee of the Hormel board of directors reviewed company labor policy (Knowlton said no), whether the board had discussed the Austin strike (it had received "updates" at four of seven meetings), whether the board had discussed the 1984 wage cut (disallowed by the administrative law judge as untimely), and how First Bank System chairman DeWalt Ankeny got onto the Hormel board. Knowlton responded that Hormel always sought input from the financial community and Ankeny's was among the best available. When MacPherson asked if there had ever been a period when there was not a First Bank official on the Hormel board, Knowlton said, "To my knowledge, no." Nor, he admitted, had any representative from the financial community on the Hormel board not come "wearing a First Bank hat."

Knowlton also acknowledged that "ultimately the board has the power" to establish labor policy. The CEO said that the Hormel dispute was never discussed at meetings of the First Bank Minneapolis board, on which he sat, and asserted that the Minneapolis bank had not been damaged by P-9's activities. MacPherson also entered into evidence a story from the Rochester newspaper in which Knowlton was quoted as saying that outside directors "have a strong influence" on Hormel company decisions. Knowlton said that he did not think the quote was accurate.

After Knowlton came Simcich, whose credentials and documentary evidence provided the strongest part of the union's case. Prior to her coming to CCI, Simcich said, she had investigated investment, tax, and personnel practices of large corporations for the Council on Economic Priorities and Corporate Data Exchange, both nonprofit research institutions, and for the United Methodist Church. Altogether, she said, she had conducted financial analyses of between 45 and 50 companies, including, with Rogers, one of the Hormel company.

During 12 years of financial analysis, she testified, "I have never seen a situation where a particular bank was so identified with a particular corporation through a multiplicity of different kinds of relationships, and the strength of those relationships," as Hormel and First Bank. Calling First Bank the "primary institution" supporting Hormel, Simcich cited links between the two entities running back to the 1920s, when the board interlocks began and George and Jay Hormel put together the capital needed to save the institution that would become First Bank Austin from failure. In 1921, the bank in turn saved the meatpacker after some serious embezzlement by a high-level officer. It did so by forming a lenders' committee that essentially ran the company. Simcich also noted that in 1981 First Bank Minneapolis and two other banks signed a major revolving-credit agreement and a $75 million long-term loan agreement with Hormel to assist in building the new Austin plant—a very unusual arrangement, since such agreements usually involve from ten to thirty banks. And she noted that First Bank managed the meatpacker's pension and profit-sharing plans, holding a total of 12.3 percent of Hormel's common stock in December 1985.

To make the case that any prohibition of such activities as the union had undertaken would represent a denial of First Amendment rights available to other kinds of groups, P-9's lawyers called three leaders of anti-apartheid and farm organizations to testify about demonstrations their groups had held at First Bank. Then the hearings recessed. Administrative Law Judge Johnston required that attorneys from both sides submit briefs of their positions by January 9.[39]

The conclusion of the hearings marked the end of the union's campaign to move Hormel by bringing pressure on First Bank; although the NLRB would not formally find the bank actions an illegal boycott till February 28, P-9 now marshalled its energies behind other tactics.[40] How, then, should we regard the First Bank strategy—as a success or a failure?

First, we must ask whether it made sense to attempt to pressure First Bank, then whether or not the pressure brought the local any relief. In an article published only a few days prior to the beginning of the strike, Professor Ken Gagala of the University of Minnesota declared the entire corporate campaign a failure. In fact, Gagala discussed only the bank campaign, which he found to be inherently flawed:

> Since seven of the 12 members of Hormel's board of directors are members of the company's management, the board is a rubber stamp for management's actions. . . . let us assume that P-9 had been able to sever the Hormel–First Bank connection. Would the campaign then have succeeded? Probably not. Hormel, according to First Bank, has no long-term debt outstanding with the bank. Instead, Hormel issues commercial paper. Moreover, even if First Bank did hold long-term debt of Hormel, it could sell its Hormel loans outstanding to a wide variety of financial institutions, thereby diffusing P-9's efforts to single out a secondary target. . . . If, in fact, First Bank is merely the administrator of Hormel pension funds, severing the Hormel First Bank connection would cost the bank its administrative fee for performing this function. But who is the loser in this transaction—First Bank or Hormel? Furthermore, could the lone First Bank representative persuade the seven Hormel managers on the corporate board to rescind the wage cut when the firm's 1984 return on equity was below the median for Fortune 500 firms?[41]

In our interview, Nyberg made similar points, noting that First Bank was not a major lender to Hormel at the time of the campaign, and that Hormel did not have much debt or need for operating capital, so "the pressure points that could be applied there would not be effective." Furthermore, he said, Ankeny was only one of 12 directors and could be easily outvoted if it came to that.[42]

As the recent spate of corporate mergers and takeovers has shown, most boards are no more than rubber stamps for a corporation's management unless forced by political or economic pressure to be something else. Hormel was no exception here. And, rhetoric aside, it is unlikely that any "connection" was going to be broken. As Simcich testified, ties between the two entities ran too deep for a real break. But Gagala and Nyberg's strictly materialistic formula leaves much to be desired. It overlooks the meatpacker's serious need for credit as recently as 1981, the key role played by First Bank in arranging for credit in that and other years, and Hormel's need to maintain support from the institutions that had historically been its creditors in order to win financing for future deals.

"You have to look at the entirety of the relationship," Simcich explained at the hearing. "And this is a case in which there are credit relationships, but there's also a very major stock relationship, there's a major relationship of interlocking directorates. . . . What is so unique is that there is a multiplicity of relationships at every level of the Hormel company's operations."[43] Such multiple and historic links meant that First Bank *did* have leverage to move Hormel, and that sufficient union pressure on the bank *could* have led to a squabble between Ankeny and Knowlton and a retreat by Hormel from at least some of its concessionary demands.

But union pressure was not sufficient to cause that friction. In a somewhat less than candid statement on the stand, Rogers said P-9's anti-bank actions were nothing more than "advertising." Clearly, under the heading of "doing everything that was lawful," he also intended for unions and individuals to pull pension funds and remove other kinds of accounts from the bank. (In fact, as the administrative law judge and NLRB pointed out, one of P-9's leaflets requested readers to pledge that "I and/or a member of my family are removing our accounts from First Bank.")

Not enough did: Before the strike, a number of Duluth building trades unions threatened to remove their funds; a Graphic Communications union local closed a $100,000 account; and the Minnesota Federation of Teachers, one of the few statewide bodies to support the corporate campaign, also removed money from the bank.[44] On the basis of letters sent to the local and to area newspapers, it is fair to say that hundreds if not thousands of individual supporters also closed their accounts. But there were not enough clear and powerful signals sent to the bank. And because of the UFCW and AFL-CIO's open hostility to the campaign, there was never a major institutional threat involving a potential withdrawal of millions of dollars from pension-fund accounts, similar to that which prompted Manufacturers Hanover Bank to dump J. P. Stevens officials from its board.

Some would argue that Rogers did not take sufficient care to avoid the charges of illegal secondary boycott activity. And it is true that during the Stevens campaign, he had chafed under the restrictions of ACTWU lawyers—demonstrators must not carry signs, or they must stand several blocks away from the banks and insurance companies, and so on. During the Minnesota campaign, he was under no such legal or bureaucratic restrictions. Moreover, since the local had fewer resources, he perceived a need to escalate the struggle more quickly, and so he tested the limits. He was only a year and a half ahead of his time: In April 1988 the U.S. Supreme Court upheld Rogers' and P-9's position that handbilling and other appeals that encourage a secondary boycott are not unlawful, since they are protected by the First Amendment. But that ruling did not come in time to save the corporate campaign against First Bank.[45]

Somewhat in contradiction to his earlier analysis, Nyberg also told me that for the First Bank efforts to be successful, Hormel executives reckoned that the union would have to violate secondary boycott prohibitions: "Unless you got to the point where you urged people to do something to hurt the company, you wouldn't be successful. Ultimately, P-9 did urge people to withdraw their money, and that's when we wound up in court under federal labor laws." And, as we have seen, the NLRB agreed with Nyberg.[46]

This does not mean, though, that "the corporate campaign failed," in Gagala's words, since by Rogers' definition a corporate campaign is a total campaign that "attacks a corporate adversary from every conceivable angle."[47] This notion is seconded by the AFL-CIO, which goes so far as to refer to such tactics as "comprehensive" or "coordinated" campaigns.[48] Today, Rogers says that the local had accomplished a lot and was ready to move on to other things anyway:

> The bank had the power to force the hand of Hormel, but I always knew that Hormel was cash rich and could withstand a fight for a long time. What if a quarrel broke out on the board, and Hormel stonewalled, saying, "We're not going to settle this thing right away, and we don't need your credit now anyway"? I figured we had to put enough pressure on the bank to alienate them from the company,

so that when we shut the other plants down, First Bank would then refuse to come to the aid of Hormel. And after we'd made such an example of First Bank, no other financial operation would want to take its place—they wouldn't want to get into the same hot water.

As evidence that worker-to-worker solidarity was always primary in his thinking, Rogers also points out that, at his urging, P-9 began its efforts at solidarity building two months before it began any bank activities.[49]

Whether or not things were moving so exactly according to plan, P-9 was, by early December, focusing more than ever on hitting the company directly. With, it appeared, the momentary blessing of the UFCW and a growing level of support from rank-and-file workers, victory seemed more possible than ever.

V

AMBUSHED

Union brothers I have many,
But you guys have touched me plenty. . . .
Kids at Christmas think of Old Santa
Mine came early from Billings, Montana.
BOILER MAKERS like you I will cheer
Next time I have a shot and a beer.
Thanks again for your time and your money
It makes these dark days a little sunny

*—Letter from P-9 member Bob Johnson to Billings, Montana,
Boiler Makers Local 599, which sent a $25 donation toward
his legal costs*[1]

Five hundred union activists from 20 states attended the
December 6–8 founding convention of the National Rank-
and-File Against Concessions. Speakers included Pete Kelly,
a longtime United Auto Workers dissident from Local 120;
Ron Weisen, president of Steelworkers Local 1397 and an
outspoken opponent of that union's capitulation to the steel
industry's program of disinvestment; Maralee Smith of the
steering committee of the Teamsters for a Democratic Union;
and David Patterson, director of Steelworkers District 6 in
Ontario. Also on hand were veterans of some of the toughest
labor fights of recent years: the Wheeling-Pittsburgh steel

111

strike; a shipbuilders' strike in Bath, Maine; and the movement to save steel jobs in Pennsylvania's Monongahela valley.

But the star attraction at the convention was the group of
seven P-9 strikers. "It's people like us who are going to decide if the labor movement is going to be past history, or if
we're going to put the *movement* back in the labor movement," Guyette told the delegates.

NRFAC had come into being when the Austin union's executive board was approached about participation in an anti-
concessions organization in early summer. In June 50 union
leaders from around the country met with Guyette and
Rogers in St. Paul to explore the idea, and in August 168
participants attended a planning meeting held in Gary, Indiana.[2]

"NRFAC grew out of our strike and the general feeling
that we needed labor folks all over," Guyette later recalled.
"One person knew somebody who'd suggested this in the
past. I certainly didn't understand all the political ramifica-
tions. It turned out that some people were involved because
they wanted to contribute, and others because they wanted
to direct and control such an organization."[3]

The "controllers," it turned out, were members of the
Communist Labor Party, only one of the several left-wing organizations that gravitated to P-9's campaign from its very
beginning. The agenda of the December NRFAC convention
had been arranged so that every panel and workshop featured at least one speaker representing, secretly, the CLP.

The Austin local's officers and members were not politically sophisticated, and it was several months before they
fully appreciated just what was going on. Pete Rachleff, chair
of another group that had leftist members but was dominated
by no one organization, the Twin Cities Support Committee,
caught on more quickly. "In June I thought there was some-

thing genuine there," he recalled. "But in December I found that the CLP controlled the convention. It was evident in the way they had limited the agenda, the way speakers were called on, and the way that the last speaker was always from the CLP."[4]

Local P-9 could not have done without the left, broadly defined. In Austin and in support groups around the country, left-leaning liberals, nonaligned socialists, and some members of leftist organizations made indispensable contributions to the local's cause—contributions that went far beyond local members' expectations. In the words of Jake Cooper, a prime organizer of the Twin Cities committee's food caravans and an open member of a small socialist fraction: "Before the strike broke, we indicated that we would help them, but they didn't actually think they'd get much from us. We gave them a lot more than they expected."[5]

And given the hostility of the official labor movement, P-9's officers felt that they were not in a position to be too choosy about those who volunteered to be allies. Some union members reacted to Marxist propagandizing with angry anti-communist outbursts. But generally P-9 officers and those of us representing Corporate Campaign observed the old maxim that any enemy of my enemies must be a friend of mine.

In the weeks that followed, P-9 would lean not only upon support committees of various cities and NRFAC, but also upon activists from the country's largest Trotskyist organization, the Socialist Workers Party. Current and former SWP members helped to provide legal assistance and to build union rallies and demonstrations away from Austin.

Rachleff would later call the NRFAC leaders "a bureaucracy in waiting."[6] The CLP followed the tactic of infiltrating the union hierarchy in order to take it over. In contrast, the

SWP seemed to believe many if not most major union officials should be ousted. CLP's politics were hidden, and its members engaged in behind-the-scenes manipulation; SWP members were open about who they were and relied heavily on circulating propaganda, especially their newspaper, *The Militant*.

Another Trotskyist group that was much in evidence in Austin, the Workers' League, viewed the SWP (from which it had split many years back) as "revisionist." The Workers' League gave over many column inches of its twice-weekly publication, *The Bulletin*, to fulminating against them and other devils.

P-9 members, who had many idle moments during the long weeks of the strike, were inundated with such left-wing newspapers, including also *Unity*, *Frontline*, the *Revolutionary Worker*, and more. These papers, which frequently contained stories about the Austin strike, may have encouraged P-9ers to view themselves as overly heroic, but they also helped members connect with other ongoing labor battles and provided an antidote to the anti-union sentiments common in the mainstream media. Local members were also no doubt impressed by the rhetoric and leadership offered them by NRFAC officers and leftists in support groups all over the United States. But no left organization developed any substantial influence over the direction of the strike: P-9's officers and members knew their own minds too well. On balance, the organized left did the local more good than harm.

Standing outside all this was the United States' largest left-wing organization, the Communist Party. Though the CP initially supported the strike in the pages of its newspaper, the *Daily World*, in time its support for the UFCW and for Lewie Anderson in particular would be made clear. What is more, the involvement of the other left organizations on the side of P-9—particularly that of the SWP—offered the CP further reassurance that it should use any influence it had against the Hormel strikers.

■ ■ ■

I was not in Austin during the month of November, the first complete month I had missed since my first journey there in March. When I returned from New York in mid-December, it seemed to me that the strike could not go on much longer. Negotiations had reconvened, Christmas was coming—surely, I felt, both sides would find a way to compromise now.

But Guyette's notes of the period show that the local's executive board members were not willing to sink to the $10.00-an-hour wage rate that the company was stuck on. Of the 12 union board members present at a December 12 meeting, four voted to propose a $10.69 rate; three, a $10.25 rate; and five, rates of $10.75 and above.

That same day, mediator Don Eaton reported to the union team that "the company is at impasse" and "Larson says he must have a complete proposal from the union." (Hormel's demand for a complete union proposal likely stemmed from concern that its own legal position of impasse—and its ability to reopen the plant with replacements working under an implemented final offer—might be put in jeopardy by any acceptance of piecemeal proposals.) He also told the union that "a dramatic move was necessary," although, he said, he was "not sure what was there."

UFCW Region 13 director Joe Hansen contributed to the pressure on the board. Time was running out, he said, and the question was how to get a settlement. He emphasized that as far as making a judgment about extending picket lines was concerned, Wynn was "setting his own course."[7]

December 13 threatened to be another nearly fruitless day. But, near day's end, Bell and Eaton announced that they had been able to get the company to agree to certain modifications and clarifications. Further alterations were made on the 14th. Joe Hansen telephoned UFCW executive vice president Jay Foreman, who questioned him about the 52-week notice of layoff, the two-tier wage scale, and the expiration date of the agreement.

Hansen reported to the P-9 board that Foreman thought the mediators' proposal was good. He added that P-9 members must be realistic, since "I don't think you're winning."

Attorney Rollins said only that the "company had cleaned up a bit," but that "tremendous ambiguity remains."

Guyette scribbled in the margin of his note pad: "Washington, D.C. Tue." He added, "changes in security, no guarantee all jobs back, no annual wage, no two-tier, 3-year contract, $10, .10 in 1987."[8]

The Washington meeting referred to would allow P-9's officers and UFCW president Wynn, Joe Hansen, and Lewie Anderson to go over the proposal together. The rest of the note is a pretty fair summation of the contract offer as amended by the mediators. The old contract's seniority clause would be replaced by the cumbersome departmental seniority setup used in Ottumwa. There was no assurance that Hormel would rehire all strikers. The guaranteed annual wage was gone, replaced by a very restricted six-month notice of plant closing, and safety improvements would be made only when Hormel deemed them to be "reasonable and economically feasible." On the other hand, there would be no two-tier wage scale: After a nine-month probation, new hires would receive the same rate of pay as everybody else. Job standards would be reviewed by a union-nominated and company-approved engineer. A few grievances would go to expedited arbitration, but virtually all past practices were eliminated. And it would be a three-year agreement, keeping the local's contract out of sync with those at other Hormel plants. The wage offer was unchanged: $10.00, $10.00, and $10.10 over three years.[9]

"The mediators' proposal was always misunderstood," recalled Ron Rollins. "It was never the objective finding of a mediator that 'this is how the dispute should be settled.' Rather, what had happened was the company was at point X, which was totally unacceptable to the union. The proposal represented the farthest the company could be pushed. The mediators were as powerless as we were."[10]

Pete Winkels noted, "The mediators' proposal didn't change much, from the Ray Rogers clause [banning "attempts to coerce the company"] to what it did to seniority. It failed to deal with any of the things that everybody felt were wrong from the beginning."[11]

But the UFCW had decided that it was enough. Bell and Eaton had gotten rid of the two-tier wage scale, the potentially pattern-setting provision most threatening to other contracts. And their proposal kept Austin workers at a $10.00 base wage for two years—the goal Anderson had always urged for the local. None of the rest mattered to the International union leaders.

Wynn did the talking for the UFCW at the Washington meeting. As Winkels recalls, "He said, 'Boys, this is the best you're going to get, and we recommend that you accept it. . . . we're not going to give you roving picket sanction or draw anybody else into this.'"

Then he bounced out of there, and we stayed with Joe Hansen, who kind of sat there pretty quiet. We walked outside the building after the meeting and Joe was giving

us a list of maladies facing the UFCW that would have
been the envy of Job. He said that the strike fund was going
broke, and that the UFCW might even have to take out a
short-term loan on its headquarters building to replenish
the fund. I thought, "What the hell kind of operation is
this? It's supposed to be the largest AFL-CIO affiliate
union." Later I found that the LM-2 [labor-management
reporting] form shows the International has a strike fund
of only $5 million.[12]

■ ■ ■

It was a double-cross, another double-cross, most members
immediately decided. The contract reopeners and concessions, the 23 percent wage cut, the missing language, the International's denunciations and regular attempts to undercut
P-9 activities: Now there was no denying that Hormel and
the UFCW had always been in it together.

"The rank and file elsewhere were behind us, and we
were ready to send pickets," Guyette later recalled, repeating
the logic of the time.

> Wynn had to move quickly to stall that off, because it
> would have hurt the company coming right before their
> big Christmas sales period. So we had a negotiating meet-
> ing as another stopgap for the company. Once the com-
> pany had its Christmas orders filled, the sanction to ex-
> tend pickets never came. Later, the UFCW took the posit-
> ion that they never would have given the sanction, since
> it would have been illegal.[13]

The UFCW helped to reinforce such suspicions with
heavy-handed attempts to cut off the flow of Adopt-A-Family
funds to P-9—funds upon which many families had come to
depend. On December 3, Wynn sent out a letter to all AFL-
CIO union presidents:

UFCW has not approved a request for financial assistance from other local unions in the AFL-CIO either by Ray Rogers or Local 9. . . . we are deeply concerned that any funds sent directly to the local would simply find their way into the hands of Ray Rogers and Corporate Campaign Inc. Clearly, after ten months of corporate campaigning against Hormel and First Bank, Rogers' strategy has been a complete failure on all major fronts. . . . The campaign has cost the members in excess of $500,000 and, other than notoriety for Ray Rogers, has produced nothing but pain, disunity, and disruptions for our members in meat packing.

Wynn suggested that any locals that wanted to send assistance make contributions to the UFCW Region 13 office in Bloomington.[14]

But what really inflamed passions in Austin was the UFCW's announcement that it would conduct a special mail-ballot vote by P-9 members on the mediators' proposal. Region 13 director Hansen told P-9 members in a December 3 letter: "The International has directed a secure, secret ballot mail referendum to provide every member of Local P-9 with an opportunity to vote in reflective privacy, free of appeals to your emotions."

Hansen's letter stressed two themes. First, P-9's members had demonstrated "courage, idealism, and tenacity," but they had been misled by Ray Rogers into pursuing a corporate campaign that was "poorly conceived and oversold," "inadequately researched," and "doomed to failure before it began." Secondly, the contract proposal was not perfect and was less than the members deserved, but "nothing measurable can be won by continuing the struggle that has cost you, your families and your community so dearly." The moral: repudiate the corporate campaign; vote, privately, to accept this "honorable, if not perfect resolution and get back to work."[15]

If the letter had not been situated in a larger context of perceived UFCW deceit and betrayal, more members might have been convinced. But in asking members to accept private ratification by way of ballots sent out from some distant, imaginably dishonest bureaucracy, he asked too much. Unlike some previous UFCW statements, Hansen's did not directly attack P-9's executive board, but the implication was clear: The local board could not be trusted to conduct a fair vote in a regular membership meeting.

Moreover, he said that the members must turn their backs on "the rallies, the balloons, and the cheerleading."[16] This meant that they must turn their backs on the community upon which a majority had come to depend. It was primarily that community, not the UFCW, that had kept members informed, united, and fed during the previous months. The majority wanted a ratification meeting in keeping with local traditions—a meeting where members showed union cards in order to receive ballots, and where they could find out what other members thought.

Anger and frustration over what they saw as conspiracy and heavy-handed manipulation led union rank-and-filers to strike out in an ill-timed action: a December 19 barricade of the entrance road to the Austin plant. Though only limited production work, utilizing the labor of supervisory and clerical workers, was going on in the plant, trucks continued to make deliveries, many not even slowing down to acknowledge the plant gate pickets. Union members felt strongly that nothing should be coming into or going out of the facility. Thus, on that day, almost two hundred members drove over to the plant at 4 A.M. and parked their cars and trucks in the middle of the perimeter road.

"Both the company and international are lying to us," one P-9er told a reporter. "The international already has the vote tallied," said member Mike Bambrick, referring to the impending ratification balloting.

As police cordoned off the entrances to the road known as Hormel Drive and began towing away vehicles, some workers resisted. One was arrested. The rest broke up the blockade at 8:30 A.M., after Hormel called off work for the day.

The members had taken care not to inform either Guyette or Rogers as they prepared for the blockade, and both leaders expressed surprise.[17] Yet it was this small and strategically unimportant blockage that allowed Hormel to seek and receive a court restraining order prohibiting any blockage and limiting the number of pickets to three at each gate.[18]

A membership meeting was set up for December 21 to discuss the contract offer, and on that day the union executive board urged the more than one thousand members in attendance to reject the proposal, which they said was inferior to contracts at other plants.

At that meeting Guyette called the proposal a sellout cooked up by the mediator and the company. "The language is inferior to what we have in Ottumwa," Local 431 chief steward Dan Varner told the members, also criticizing the pact's out-of-sync expiration date. "All they're going to do is pit one plant against another." All executive board speakers and a great many rank-and-file speakers denounced the proposal.[19]

Winkels later recalled, "I spent over 16 hours going over the very confusing seniority language."

The old seniority, which had taken 50 years to construct, was perfectly clear. If the gang got cut, it was "the oldest can and the youngest must." But under the new seniority, if you got cut out of your job, you'd have to assume the youngest man's job in the department, and if you couldn't do that, you'd go out into the plant, to the youngest man's job in the plant. If you couldn't do that, you'd be laid off. We talked to Ottumwa, where they'd been working under this same language for seven or eight years, and they told us it still caused a lot of confusion. There, the company did pretty well as it pleased. What's more, we had still had past practice governing seniority, and this proposal would have done away with even that.

Anyway, during the meeting to explain the mediators' proposal I drew a diagram and went over as best I could what would happen in case of a departmental layoff or plant closing. Then I told them, "If you don't understand that, neither do I." We were looking at a situation that would only be clarified after one or two grievances took several years to arbitrate.[20]

The local executive board decided that, in addition to the International's mail-ballot vote, scheduled to be tallied on January 3 by the Federal Mediation and Conciliation Service, there would also be a local vote conducted in the usual manner on December 26 and 27. Guyette told the press that if the members voted down the proposal in the local's vote, the executive committee had approved a plan to send roving pickets to other Hormel plants in spite of the UFCW's refusal to give sanction.[21]

Union leaders' opposition to the contract proposal led Austin mayor Tom Kough to call upon both sides to sit down with former state labor conciliator Kenneth Sovereign and St. Paul mayor George Latimer to work out some changes in four areas: seniority, worker callbacks, the 52-week guaranteed annual wage, and the grievance procedure and past-practice clauses. P-9 leaders agreed, but Hormel refused. Nyberg said that the company "has gone the last mile with Local P-9." If the mediators' proposal was rejected, he said, the company would reopen the plant and invite P-9ers to return to work.[22]

Wynn attacked the local for conducting its own vote in a telegram to the executive board, saying "telephone calls to headquarters describing a physical and psychological gauntlet that the members had to pass in order to vote in the local's balloting only confirm our judgment."[23] But four local ministers who witnessed the balloting described the process in writing, noting "we observed no attempts to intimidate and coerce, or influence the vote in any way in or near the polling place by any persons."[24]

The proposal was rejected in both votes. Both appear to have been conducted honestly, though a somewhat out-of-date International mailing list meant that some retirees and other nonworkers received mail ballots. The local announced its vote results on December 27, saying that P-9 members had rejected the proposal by 61 percent. In the International's mail ballot, 755 voted no and 540 yes, as announced by the Federal Mediation and Conciliation Service on January 3.[25]

Hormel then announced that it would reopen the plant on January 13, and any strikers who did not return would lose their jobs to "permanent replacements." Guyette said that the local would be sending pickets to the other plants, and that the company should "expect us anywhere."[26]

■ ■ ■

Christmas had brought yet another food delivery from the Twin Cities supporters: On December 21, a caravan led by

Cooper's tractor trailer delivered over twenty tons of food and toys to the P-9 hall, where a kids' party complete with Santa Claus and a juggler was in progress. Twenty-four locals of various unions, along with the Minnesota Education Association, contributed to the effort.[27]

But for many other observers of the Austin labor war, the new year brought only dread. With the company insisting that the local leaders had misled the members—"We feel Mr. Guyette and the executive board did everything they could to distort and discredit the proposal by the disinterested federal mediator," said plant manager Deryl Arnold after the voting[28]—state and local officials became very active in proposing a variety of "fact-finding" investigations and possible re-votes on the proposal.

First, St. Paul mayor Latimer and labor conciliator Sovereign met with Mayor Kough and the P-9 board. Nyberg greeted the news with the statement: "We will not allow outside parties to inject themselves into the dispute."[29] On January 5, Sovereign advised the Austin city council that a settlement was possible if ambiguous terms in the mediators' proposal were cleared up: He pointed to six areas in need of change, including the language governing seniority, use of temporary workers, arbitration procedures, starting wage levels, and references to the elimination of past practices. Sovereign asked that a committee of the council meet with both sides and seek changes in these areas. But nothing came of this recommendation.[30]

Next, Governor Rudy Perpich recommended that a neutral fact-finder review the contract and resubmit it to a union vote. At first both sides spoke positively of the idea, and the company said that it would delay reopening the plant until such a vote was taken. But the idea was abandoned when P-9 made it clear that it would accept fact-finding only if that

meant further negotiations, not simply another vote on the
same proposal. State officials continued to seek out a mediator, nonetheless.[31]

On January 10, Nyberg and Guyette agreed to another
meeting during a live broadcast of St. Paul public television
station KTCA's news program "Almanac." Guyette pressed
Nyberg to head up the Hormel negotiators personally, com-
menting that "the people we dealt with prior to the strike
didn't even know their own proposals."[32] But nothing was
achieved in a January 11 meeting, the first attended by
Nyberg.[33]

It was the last chance for a breakthrough before the company implemented its plan to reopen the plant on Monday,
January 13.

On Sunday, Pastor Henry Mayer of the Grace American
Lutheran Church prayed for those affected by the depressed
farm economy, the closing of businesses, and the effects of
the strike, and urged that there be no violence. A three-panel
cartoon in the *Minneapolis Star and Tribune* showed a wor-
ried-looking P-9 picket standing in the snow, an anxious
Hormel executive, and a pacing Governor Perpich. Each
character was thinking the same thought: "I hope Monday
doesn't come."[34]

That afternoon, three thousand P-9ers and their relatives
came to the Austin High School to hear retired federal judge
Miles Lord announce the beginning of an investigation into
the Hormel Foundation. Local union members and Corporate Campaign had raised the issue of the foundation back in
the summer, noting its voting power over almost 46 percent
of company stock and the failure of foundation board members to act in accordance with the foundation's original mandate to be a protector of the community.[35] A union study
committee had continued to publicize the questions sur-

rounding the foundation, ultimately enlisting Lord's support. The judge warned that the legal costs of providing information that could get the state's attorney general, Hubert H. Humphrey III, to act could run as high as $100,000.[36]

At the rally, Lord talked at length about the foundation's responsibility to the town. He pointed out that Hormel was withholding $800,000 in profit-sharing money from the Austin workers—money that had been paid at the other plants—"so that women and children will suffer." Finally, he said what was on a lot of minds in the audience: "If you are not going back to work, you should all stay out."[37]

■ ■ ■

The reopening of the plant brought news reporters to Austin in droves. William Serrin of the *New York Times*, who had traveled to Austin for earlier rallies, came, as did a reporter representing the *Wall Street Journal*, several from the Twin Cities and Rochester newspapers, and a host of national and local television reporters and technicians. Minneapolis television station WCCO moved its satellite-relay truck down so it could send live feeds. ABC television reporters arranged to fly in each day from Minneapolis by helicopter. According to Police Chief Don Hoffman, during peak periods over 170 reporters, technicians, and camera and sound personnel came to town to cover strike events. "It was another case of herd journalism," said Serrin later. "You got a gang of guys there and everybody's saying, 'C'mon boys, let's ride.' "[38]

The company had prepared a show for them, as had P-9. In spite of near-zero temperatures and darkness, a milling crowd of 350 strikers gathered in the icy field across from the plant's south gate at 6:30 A.M. on Monday morning. The mood was optimistic and even cheerful: Since the injunction had limited the number of pickets at the gate to three, many strikers carried fishing poles, some with cardboard fish attached to the lines, saying that they were there to do a little "ice fishing." Across the road, plant security staff were massed at the gate. But only about a dozen cars crossed the line. Local leaders later said that only seven members had crossed.

P-9 members told reporters that they were proud that so few of their members had crossed, and that photographs taken of those driving through the line showed most to be security guards trying to create the impression that members were going in. The company said that it would begin to interview new workers to take the strikers' jobs on Tuesday.[39]

That day, hundreds of cars from as far away as Florida, Wyoming, and California crossed the line to get application forms, and the company announced that over a thousand people had applied for jobs. (Pickets later reported that they recognized some drivers as workers from Hormel headquarters, who must have been told to drive through the plant gate over and over to contribute to the show.) Again hundreds of union members gathered across the road from the south entrance. Strikers yelled "scab" and "lowlife" at those who drove in but did not try to block their path.

A great many of the cars that crossed the picket line had Iowa license plates, encouraging the strikers' dormant Minnesota chauvinism. Most autos contained more than one person, and some had as many as six inside. Either because of the drivers' poverty or fear of picket line violence, there were many rusty, dented vehicles, and three cars were ticketed for having no license plates at all. One woman walked in, and another tried to climb the fence to avoid facing the pickets. After picking up an application, many tried to make a quick getaway: Hurrying to escape, one driver slammed into a police car.

"I'm desperate, I got to save my house and family," a California driver told a television reporter. The same report caught striker Jim Getchell crying. "My mom and dad together worked 70 years for the company," he said, "but Hormel just don't care about our families any more."

"It doesn't end when we go back," said striker Joe Stier. "They're gonna be a scab and have to live with that—their families are going to have to live with that all their lives."

Dan Allen, a firebrand who frequently drew the attention of the television cameras, said, "A lot of our people may follow some of these scabs home to tell them what our fight is about and how our community is being ripped off by the company and the foundation. But we're going to try to be peaceful."[40]

And almost everyone stayed peaceful, largely because of the counseling of Ray Rogers, who insisted that strikebreakers were only misguided and unemployed workers and that P-9 should "take out its frustrations on the ones who are truly culpable."[41]

"I had been to picket and had taken my boy along, just so he could see what his dad was going through," Darrell Busker told me.

As we left, a guy passed by waving his application out the door, just rubbing it in my face. So I followed him to his house, and he ran into his garage and grabbed a baseball bat. "You get out of here, or I'll bust you," he said. But I told him I just wanted to talk. Gradually, he came over and talked. Then he looked in the car and saw my son crying. He just ripped up the application. "I can see what you're going through, and I won't take your job," he said. The guy was on welfare, and from what I could tell, the welfare agency had pushed him to go to Hormel.[42]

◆

There were in fact many stories that welfare and unemployment compensation agencies in neighboring states were
pushing people to apply for jobs at Hormel.

On another occasion, a carload of union members chased
a car filled with scabs, doing 90 miles per hour down the
highway. "We were in the lane next to them," a participant
remembered. One P-9er was "hanging halfway out the front
window, shouting and waving his fist at them—they had to
be doing 100 just to get away." Again, only words were exchanged, not blows. When a "scab hunt" ended with the
crossover's car being surrounded, his car hood was pounded
and angry words were exchanged, but little else of a physical
nature ever occurred.[43]

In fact, many P-9 members were saddened by the specta-
cle. But Hormel remained as belligerent as ever: That day it
announced that CEO Knowlton was getting a $236,000 raise.
Nyberg justified the move, saying that "it was the feeling of
the board that his salary should be competitive."[44]

■ ■ ■

Union members packed the hall that Tuesday evening for a
strategy session. Rogers told the gathering, "What you've
done for two straight days is to show the company and the
rest of the country that P-9 is sticking together." He encouraged everyone to remain nonviolent, adding that it was certain that the company would soon bring in professional agitators to try to provoke a mob scene. Members reassured
themselves that no one was taking their jobs yet; they were
just getting applications. Of the seven who had crossed the
first day, Rogers said, three had been persuaded not to cross
on Tuesday.[45]

Those who had crossed received hand-delivered letters,
phone calls from friends, and visits from executive board

members, all encouraging them to come back to the union fold.

But on Thursday the UFCW sent a public signal encouraging strikers to cave in and cross the picket line.

In his late December telegram protesting against the local's voting procedure, Wynn had said that "if the proposal is rejected, we will direct Director Hansen to stand aside and let representatives of Local P-9 see if they can negotiate more than we could together."[46] But there was to be no standing aside. Three days after the plant reopened, television stations and newspapers were reporting on another UFCW "telegram." "Suicide is not an acceptable alternative," Wynn wrote.

> You may choose martyrdom for yourself. But as a leader it is your responsibility to make sure that 1,500 loyal and true union members don't also become martyrs. . . . Your goals are unachievable. It is within your power to prevent the imminent total defeat and the loss of 1,500 union jobs in Austin.

The message also contained another refusal to sanction extended P-9 pickets.

Since, like other P-9 members, Guyette first got this message from the news media, it was clearly meant as a public denunciation of the strike, rather than as an executive board advisory.[47] Lengthy citations from the message were broadcast on television, along with a daily accounting of how many union members had crossed. On the day of the Wynn blast, Austin's KAAL-TV said that 70 P-9ers had gone back and that, according to the company, 2,000 people had applied for jobs. (The next day the station reduced the first number to 55, while the *Minneapolis Star and Tribune* put the number at 80 to 100 at the end of the week.)[48]

The next week would be pivotal for P-9, the ever-watchful reporters said. No longer merely interviewing, the company would attempt to bring in "replacement workers" to run the Austin plant, while Austin union members would be traveling around the country trying to close the company's other plants.

But a weekend Minneapolis support meeting more correctly foretold that, for the moment, the action would continue to be in Austin. Guyette urged the several hundred people who turned out at the United Auto Workers Local 879 hall to bring down as many union people as they could the next day and each day that week. Four hundred fifty of them signed up for a "Labor Solidarity Brigade."[49]

At 7:30 A.M. on Monday the 20th, a huge traffic jam blocked all access to the Austin plant. P-9 members and supporters drove their cars onto the plant perimeter road, Hormel Drive, and switched the engines off. Minneapolis supporters carried UAW flags and American flags, and one even displayed a worn "Professional Air Traffic Controllers On Strike" placard. Anyone who tried to drive through the area found his car surrounded by angry protesters shouting, "Get out of here and don't come back!"

Hormel videotaped and photographed everything. The only injury of the day was that of a Hormel photographer who unwisely confronted a striker. News reports said that he was taken to the hospital and released after being "kicked in the groin."[50]

That afternoon plant manager Deryl Arnold flexed his talent for hyperbole. "There has been a complete loss of law and order at the company's Austin, Minnesota, plant," he said, reading a prepared statement to reporters. "The police are powerless to control mob violence, mass picketing, and wanton destruction of property, and mob psychology has taken over. . . . We have called the governor and told him that the mayor is ineffective and the police not in control, and we have requested help from the governor."

Documents obtained from the state Department of Public Safety reveal that Hormel's Knowlton called Perpich at 9:30 A.M. to request that the State Patrol be dispatched to Austin in order to prevent violence and allow the plant to reopen. Public Safety Commissioner Paul Tschida and the governor's chief of staff subsequently called Knowlton and Nyberg and informed them that the State Patrol could not by law be used in conjunction with labor disputes, but that the National Guard could be so used. A request for the Guard, however, must come from local officials "indicating that local resources were exhausted and not capable of dealing with the threat to public safety," they said.

By 3:00 P.M., Tschida had received such a request in the form of a conference call from Austin Chief of Police Hoffman, Mower County Sheriff Wayne Goodnature, and Mayor Kough, a union member who could never decide whether to behave as a militant striker or as a neutral public servant. The call was backed up by a letter that alleged:

> During the early morning hours, a citizen was assaulted at the scene. Several vehicles had their tires slashed, two windshields were broken at or near the employees entrance. . . . Another incident happened about 11:00 a. m. involving a new applicant for work who was followed by unknown persons that fired a shot at his vehicle. No one was injured in this incident. . . . We are beyond the point where we can handle this lawlessness with our resources.

A telegram sent to the Bureau of Criminal Apprehension reported the same occurrences, committed by "a mob of 400 to 600 union sympathizers."

In response, Perpich cited his "constitutional responsibility to protect the lives and safety of Minnesota citizens" and called up the National Guard.[51]

■ ■ ■

I was at the P-9 hall when I first heard the news. It was late afternoon, and the building was mostly empty. Ed Allen, his face flushed from the cold, burst in through the front doors. "The National Guard is on its way," he said. "Carole Apold says she heard on the radio that they're supposed to be here in about half an hour."

It was a moment of great anxiety. Could P-9ers fight the National Guard?

Three hours later, a majority of the union executive board decided to end the strike.

I had left the building for a few hours. When I came back, Allen told me that the board had caved in, that he had heard that they were going to cut some deal with the UFCW. Union members were beginning to come into the hall for the nightly meeting. We stopped Pete Winkels, who wouldn't tell us anything. Rogers, distracting himself with some minor organizing details, was equally laconic. Minneapolis support committee activists Tom Laney and Paul Wellstone were around and said to be counselling retreat. Guyette acted as though nothing had changed, and said he wasn't giving up. But as we discovered by cornering other board members, Guyette and Vice President Lynn Huston were pretty much alone in wanting to continue.

By 7:30 the auditorium began to fill up as members and their families continued to arrive. Soon, nearly a thousand people packed the hall. Those who could not get a seat stood crammed into the back of the room and out the fire exit onto the street.

I drifted back and forth between the auditorium and the little *Unionist* office down the hall that Rogers had claimed for himself. I stood there waiting for some direction, some indication of what to do. Suddenly there was an explosion of voices, angry shouts, and the sound of furniture being violently shoved about in the big room. A dozen red-faced men—the so-called P-10ers, who had been vocal opponents of Guyette and the corporate campaign from its beginning—trooped by the doorway and out of the building. Drunk and cursing everyone else, they had announced that they were going back. The next day they would try to cross the picket line as a group.

The people who remained in the auditorium were far from being broken. Their determination to press on was apparent from the change in their mood from anger to joking good humor. What would the company do next, somebody said—use nuclear weapons? Everyone seemed eager to find out what the next thing would be, certain that they had not lost so long as the company had to keep raising the ante.

The executive board filed onto the stage late, and no one seemed to want to be the first to speak. Soon there was a lot of discussion, with members of the audience standing up and shouting out their defiance of the company, the UFCW, the governor, and the Guard. Should they all go back in together and, as some outside sympathizers were urging, "work to rule" until the other Hormel plant contracts expired in the fall? The majority felt that it was better to throw up pickets now at the other plants—the iron might never be so hot again. Finally, Winkels went to the podium.

"A half-hour ago I'd have said it was all over," he began. "Now, I see that it's not.

"This is the orneriest group of people I've ever seen," he said. The hall erupted with cheers and applause.

Some months later Lynn Huston recalled the events of the evening. "There was some pessimism on the executive board at the time," he said.

> Floyd Lenoch was saying it was all over. Winkels was crushed—he really caved in. There was a lot of argument about going back in, and a majority of the board said we should just go back. At the general information meeting, the rank and file wanted to poll the executive board. Initially, Pete refused to sit up on the stage. Well, during the meeting we really hashed it out, and 90 percent of the members didn't want to go back. We could tell that some members were missing at the meeting, and we knew that those were the ones who had made a decision to go in.[52]

The events of the next day seemed to confirm the rank and file's faith that P-9 could take on anyone. Five hundred National Guardsmen began arriving at 2:30 A.M. But when they went to the plant at 4 A.M. to take up their positions near the south gate, they found the union already there in force. The weather was warmer than it had been, and an eerie, dense fog lay close to the ground. The roads all around the plants were blocked up, hundreds of union members filled the streets, and those who wanted to cross had no way to get through.

The executive board had left Rogers to direct the action. But when he arrived at the south gate at 4:30, he found the scene frightening and chaotic.

> The police had the corners cordoned off. There were all these union people milling around and running back and forth. The Guard, dressed in combat gear and armed with big clubs, kept arriving. They were doing all these fancy marching formations—probably intended to intimi-

date—and it looked serious. I knew National Guardsmen hadn't behaved well in other situations, and I was afraid from the way they were acting that they were going to move on the strikers. I got ahold of a bullhorn and said, "If the Guard moves on you, head for the union hall."

Adding to Rogers' sense of foreboding were the questions asked by a couple of ABC cameramen just as he arrived. Had Ray seen Mark and Joe, the network correspondents who had been covering the story? The reporters had left Minneapolis in a helicopter at 3 A.M., and nobody had seen them since. It later turned out that their copter had crashed, and both men and their pilot had been killed.[53]

I didn't know about that, and when I arrived at 5:30, what I saw appeared more comical than threatening. Rogers was crouched beside a police car, using the on-board public address system to communicate with both the forces of law and order and the demonstrators. It seemed that even the police were openly admitting that the streets belonged to the people.

The results of the day were, television reporters admitted, "much the same on Tuesday as on Monday, despite the presence of dozens of National Guardsmen." The pickets had prevailed, and at 8 A.M. the head of the Guard, the chief of police, and the union agreed to keep the plant closed in exchange for a reduction in the number of union demonstrators. There were just not enough troops, it seemed, so four more companies were called up. That meant that there would be 800 total troops there the next day to assist local police and sheriff's deputies.

Plant manager Arnold continued to speak as if blood were flowing in the streets. "You are seeing the result of Mr. Rogers' policies of confrontation, harassment, intimidation and threats," he said. "Local P-9's leaders and Rogers talk about nonviolence apparently with their tongue in cheek [*sic*]." Generally, his equation of the street blocking with violence—and an open plant with nonviolence—was accepted by the media.[54]

On Wednesday, the Guard, State Patrol, and local police finally managed to get about 150 strikebreakers into the plant using a tool not faced by previous generations of strikers: the Interstate Highway system.

I-90 passes just north of the plant, and an exit ramp feeds into a street only a few hundred yards from the north gate. At 3 A.M. Guardsmen massed along the street, and local police on the Interstate directed those with orange Hormel stickers on their windshields down the exit ramp and in through the plant gate. Cars without the stickers were turned away from the exit. Initially outflanked, P-9ers caught on that the action was no longer at the south or west gate and attempted to block up the Interstate by driving very slowly or stalling their autos. But the State Patrol, supposedly barred by law from any involvement in a labor dispute, prevented P-9 "breakdowns" from blocking the highway. In two cases where union members stopped their cars, locked their doors, and refused to move, local police broke car windows, arrested the drivers, and drove the cars away. The south and west gates, scenes of the previous days' activity, remained closed.

Union members conceded the setback, but maintained that the police were only able to open the plant by using terror tactics against the public and denying citizens access to city streets. The Guard, Rogers and local officers said, was acting as a private security force for Hormel and should be withdrawn. Taxpayers should not be footing the bill, estimated at fifty to sixty thousand dollars each day the Guard was in town, to run strikebreakers into the plant, Guyette added. Nyberg responded that since the company was "under siege," it was appropriate for the Guard to be there. And

Sheriff Goodnature moved the town a step closer to a police state with a note to Mayor Kough, which he read aloud to reporters on January 22. "I am taking control of the police," he wrote, "and because you are a P-9 member, you will not be involved in any strategy sessions."[55]

Late in the day, a tractorcade of about a hundred militant farmers who had been at a protest rally in St. Paul arrived in Austin to lend support to the strikers. Giant earthmoving vehicles, carrying signs reading "Farmers and Workers Unite," paraded past a crowd made up of P-9 members, leaders of the American Indian Movement, including Vernon Bellecourt, and UFCW Local 6 members from the Farmstead meatpacking plant in nearby Albert Lea. At about 7 P.M., just before the union's nightly strategy meeting, hundreds of P-9 members and supporters decided upon a show-of-strength drive around the plant. At the north end of the plant, the farmers drove their tractors right up to a rank of National Guardsmen, who were still standing in formation.

It was the second dicey moment in two days, as union members and supporters left their cars and strode up to the troops. "Get out of here, just get out of here!" one woman shouted to the Guardsmen as they fondled their riot sticks. "Have we come this far to turn back now?" one man, not known to me, cried. Television crews turned on their spotlights and prepared for action. Then the demonstrators turned back. We had thrown such a scare into the Guard that the next day it brought in two armored personnel carriers. The cooler union heads had prevailed, though, probably because the majority felt that they had a better plan than fighting the Guard.

For P-9 had begun to move on the company's other plants. A team of 75 Austin strikers had thrown up a five-hour picket at Hormel's Ottumwa plant on Tuesday, and almost all of the 850 workers there stayed out until the pickets left. Truck drivers also honored the line, parking trailers filled with live hogs outside the gate. On Wednesday, contingents of roving pickets traveled to small Hormel facilities in Algona, Iowa, and Beloit, Wisconsin, where they were less successful.[56] These were only intended as a testing of the waters, further preliminaries to the real extension of P-9 pickets, which local leaders still said was coming soon.

There were strong indications that the company needed production, and that disruptions anywhere would hurt it. The *Wall Street Journal* quoted Knowlton as saying that "company inventories are 'down to the bare walls' " and that "Hormel needs to resume production of its sausages and bacon" or risk losing business to the thirty other packers that were ready to grab part of its market.[57]

Things were also moving quickly in the state capital. Twin Cities Support Committee members began a noisy and highly publicized sit-in at the governor's office, demanding withdrawal of the Guard. It was widely appreciated that Perpich, running for re-election in a few months, could suffer politically as a result of his use of the Guard. The governor scrambled and got both sides to agree to meet with his fact-finder, Arnold Zack.[58]

It was a critical situation. Each day brought another desperate battle. We seemed to be on a see-saw: One day we would be victorious, the next defeated; one day elated, the next downcast; and ultimately I just felt numb. In the back of my mind, I knew that if I were calling the shots, I would have given in long before. At the same time, things were moving so quickly—and those who were taking the biggest risks seemed so sure of their actions—that I hardly allowed myself to make judgments. Would the see-saw ride continue? And if it did, which side would be worn down first, and which would end up on top?

VI

CLOSING RANKS

If you had to trust your life or your country to a scab or a striker, which would you chose? Ask the police and National Guard. . . . Stand strong and the worst that can happen is they take your job. Cave-in and they will forever have your soul.

—Letter of fired PATCO striker to P-9 members[1]

'm still surprised about what I saw in that little meatpacking town," William Serrin told me two years later. "I remember those farmers and the Indians, and I'm still surprised about the depth of what they were doing and the coalitions they were making."

> I called Rex Hardesty of the AFL-CIO, and I told him, "It's just amazing up there." He said, "Oh, naah." The established labor movement was incapable of recognizing what was there and of building upon it. A guy like Walter Reuther would have been in there in a minute to capitalize on it.[2]

The farmers and the Indians were as excited as the Austin workers about their incipient coalition: Wabasso farmer Gene Irlbeck, who came up with the notion of bringing the tractorcade to Austin, told the gathered P-9ers that evening,

"Farmers will not cross any picket lines." Groundswell founder Bobbi Polzine, speaking at the same meeting, said: "I saw the sons of farmers and of labor on the National Guard lines. They've set blood against blood. It's rotten wrong, and we're not going to stop till we get them the hell out of here." Then Chippewa and AIM leader Vernon Bellecourt declared, "The American Indian, farmer, and worker should lock arms and close ranks."

Workers from across the country came to Austin to see what they could do and to testify before the always crowded nightly union meetings. Two women members of Nashville UFCW Local 405 told the strikers, "P-9 has opened our eyes; when we came here we told our husbands that we wanted to be with those people because they are fighting, and we want to fight with them."[3]

The union local was receiving thousands of letters of support. During the month of January 1986, 250 such letters arrived, followed by another 412 in February, and over a thousand more in March and April. The majority were from union locals, but between a third and a half were from individuals who felt the need to reach out to the strikers.

But labor's leadership wasn't having any of it: Few union officials would "meddle" in the affairs of another union without first getting permission from the top—namely, UFCW president Bill Wynn.

So, although many labor officials must have been shocked to see Lewie Anderson, rather than a Hormel executive, debating Jim Guyette on the January 24 ABC News program "Nightline," few said anything. It was left to moderator Ted Koppel to express his own astonishment: "Mr. Anderson, in the past unless a local really did something outrageous, the parent union would have defended it; otherwise the whole labor movement starts coming apart at the seams."

To the likely puzzlement of "Nightline" viewers nationwide, Anderson stuck to his argument about the need to
bring wages down in order to win a national wage rate. (Koppel to Guyette: "You heard what Mr. Anderson said—what
he's worried about is . . . if you guys in Austin move up too
high, then all the other plants, those 13,000 other meatpackers are going to say, 'Why not us?' ")[4]

But Anderson presented a less one-dimensional argument in a "Fact Book on Local P-9/Hormel" distributed within the UFCW and to the press three days earlier. There he
revived the charge of "breaking with the chain" and cited the
UFCW's history of fighting concessions, while accusing P-9
and Ray Rogers of initiating an "unceasing hate campaign"
against the UFCW that had undone organizing drives, encouraged disaffiliation, and helped to perpetuate an anti-
union climate. P-9, he said, had bankrupted its treasury to
embrace Rogers' irresponsible position of "100% victory or
100% defeat."[5]

It was the end of a week that saw the use of the National
Guard against Minnesota strikers for only the third time in
the 20th century. Still no labor leader of national standing
had spoken out against the deployment of the Guard, and
state AFL-CIO president Dan Gustafson had actually endorsed the governor's decision.

Few labor officials ever spoke against Perpich—the
UFCW saw to that. Nevertheless, the presence of the Guard
encouraged a broadening of support for the local, and political opposition was building: The head of the Minnesota
Democratic Farmer Labor Party called his own governor's act
"politically undesirable." Perpich seemed to have no idea
how to get out of the dilemma except to encourage the fact-
finding process and hope for the best.[6]

■ ■ ■

Local union leaders and Hormel executives met with fact-finder Arnold Zack on January 23 and 24, though Hormel discouraged any high expectations. Nyberg told reporters that the meeting was "definitely not a negotiating session—there are people in the plant who are permanent employees, and there's nothing in any agreement going to change that." Later he added that what was going on was "not negotiating, not mediation, it isn't arbitration—it's pure and simply fact-finding."[7]

But P-9 leaders were treating it as negotiation, raising topics not dealt with in the mediators' proposal and drafting and submitting complete proposals to the company. Zack asked union negotiators if the annual wage was a key, and Rollins called it "a threshold issue," along with job security and seniority. Board members Huston, Retterath, and Kenny Hagen told how much the annual wage had meant to Austin historically, offering family security and a stable, nontransient work force. Rollins asked company negotiator Dave Larson why it was important to change the annual wage; Larson would only say that business was better served without it.[8]

With the board thus occupied, the members and Rogers were planning finally to pull the string with extended picketing. On Friday evening, several carloads of pickets departed Austin for Fremont, Nebraska.

Then the executive board flinched.

"Some of the board members had been in touch with their wives, who said their phones were ringing off the hook," Winkels recalled. "Wives of the members who'd gone to Fremont were calling, panicky, to ask if anything positive had occurred in the talks. We decided to hold back." Lynn Huston added:

> We had so much trouble making decisions that we had given a lot of responsibility for the pickets to Ray. Floyd for some reason was afraid of sending out the pickets, and of course Keith Judd and Kenny Hagen were pissing in their pants the whole time. Jim and I really wanted the pickets to go. Well, the board decided they should go. Then Jim and I went off to the "Nightline" program. They talked it over some more and decided it was too rash, that we had to make a good-faith move. So, while Jim and I were gone, Pete called Ray's house to get him to pull back the pickets.

Ray wasn't there; only I was. I telephoned the union hall. Rogers told me it was too late—the pickets had gone, and there was no getting them back.

Rogers came home about midnight. At 3 A.M. the phone rang, and it was Winkels again, insisting that the pickets be called back. Rogers took the call and soon, with the help of numerous operators, had a four-way long-distance debate going between himself, Winkels in one Minneapolis hotel room, Guyette in another, and pickets Jo Ann Bailey and Cecil Cain at a 24-hour store in Fremont. The discussion went on and on, but the exasperated Rogers could not talk the board out of calling the pickets back. They had ruled, and a majority had gone off to bed. "The people in Fremont were real pissed off," Huston remembered. "They had driven for hours to get there and were ready to go."[9]

But, like the crippled atomic bomber plane in the movie *Dr. Strangelove*, some pickets got through anyway, as Jim Getchell recalled:

Five of us in one van got separated from the rest. We sneaked into Fremont the back way. We got to the plant about 4:45 A.M. and found about fifty deputy sheriffs and Highway Patrol waiting for us. The Highway Patrol lieutenant said,"Don't worry about us,"; he'd remembered how Nyberg had said nasty things about them in the summer. Well, the five of us pickets kept over two hundred people out—they didn't cross but instead went to the union hall. Then somebody from the caravan showed up and told us we were supposed to back off. We'd have had the whole work force. As it was, we shut them down for about two and a half hours.[10]

The memory of the incident still torments union participants, perhaps more than any other. In their minds it remains a golden might-have-been moment that could have turned everything to P-9's advantage.

"I voted to pull the pickets, and it was one of the biggest mistakes we ever made," recalled Carl Pontius. "But the board wasn't 100 percent behind the idea."

"The fact-finder had made a major pitch for a good-faith gesture," Guyette asserted some time afterward. "Until recently I thought the board had gotten cold feet, but in fact they were sucked in. It's too bad, because at that point the pickets would have been honored: At that time Rosenthal hadn't been intimidated, but when we went later there was a tremendous change in attitude."

Even Winkels, who led the retreat, now regrets the move. But he recalls that the board always tried to get consensus before taking any dramatic step. And he says that a number of board members kept holding back out of fear that too strong a union play might "hurt the company."[11]

Most adamant that this was the key blunder of the entire campaign is Rogers: "We had the whole thing in the palm of our hand, and the board threw it all away."[12]

On Saturday morning, both the union and the company made noncommittal public statements about the fact-finder's report. According to Huston, Zack had been unhappy about even the "Nightline" appearance and urged maintenance of the "status quo." (At one point, according to Guyette, the "Nightline" staff called to confirm his appearance, and Zack took the call to say that Guyette could not make it. "He was real arrogant—with both sides," recalled the P-9 president.) In order to maintain that "status quo," P-9 went so far as to remove its pickets from the Austin plant, though 500 members and supporters from 40 other unions picketed the governor's mansion in minus-20-degree weather. Zack's report was to be ready in 48 hours for presentation to the union membership.

That evening the board told the gathered members that they should not expect a lot that was new in the fact-finder's report. It would really only be another bite at the apple of the old mediators' proposal that they had voted on before. And it was unclear how it would deal with the huge problem of getting rid of the replacement workers. In response, enraged rank-and-filers told the board to stop hedging on the roving pickets. They also voted to call for a nationwide boycott of Hormel products, in spite of the lack of International union sanction.[13]

So on Monday little attempt was made to block the Austin facility. Instead, 200 P-9 members finally extended the local's picketing to five other plants: Hormel's two other key slaughtering facilities in Ottumwa and Fremont, the FDL plant in Dubuque, and small facilities in Dallas, Texas, and Algona, Iowa.

In Ottumwa, it worked to perfection. Both shifts, comprising some 750 workers, stayed away. In Dallas, the entire 52-person work force also stayed out, closing down that operation. Fremont, though, was a bust: This time only seventy-odd workers out of 850 honored the lines. And at FDL, only 30 of 900 workers observed the line.

From Houston, where the annual stockholders' meeting was in progress, Hormel executives responded immediately: By mid-day they had announced that 500 workers in the several locations would be fired and permanently replaced, in spite of the strong contractual position of the union members in Ottumwa and Fremont.

The governor appeared inept and powerless. He urged the company to stop hiring replacements and the union to "stabilize its campaign" until both sides had time to study the fact-finder's report. Joe Hansen, silent since the mail-ballot vote on the mediators' proposal, told reporters, "It appears they're trying to spread the misery that they have created in Austin to the other locations."[14]

■ ■ ■

"Right away we had 100 percent in Ottumwa," Huston remembers.

People on the Ottumwa executive board and Dan Varner felt no more than 10 to 15 percent of them would honor the line. But Bill Cook told me, "Hey, we can pull this off." That morning we let Bill and 20 other solid people know we were coming. We got our picket line up on the road by the freeway and had people with bullhorns at the gate. Bill got all of his good people to drive down there, stop their cars in front of the main gate, and block the road. They were the first ones there, and they stalled for time as the traffic built up behind them. They got out and talked to the people. Then they drove down to the union hall. And Bill was 100 percent right: Since no one in front of them turned in, each driver did not turn into the gate either. Nobody wanted to be the first to turn in and cross the picket line.

At about 5:30 A.M., Local 431 business manager Louis De-Frieze came to the hall, arranged for witnesses, and formally asked Huston to remove the picket line. Huston refused. De-Frieze went through the same motions down at the picket line. Then he returned to the union hall, and every 15 minutes got up and read a statement to the effect that members might lose their jobs for honoring the picket line. Each time he spoke, Huston responded. "We went through this about 15 times," Huston said. But no one went in. Second-shift members came to the hall and also decided to stay out.[15]

One of the Ottumwa militants, Larry McClurg, said that there was a simple reason why Ottumwans honored the line: "A lot of people said, 'We've been screwed for 10 years, and now's our chance to get back.' "[16]

But in Fremont, the second picket in three days brought all the old frictions between Local 22 members and P-9 to the surface. P-9's faith that, in Huston's words, "the Fremont guys would honor the line for sure," particularly the former Austin workers who were led by Jerry Rosenthal, proved unfounded.

A strong majority did back Austin, according to Bob Langemeier, but too little was done to keep their morale up: Months would go by without a visit from the Austin strikers, who worked a lot harder building support in Ottumwa. Meanwhile, the news media, the company, and local president Skip Niederdeppe kept warning Local 22 members that they might be fired for honoring any extended picket.[17]

On the first day, therefore, only 70 or 80 stayed out, with some of these calling in sick. That number eventually dwindled to 26. "If we had leadership here, we'd have been as strong as Ottumwa," Langemeier continued. "Perhaps we did lead Austin astray, letting them think that they didn't have to do much to get our support."

> Rosenthal did have a following in the hog kill, and he did lead some across the picket line. But the kill starts an hour later than other operations, so many had already gone in by 8 A.M. Meanwhile, he was at the union hall, pacing the floor. I always thought he was wishy-washy. He had been getting weaker and weaker, in the end becoming a spy for Niederdeppe. Finally he said, "I guess we got to do it."[18]

After Rosenthal went in, "it was like an avalanche," noted Winkels. "Everybody was looking for someone from the board leadership to support us, but when it got down to it, nobody did. You didn't have a rebellious executive board there, just a rebellious faction with nobody in control."[19]

In Dallas and Algona, local union officers encouraged the members to go back in, which they did after being threatened with firing. In Dubuque, Business Agent Mel Moss also urged members to cross. The surprising thing at these locations is not how many crossed, but that anyone stayed out given the absence of strong, pro-striker leaders. Nevertheless, by Tuesday pickets were up at four more Hormel plants: Houston, Texas; Stockton, California; Renton, Washington; and Atlanta, Georgia. And on Wednesday, Perpich began withdrawing the National Guard from Austin.[20]

■ ■ ■

The shutdown in Ottumwa energized the Austin strikers, and the subsequent firings established a bond between the two locals. The events also sent shockwaves through the labor and farmer communities in Iowa and set up a second center of strike activity.

On January 29, over two thousand family members and supporters of the Hormel workers marched through the streets of Ottumwa to demonstrate in front of the plant. (Workers who had honored the picket were instructed by their lawyers not to march, so they watched from the sidelines.) Demonstrators included UAW members from the local John Deere works, Teamsters, Steelworkers, city workers, Hormel and Morrell retirees, fifty P-9 members, and Mayor Jerry Parker.

"If Hormel is going to be an integral part of this community," the mayor said, "they'll have to take these workers back." Signs read "Stand together and fight for what is right" and "Citizens of Ottumwa support working people."

Local 431 members began building committees like those in Austin: They established a food committee to feed those honoring the picket line, set up a kitchen and child care facilities at their union hall, and sent the faithful to Fremont to urge support for the picket line there. The Ottumwa citizenry showed greater backing for the union than did those in Austin: Reverend James Grubb allowed P-9 pickets to sleep on the basement floor in Sacred Heart Church, and many grocery stores began spontaneously removing Hormel products from their shelves.

On the day of the march, from the company stockholders' meeting in Texas (also attended by Guyette and about thirty strikers), CEO Knowlton said that the company would review all the cases and would probably reinstate some of those fired.[21]

The extended picketing also prompted another outburst from Wynn in the form of a telegram to all union locals: "I strongly urge you to inform every member of the consequences of risking their jobs in order to help Rogers save face," he wrote.[22]

Then the UFCW did something more than verbally attack the strikers and their backers. It sent in a "special organizing team" to Hormel locations across the Midwest. Ostensibly, the team was sent to help file grievances for and provide assistance to those who were replaced or disciplined for honoring the Austin lines.[23] But in time "the program," as some team members referred to their work, became primarily concerned with spying on strike activities, with the ultimate goal of placing the Austin local in trusteeship and breaking the strike.

Later trusteeship hearings would reveal that beginning on January 31, organizers from as far away as San Francisco and Massachusetts were sent to Austin, Algona, Ottumwa, and Fremont. These representatives reported to the assistant to the International director of organizing, Larry Kohlman, who moved between Washington and the Region 13 headquarters near Minneapolis. Operations were overseen from afar by Organizing Director Doug Dority and Executive Vice Presidents William Olwell and Jay Foreman.

Most of the reps testified that they were in Algona, Fremont, and Austin to "return phone calls" and help union members in need of assistance with unemployment insurance and getting on Hormel's recall list. When pressed, though, one admitted that he could not really "answer a lot of questions about unemployment." Representative Larry Plumb avouched that as early as the first week of February he was sent by Joe Hansen to "witness pickets in Austin."

The six to eight organizers who spent time in Austin also acknowledged that they were in frequent contact with former P-9 business agent Richard Schaefer and "P-10ers" John Morrison and John Anker, both of whom had crossed the picket line. Plumb, who was originally from Philadelphia, said that he and Massachusetts representative Bill McDonough met with Schaefer and the P-10ers individually rather than as a group. The contact with Schaefer was not a superficial one, though, Plumb said: They had spent enough time together to become "good friends."[24]

One might have expected the UFCW to be secretive about its contacts with those who had crossed over. It was not. On January 24, UFCW public affairs director Al Zack told the *Austin Daily Herald* that "it's been reported to us by those strikers who have gone back to work" that supervisors are treating them much better and saying "they learned their lesson."

Then Zack dumped a bombshell: He said that he had recommended the use of fact-finder Arnold Zack to Perpich's staff, and he told the Austin reporter that Arnold Zack was his cousin. "I said that it's going to be controversial. I said, 'You ought to be careful about the name. It may cause some people some problems.' "[25]

A few P-9ers rose to the bait and denounced the fact-finding process as another plot against them. Apparently, UFCW officials were ready to recognize the scabs as the new union, and thus wanted to ensure that the fact-finding process had no chance of success. The director of the state's mediation services, Paul Goldberg, expressed fears that Al Zack's statements would have this effect. He quickly announced that the International union had nothing to do with the selection of Arnold Zack. Later, Arnold Zack denied that he was any relation to the UFCW's media man.[26]

■ ■ ■

The initial picketing had failed in Fremont and Dubuque, but Austin pickets remained on the scene, hoping to persuade workers there to change their minds. "We only need to get one more big plant down, and the rest will fall like dominoes," Rogers explained, repeating the hopeful logic of the board.[27] P-9 pickets also hung on at the small Beloit, Renton, and Stockton plants, where workers also ignored their lines.

Meanwhile, Perpich responded to the criticism from his own party—one DFL leader told a reporter that the Austin situation "is completely un-American, more like Eastern Europe"—and withdrew the Guard. (On the 28th, Mayor Tom Kough also opted momentarily to side with the strikers and unhappy Austin townsfolk and wrote to the governor asking that he "move the National Guard from blocking the city streets"; by the 30th, though, he was back on board with Hoffman and Goodnature, urging that the Guard stay.) Around 380 of the troops left Austin, and the remainder were pulled away from the plant and stationed at the town armory.[28]

As soon as the troops were away, P-9 shut the Austin plant down again.

At 4 A.M. on the 31st, over 400 union members and out-of-town supporters tied up the north entrance with a massive traffic jam. One woman attempted to climb over a fence to enter the corporate headquarters and immediately became the object of a tug-of-war, with union people pulling on one foot, crossovers pulling on the other. Although local police attempted to guide cars through the wall of strikers, few strikebreakers were able to enter the plant. The company never declared the facility closed, but police soon began turning strikebreakers away, and security guards locked the gate.[29]

Police Chief Don Hoffman said that the troops should return. Sheriff Wayne Goodnature called it "the worst day of my life," the first time he had ever been unable to enforce the law. His exaggeration rivaling Arnold's, the sheriff summoned up pictures of gunplay and death, saying that he had called his men back because "I didn't want to lose a law enforcement officer or lose a number of strikers." Knowlton telephoned

Public Safety Commissioner Tschida, who was also visited by a group of company executives urging that troops be returned. But an aide to Perpich indicated that the governor would not again be manipulated by loose talk about mob violence where none existed: "The bottom line is always public safety," he said. "It's not the comfort of the union, and it's not the comfort of the company."[30]

Hormel now maintained that it had 750 working in Austin, including 305 P-9 crossovers, and that it needed only 1,025 "to resume full operations."[31] Subsequently released hiring lists show that the company was hiring at the rate of 40 to 50 a day between January 20 and February 24.[32] But the real question seemed to be whether, without the assistance of the National Guard, Hormel could keep open the plant it seemed to regard as vital.

Objectively, both sides were now violating laws. No one had been seriously injured in the plant gate incidents, so P-9's lawbreaking really consisted of traffic infractions, violations of the injunction that limited the number of pickets at the plant, and possibly some minor destruction of property. Hormel, on the other hand, was refusing citizens access to the public roadways and denying them their constitutionally protected right to demonstrate. Referring to the injunction, the company entered a steady stream of contempt motions against the local, Guyette, Rogers, and a great many union members whom company attorneys attempted to identify in hours of videotapes shown in the courtroom of Bruce Stone, a semi-retired judge brought in to handle the issue. As attorney Winter recalls:

> One motion would just begin to be heard, and they'd bring a new motion. They really focused on the few people of color in the plant, whether or not they'd been in-

volved in any demonstration. We kept getting the company's motions thrown out because they'd name people
not shown in their videotapes. But their many motions
made things monstrously complicated, and led to mass
confusion. Hearings on the various motions started
overlapping.[33]

So certain of the primacy of its rights was Hormel that company spokesmen talked of the need to further limit the constitutional rights of the strikers: "Deprivation of individual
liberties" was "one of the unfortunate tradeoffs," said
Arnold.

"It could be equally said that risks of traffic jams are one
of the unfortunate tradeoffs of free use of public streets,"
quipped labor reporter David Moberg. "The right of management to run its business emerges as paramount."[34]

The law, of course, belonged to the strong. Hoffman and
Goodnature regularly said that they were not favoring either
side. In the same breath, Hoffman would reveal his department's bias, saying, "There seems to be a real loss of support
here [for the strikers] . . . plus there are more workers going
back to work. That in itself is going to determine how much
manpower we need to maintain law and order."[35]

The same bias that equated loss of support for the union
with progress for law and order led to police surveillance of
union meetings and repetition of rank hearsay that placed
union intentions in the worst light. Austin resident Denise
Bahl sent the following memo to Hoffman:

My husband, Dennis, talked to a friend who attended the
union meeting on 2-1-86. He stated to Denny that Mr.
Guyette tabled anything having to do with settling the
dispute and proceeded to tell the members that they were
going for broke. They were calling in other unions for

Monday morning and under no circumstances are the
gates to open. They are done being nice. He advised the
Local P-9 to stay in the background and let other unions
take the lead. Arrests were not a problem as they would
be RPR'd [released on personal recognizance] and out in
a matter of a short time. . . . The governor will not release
the Guard because of the pressure that the Public has put
on him and he would be going against Labor. All they
have to worry about is local Law Enforcement and they
don't have the people to deal with it.

This third-hand report was condensed, supplemented with
the information that "Teamsters union have been in contact
in the past and supplied lists of radical members" and that
"union council now appears to be making all decisions;
membership not having much say in what is going on," and
sent to Tschida and Bureau of Criminal Apprehension super-
intendent John Erskine.

In other memos forwarded from Hoffman to Tschida, policemen reported having heard that "some of the P-9er's [sic]
have some type of puncture or razorblade type object on the
toes of their boots" and that "P-9 had bought an old garbage
truck," perhaps intending "to run a Hormel gate." A report
on a mid-February rally noted the places of origin for out-of-
state automobiles, adding that "there was only one car noted
from Nebraska," a fact that "would appear to affirm the lack
of sympathy for P-9 at Freemont [sic]." Police may have even
tapped the union hall telephone: A word-for-word transcript
of a phone conversation between Rogers and Minneapolis
supporters, obtained from Hoffman's files, suggests that such
a tap existed by late April.[36]

Documents obtained from the Minnesota National Guard
show it to have been anything but a neutral "peacekeeping"

force. Every army must have an enemy, and the National Guard's enemy was clearly not just "disorder," but Local P-9.

The Guard kept a log of each day's occurrences, supplemented by observations and speculation about the union's current strength, morale, base of support, tactical options, access to publicity, and fundraising ability. Between January 22 and February 10, for example, the log-keeper regularly observed that "P-9's strength is continuing to dwindle." On January 27, after roving pickets had shut down Hormel's Ottumwa facility, the log notes that "increased activity of P-9 on several fronts will probably raise moral [sic] of P-9 members who remain off the job," while media coverage may enable the union to raise more money. But on the 29th it says, "Sources report people in union hall are despondent."

That same day's log contains a curious entry: "P-9 remains capable of strong political influence, but this capability may be lost in the event of the illness of the mayor, if he leaves town, or if he returns to work." By February 3 the union was said to be "grasping at straws," and later in the month, "becoming desperate."

No similar assessments were made of company executives' morale, base of support, or financial health. No record was kept of their daily activities, nor did the Guard receive police informants' reports of discussions held in Hormel's executive offices.

Such one-sidedness was doubtless encouraged by the Austin Police Department's portrayal of P-9 as virtually a terrorist organization. The Guard's log frequently refers to the activities of "20 to 30 radicals" and "ultra-radicals," a list of whom, it says, was supplied by the police. On one occasion the log alleges that certain union activists have purchased axes for use against crossovers; on another, that P-9ers may soon get the support of a representative of the right-wing

Posse Comitatus; then it warns that "there are a few abandoned vehicles near the Hormel plant that are to be blown up
for effect." (None of these predictions, of course, ever panned
out. The Guard also regularly received "incident reports"
from Hormel's private security, California Plant Protection
Services. But not everyone can perceive the union's terrorist
leanings, the log says, since its members work hard "to de-
ceive the public into thinking they are a peaceful, non-violent
group."[37]

P-9 members saw the partiality of the local police, but
spoke of this as if it were a matter of prejudiced individuals,
not a problem of the larger system. For many months they
did not absorb the larger lesson that far beyond Austin, the
original promise of the National Labor Relations Act had
been undermined in, as David Moberg put it, an era of "labor
law by injunction."[38] It seems now that local members' willingness to go along with Rogers' program of nonviolence
grew less out of a belief in the effectiveness of that approach
than out of a feeling that, after all, this was America and that
some larger forces would intervene to make sure that Right
and their rights would prevail.

On Saturday evening, February 1, 900 P-9 members voted
not to vote again on the mediators' proposal, as "clarified" by
fact-finder Zack. Members were unpersuaded that a "seniority board" would resolve all the thorny problems created
by new seniority language, and unreconciled to the proposal's failure to address their original concerns.

This vote, and alleged threats from the crossovers (as reported by Goodnature) that they would use weapons to gain
access to the plant, led Tschida and Perpich to return 800
Guardsmen to the north gate. There, on Monday, the Guard
re-enacted their previous tactics, blocking off city streets and
again escorting strikebreakers into the plant. Tuesday, Stone
found both Guyette and Rogers guilty of contempt for violat-

ing the injunction, fining each one $250 and sentencing them
to 15 days in jail. The sentences were stayed pending another
violation.[39] In Mower County, obeying the law meant
surrender.

■ ■ ■

Rogers determined that there was nothing to do but make an
issue of the contradictions in the law. Civil disobedience had
forced southern states to abandon their segregationist laws
and comply with larger constitutional principle. Perhaps
civil disobedience could force the abandonment of laws that
said strikers must allow companies to fill their jobs with
strikebreakers.

On the day the Guard returned, Rogers went to the Austin
Law Enforcement Center and told the sheriff that it was obvious that other efforts would be made to block the Hormel
plant. Fearful that the police might turn violent, Rogers was
looking to work out an understanding whereby mass arrests
would be carried out in a peaceful, orderly fashion. Goodnature chose to take Rogers' statements as a threat and refused to discuss the matter.[40]

On Thursday the 6th, Rogers led about a hundred union
members and backers over to the north side of the plant at
5:45 A.M. This was not meant to be the blockage he had discussed with the sheriff, but rather a public testing of civil
liberties. No one tried to block the gate. Instead, groups of
five and six challenged the police by attempting to walk
down the streets around and under the I-90 exit ramp, and by
assembling away from the gate area. After a while, individual
strikers approached police and Guardsmen and told them to
give way or else they would be subject to citizen's arrest for
blocking the public streets. Police, in turn, arrested and
handcuffed Rogers. As he was being led away, Rogers announced through a bullhorn that demonstrators should "al-

low them to arrest each one of you." But the police arrested only 26 people, none of whom were union executive board members.

"We absolutely didn't do anything to justify the arrests," recalled Rod Huinker.

> There was the injunction, but also it seemed the police chief, Don Hoffman, was trying to interject his own rules. We had no plans of shutting the place down—we didn't have enough people. A police officer let 26 of us go through the underpass toward the front of the plant, then he held the others up, saying, "Those who went through are going to get arrested." Only then did they tell us to leave the area—I was the fourth to get arrested.[41]

All were charged with obstructing justice, a misdemeanor carrying a maximum fine of $700 and 90 days in jail. After a day of mulling over their options, Mower County authorities also charged Rogers with the felony of "criminal syndicalism." Reading the statute to the news media, Goodnature stumbled over its archaic terminology. "It is 'the doctrine which advocates crime, malicious damage or injury to the property of an employer, violence, or other unlawful methods of terrorism as a means of accomplishing industrial or political ends.'" Those who advocated such a doctrine, joined a group or assembly that advocated the doctrine, published, sold, or displayed any writing that advocated the doctrine, or allowed the use of facilities to those advocating the doctrine could be imprisoned for up to five years and/or fined up to $5,000.[42]

Criminal syndicalism: The very words betray the law's antediluvian origin. At one time criminal syndicalism statutes existed on the books of 23 states, a product of the latter days of the Industrial Workers of the World. While the federal government attacked that radical workers' organization obliquely for its part in organizing resistance to World War I, in 1917–20 local legislatures struck head-on. In the words of the historian Melvyn Dubofsky, the legislation "defined almost every fundamental tenet of IWW ideology as a crime against the state, and hence anyone who advocated the Wobbly creed by speech, writing, publication, or display became *ipso facto* a criminal."[43]

In virtually every state that enacted such legislation, the impetus came directly from business interests in industries where the IWW was organizing. Hundreds were sent to prison under the laws, including Local P-9 founder Frank Ellis.

Minnesota was the second state to outlaw criminal syndicalism and the first to successfully prosecute under the law, sending lumberjack Jesse Dunning to prison in 1917. But the statute had neither been invoked in 60 years nor interpreted or narrowed since 1921. Moreover, it was virtually identical to an Ohio law declared invalid by the U.S. Supreme Court 15 years earlier. Statutes remained on the books in only nine of the original states.[44]

It was Rogers' first time behind bars. His clothes were taken away, and he was issued a day-glow orange jumpsuit. At first he shared a cell with P-9er Ray Goodew; then he was put into a cell by himself. Unlike other political prisoners facing their first jailing, he claims to have experienced neither a sense of embarrassment nor one of defeat. Instead, he announced that he would be on a hunger strike until he was released. "I didn't want anybody to forget I was in there, and it was a way of declaring that the authorities weren't totally in control," he explained. He also used one of his two phone calls to tell *Times* reporter Serrin that P-9 was ready to carry its strike "into the summertime."[45]

Moderate bail was arranged for the arrested rank-and-filers. But Mower County attorney Fred Kraft asked that criminal syndicalist Rogers' bail be set at $10,000. Though the judge set bail at $2,500, Rogers chose to spend the weekend in jail and be bailed on Monday, "in order to get some rest."[46]

■ ■ ■

The arrests signaled the beginning of a new phase in the campaign: From now on, it would be a struggle waged primarily against the judicial power of the state, which became Hormel's first line of defense. It was, perhaps, the arena for which we were least prepared.

The local had a number of attorneys assisting with negotiations and the secondary boycott charges, including Ron Rollins and Rick MacPherson. Now, with the force of the courts and criminal charges being used increasingly against the entities Local P-9 and Corporate Campaign and against individual participants, more legal assistance was needed.

MacPherson and Winter were already working on the contempt motions. Austin attorney Robert Leighton volunteered to assist the local people. And the bizarre criminal syndicalism charge brought further help from New Yorkers Emily Bass and Linda Backiel, who, with backing from the National Emergency Civil Liberties Committee, would write a brief against the charge, and Twin Cities attorney Mark Wernick.

At the same time, with the company announcing that it would soon have its full quota of workers, the problem of P-9 crossovers became ever more acute. Striker Ray Moloney told a reporter, "It bothers me real bad. I've got a lot of good friends in there, and, to be honest with you, I don't know how I'll treat them when I see them again. Some are guys that really fought hard when we started out on this rocky road— guys I thought would be with us till the end, and they've deserted us."

The early crossovers had been weak and desperate people or opportunists like Bob Dahlback, an alderman and

"P-10er" who opposed Guyette's leadership and the corporate campaign from the beginning. Asked by a television reporter about P-9's emphasis on winning "dignity" from Hormel, Dahlback beamed as if he had been the most steadfast of strikers and said that the company had learned its lesson. "We've got [dignity] now," he said. "It's a total different atmosphere in there. The people are more friendlier [sic], the foremen, management, and everybody you talk to. I've never heard 'good morning' as many times as I have in the last month that I've been back to work."[47] But those who were now deciding to cross the line were a different breed: people who felt that they had given the strike their best shot and had simply been defeated; men and women who no longer had an answer for the wives, husbands, parents, and other family members who were insisting that they return to work.

"Shorty" Wilson was among these. A small man in a land of Scandinavian giants, he always came across as an agreeable and likable guy. He had been an eager participant in caravans and trips across the Midwest and had taken part in the Fremont picket that was called back and in the shutdown of Ottumwa, where he spent a lot of time. In early February, he was frequently at the union hall, one of those who would go along on any job that was needed.

When a lot of members began crossing, the local held a membership-only meeting at the junior high school to consider what to do. The executive board asked for an honest reckoning: Were people going to cross? Was anyone going to cross? Of the 1,000 P-9ers there, no one spoke in favor of going in. Many spoke passionately for sticking together and staying out, among them Wilson, who said that Austin now had a grave obligation to stand behind the Ottumwans.[48]

The last time I saw him he gave me a lift from my house to the union hall. He didn't have a lot to say—we talked about how rotten the cold was—but he seemed untroubled. Two days later I heard he had gone back. It was nearly impossible to believe: I could still envision him outside the Ottumwa plant the previous August, waving his P-9 cap and cheering as passing trucks honked their horns in solidarity.

"I couldn't believe it, but I'd noticed he was getting discouraged during the caravan to Milwaukee," recalled Rod Huinker, who had known Shorty well. "Like a lot of people, he was pressured by his family. A lot were given an ultimatum: Either go back to work, or pack your bag."[49]

Another crossover, whom reporter David Moberg referred to only as Roger, said, "It's the worst thing that ever happened to me, going across that picket line, but number one is your family." Ironically, Roger had not been convinced by the International's indictment of the strike as a suicide mission. Rather, he felt that he had to admit the local had lost because Wynn, not Jim Guyette, was the UFCW president—and the International had sold the members "down the river." Moreover, a physical disability, common among Hormel veterans, made Roger fearful that he might never get another job.[50]

Furthermore, regardless of the rhetoric of Groundswell and other farm organizations' leaders, the farm crisis played its part in compelling formerly loyal P-9ers to cross. Some had gone to work in the plant in the first place in order to save their less-than-flourishing farms. Then they were whipsawed by the wage cut and by the effects of being on strike. They had started off in a bind, and things just kept getting tougher.

As soon as they went in, each man became just another "lowlife" in the rhetoric of the most ardent unionists, just another goddam scab. But it could never be that easy: The strikers who had been friends of those who were now abandoning the union community were inevitably left questioning the wisdom of continuing the fight.

P-9 negotiators had held back from reducing their wage demand below $10.69. But on February 11 they succumbed to the logic that said compromise could come only on the company's terms. The union proposed a one-year contract with a $10.05 wage rate, accompanied by amnesty for all strikers, everyone returning to work in Austin, Ottumwa, and elsewhere, and all legal actions being dropped. But it insisted on keeping the annual wage and old seniority language, and asked for expedited grievances and baseball-type arbitration on work schedules and standards.

The company said no. The permanent replacements were indeed permanent—the union would have to negotiate its people back as vacancies occurred. Moreover, there would be no annual wage, Hormel would have to think about dropping the legal actions, and the contract would be for three years, leaving Austin out of sync with the rest of the chain contracts.[51]

Hormel had made it clear that there would be no compromise. The negotiations had no result other than to provide Nyberg with an opportunity to gloat: Afterward he said, "It is unfortunate that union members have only now come to recognize the economic realities facing the meatpacking industry."[52]

Later, Lewie Anderson told me that "the company never changed their position."

> They felt that they had walked the local into position to clobber them, and at that point they had no desire to negotiate in good faith. And there came a point where the straight vicious bastards—Krukowski—ended up being substantially influential in the company's tactics.[53]

P-9 really needed a show of support from somewhere. *USA Today* announced that February 11 marked a "pivotal

point in [the] conflict," as the company reopened the Austin
hog kill and announced that it had reached its full workforce goal of 1,025 replacements, including 450 returning
strikers. (In fact, later-released company records would show
that Hormel continued hiring until February 24.) On February 14 the New York Times would editorialize about "the
strike that failed," calling P-9's efforts "less a labor action
than a defiant shaking of fists at large economic forces" and
quoting energetically from UFCW broadsides.[54]

But labor supporters around the country did not believe
that the strike was over. On February 7, a half-dozen officers
of influential New York Teamsters and Communications
Workers locals came to Austin. Their "fact-finding mission"
was part of a New York effort that had been announced on
February 6 by CWA international vice president Jan Pierce
and 30 other area labor officials.[55]

These "fact-finders" brought high union spirits and a
much needed demonstration of reality: Their presence showed that there was somebody out there other than enemies. Bill
Henning, an enthusiastic CWA local vice president, brought
good wishes from Pierce and his union and announced that
CWA locals would be adopting many P-9 families (over a
hundred, Pierce would later declare). Henning and Bill
Nuchow and Dan Kane of the Teamsters, among others, joined
in the life of the P-9 community at the hall, in members'
homes, and at Lefty's Bar. Then, along with 300 P-9ers, they
traveled to Ottumwa, where 3,000 unionists, farmers, and
community backers rallied on February 9 on behalf of the over
400 fired Local 431 members.

The Iowa town had become less favorably disposed to
union goings-on in the weeks since the shutdown. Hormel
had threatened to close its plant permanently, and company
officials began telephoning area farmers to say that it might

have no further need for their hogs because of the demands of greedy workers. In turn, the parish council of the local Catholic church told Father Grubb that he could no longer allow P-9 pickets to sleep on the church basement floor. The Chamber of Commerce took out an advertisement in the local paper thanking those few Hormel workers who were continuing to report to work. And Ottumwa's town council refused to give the union a parade permit or allow it to use public auditorium space. The union members and supporters decided to hold their rally outdoors in a park in near-zero-degree weather.

Mayor Parker still stood with the union members. "I've read your contract," he told the gathering, "and you have the right not to cross picket lines." So did a large gathering of farmers. Dixon Terry of the Iowa Farm Unity Coalition announced, "We will not tolerate these divisive tactics to turn brother against sister, neighbor against one another."

Representatives of 36 unions from across the state showed their colors. The UAW's Iowa political director, Chuck Gifford, reported that his members were busy getting Hormel products removed from grocery shelves. The New Yorkers again described the support that was building in the East. Even Gregory Hormel, great-grandson of George A. himself, sent a letter saying, "It is sad to me that the company that bears my family name is acting this way."[56]

But even this show of strength was outdone on February 15, when 4,000 supporters from around the country—including a delegation of 30 from various New York unions—converged in Austin.

The day before, Judge Stone amended the December injunction placing even further limitations on plant gate picketing. At a hearing held to determine whether Rogers and Guyette had breached the earlier injunction for a second time, the judge announced that only three picketers and six other demonstrators would be allowed within a 50-foot perimeter of the facility. (In effect, this ratified the practice that police instituted on February 6, when Rogers and 26 others were arrested.) Then he said that he would send Guyette and Rogers to jail unless each signed a statement that they would abide by the new rules. Stone admitted that this was "a curtailment of your First Amendment rights, but there comes a time when a judge has to do something he thinks is fair." Hormel's attorney asked for immediate jailing under the February 6 stay of sentence. But Stone allowed Guyette's and Rogers' attorneys, Winter and Wernick, a week to appeal.[57]

The amended injunction—and Hormel's apparent need for it—provided rally speakers with proof that the strike remained powerful.

"Your struggle embodies the feeling of working people everywhere," Henry Nicholas, president of the National Union of Hospital and Health Care Employees, told the over twenty-five hundred who jammed into the high school auditorium. "P-9 is enduring the crucifixion that will be the resurrection of the labor movement. It is the litmus test for organized labor."

Nicholas was one of two labor leaders of national stature who braved the UFCW's injunctions against getting involved in the Austin strike and came to the rally; Pierce was the other. Since his union was already facing AFL-CIO sanctions, because of disputes with other unions, Nicholas told the crowd that he had nothing to lose by being there, unlike Pierce, whom he commended for coming. He criticized the AFL-CIO leadership for not backing the strike, and he likened the injunction's limitations to the curtailment of rights in South Africa.

Pierce had arrived in Austin the night before, one week after the contingent of other New York unionists. A tall and

vigorous fellow-midwesterner whose smashed-around nose
was the result of previous passionate stands for labor, Pierce
later told me that he had expected the mood in Austin to
match the wintry weather. He came because "it dawned on
me that five years before we'd sat on the sidelines and
watched PATCO go down the drain—here was history repeating itself."

Instead of a broken and discouraged handful of strikers,
he found a rowdy 2,500-plus throng of fired-up workers and
their families. "I got choked up," he said. "I hadn't seen this
sort of expression of militancy and union-building for 20
years."

In an extremely emotional speech, Pierce told the crowd
that when he had looked out his hotel window that morning
into the cold, gray sky, he could feel Hubert Humphrey looking down with a tear in his eye at what had become of his
state and the labor movement. He said he had been swept
from that feeling to his own anger at the scabs. "I told them I
could see these pigs who, if you've ever looked at them, have
some pretty sorrowful eyes, and I thought how even a hog
deserves a better fate than being slaughtered by a no-good,
low-down, yellow-bellied, scum-sucking scab." He quoted
the late New York transit union leader Mike Quill, whose
widow Shirley, had also come out from New York, to the
effect that the injunction-wielding judge should "drop dead
in his black robes."

Then Pierce delivered the most emotional gesture of all:
At the end of his remarks, he walked to the edge of the stage
and jumped off, six feet down into the audience, where he
began embracing strikers.

Other speakers found it a hard act to follow. On the up
side, Ottumwa steward Dan Varner described developments
in that city, where he said Hormel had hired only four replacement workers, though it claimed that over four hun-

dred union members had been fired for engaging in a sympathy strike, rather than honoring an authorized picket as their
contract allowed. Twenty thousand dollars had been raised
by the "terminated workers' fund," he noted. On the down
side, Frank Vit, one of the few who had honored the line in
Fremont, said that there was "a hell of a battle" going on in
that local, adding, "With the help of the good people of Austin and Ottumwa, we'll get them people out." Marsha Mickens and Bob Brown, leaders of NRFAC, which had called the
rally, told how local support committees were building the
Hormel boycott in Detroit and Philadelphia.[58]

The rally gave P-9ers the boost they needed to continue
with their only alternative—keeping up the fight. Two days
afterward, Rogers organized what he called a "mystery ride"
for union members and many out-of-town supporters who
were still in Austin. There was no mystery about what they
would be doing—everyone knew they were going somewhere to try to shut down another plant. The only mystery
was where they were going when their two busses pulled out
of Austin in the middle of the night.

It was Dubuque. The next morning, the 150 pickets found
themselves in front of the FDL slaughtering facility there,
upon which Hormel was now very dependent. And several
hundred FDL workers observed the picket, thoroughly dis-
rupting production.[59]

In days to come, union retirees made themselves a regular
part of the action, pressuring merchants to observe the boycott and traveling to the state capital in St. Paul, where they
picketed state buildings and the governor's office. "Workers
can't negotiate at gunpoint," their signs read.

And five days after the rally, 300 children of P-9 families
staged a walkout from school and a demonstration at the corporate headquarters. Carrying signs that read "We're tired of

Hormel High" and "We don't want to grow up to be scab labor," they demanded to meet with CEO Knowlton and, when turned down, moved over to the plant entrance, which they blocked until threatened with arrest. Later, the students announced that they would be going to the state capital, where they would demand to speak with Perpich.

The student protest was partly motivated by the prohibition of any discussion of the strike in city schools. Officials argued that the schools should be a strike-free zone to allow children some relief from the stressful situation. But they could not isolate these institutions from the larger social reality. In days just prior to the protest, several students had been given in-school suspensions for wearing P-9 buttons.

The student actions were extremely controversial among P-9's ranks, with some disapproving union members hearing echoes of 1960s student rebellions against authority. The union executive board took a hands-off position. But most parents of the students supported them, and the kids themselves had no ambivalence. "It helped a lot for us to do this," said junior Chris Klingfus. "Our future is at stake."[60]

Families fighting back: support group member Sandy Titus (center) with her parents, Billie and Ray Goodew. (*Hardy Green*)

Rally at Austin junior high school, January 1985. (*Bob Gumpert*)

Local P-9 president Jim Guyette at the January 1985 rally. (*Bob Gumpert*)

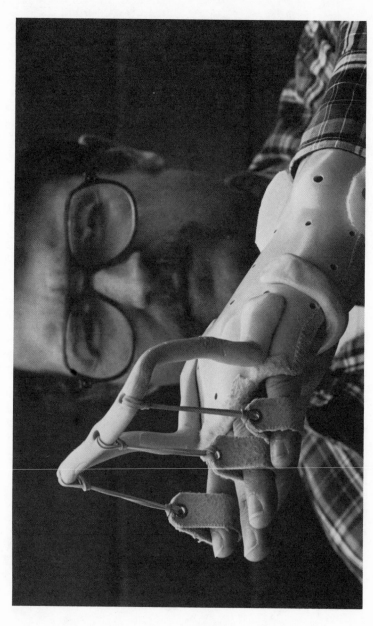

Legacy of pain: On-the-job injuries inflamed union passions against the company. Pictured is James Krulish, whose hand

Dubuque, Iowa: Ray Rogers and P-9 members protest First Bank's ties to Hormel, August 1985. (*Hardy Green*)

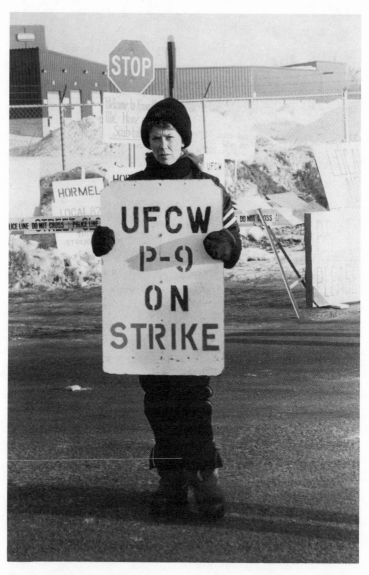

Striker Cheryl Rawn pickets in front of the Austin plant, January 1986.
(*Hardy Green*)

Austin union members face the Minnesota National Guard, January 1986. (*Hardy Green*)

Minnesota farmers bring their equipment and join Austin strikers on the picket line, January 1986. (*Hardy Green*)

Striker Merrell Evans tells the local business agent at Dubuque's FDL Foods that he should stand with the

A 30-year FDL worker pauses to consider the extended picket line that P-9 has thrown up in front of his Dubuque plant—then decides not to cross. (*Nancy Siesel*)

Over 4,000 supporters from across the country march through Austin's streets in support of P-9 on

Police charge into P-9's human blockade of the Austin plant, April 1986. (*Alex Rottner*)

Strikers flee police tear gas, April 1986. (*Hardy Green*)

Rev. Jesse Jackson arrives at the Austin airport, April 1986. (*Hardy Green*)

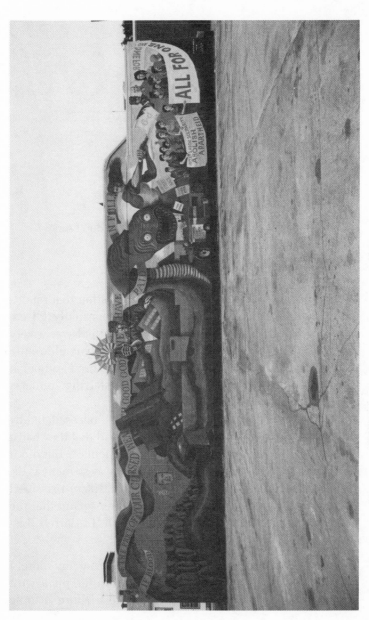

P-9ers' mural commemorating the strike and dedicated to jailed South African liberationist Nelson Mandela. After Local P-9 was placed in trusteeship, the UFCW first sandblasted, then painted over the mural. (*Hardy Green*)

VII

DISOBEDIENCE

You can question a lot of things about me, but don't screw around with my integrity.

—*UFCW president William Wynn*[1]

Was the strike broken? That was the question that reporters, politicians, and labor-watchers repeatedly raised. There was no reason why it had to be. Hormel was a very rich outfit, and, if it felt compelled to, it surely could rehire the 800 "replaced" Austinites and the 500 "fired" others at some compromise wage rate, perhaps transferring "replacements" around to various plants.

Hormel always justified its decisions as "necessitated by business conditions." Its spokesmen also said that they had a legal obligation to the "permanent replacements."[2] But did it really make good business sense to throw away so many skilled and experienced workers? The loyal strikers reassured themselves by saying that it didn't make sense and that the inexperienced scabs couldn't run the plant. In Darrell Busker's words:

> When the company said they weren't hiring any more, I said, "Fine—let them see if they can run the plant with that slime." New hires they'd rejected before. People

who'd been abusing the workers' comp system, claiming
to be disabled. And 30- to 40-year people who went back
just to finish up and get their retirement. It wasn't a dedicated work force. My mom and dad had over 50 years in
with the company, and young workers like myself could
have really given something to them. But I vowed not to
go back till every one of us went back.[3]

It seemed there must be some unknown reason for
Hormel's intransigence. Some strikers said that the company
now was fighting for the industry as a whole, possibly with
material backing from the Meat Institute or some such industry organization.

Others strikers said no; at this point the company was
fighting on behalf of the UFCW, whose leaders could not sur-
vive a P-9 victory.

Far from the ice patch where such topsy-turvy logic
seemed plausible, the elected leadership of the American
working class prepared to hold its annual winter executive
council meeting. For decades AFL, then AFL-CIO, leaders
had repaired to southern Florida for a couple of mid-winter
weeks of sun and speechifying. Just as ritualistically, a corps
of reporters trailed after them, unoptimistic but eager for
some printworthy tidbit. This year the AFL-CIO intended to
spoon-feed them lots of information on how it was revitalizing the labor movement, in accord with a superficial but
much-advertised plan adopted the previous year, "The
Changing Situation of Workers and Their Unions."

The UFCW's national officers saw the Bal Harbour meeting as a chance to slam the door on the strike. The gathering
would be a rare opportunity to promote the UFCW's version
of events among the heads of other unions, who would all be
there, and with the press corps. Thus, Al Zack and other

union staff labored for some weeks before the gathering to put together a definitive "Special Report" on the Austin situation, "UFCW Local P-9 Strikes Hormel: The International Union's Perspective." They planned to circulate thousands of copies of the report at the meeting, and to back it up with press conferences featuring Anderson and Wynn.

Word of these plans also reached Austin, Minnesota. Reporters who admired P-9's spirit—and who hated the thought of wasting time at another AFL-CIO meeting where nothing happened—urged the local to send representatives to stand up to what would otherwise be an unchallenged UFCW media blitz.

I pressed Guyette and Rogers, and reluctantly they agreed to go. After looking over Anderson's "Fact Book on Local P-9/Hormel," we hastily put together our own special report, "The Controlled Retreat: The Crisis of Leadership at the United Food and Commercial Workers Union." We arranged for a meeting room at the Seaview Hotel, only a block away from the Sheraton Bal Harbour, where the convention was taking place, and announced that a press conference would take place on February 19.

Florida was indeed another world of sunlight and warmth, as the three of us realized as soon as we arrived at the lush Miami airport on the 18th. The next morning, prior to our press conference, Guyette would go on the nationally televised "CBS Morning News" for another debate with Anderson, who stressed the International's new theme of attack: P-9's "irresponsible" loss of over a thousand union jobs.[4] (The UFCW's "Special Report" said that P-9's "gallant members" had "become cannon fodder for a self-proclaimed 'master strategist' bent on attaining symbolic victory or glorious defeat at the expense of hundreds of workers' jobs, divided families, a broken community, and labor solidarity.")[5] Meanwhile, Rogers and I went on to the Sheraton to make sure that members of the press had really gotten word of our press conference.

There was no problem about that. Virtually every member of the press who was in town to cover the convention turned up, along with several local television crews who gravitated to the display of intra-union conflict, as rare at an AFL-CIO convention as sharecroppers at the Sheraton Bal Harbour. Also in the room were Victor Kamber, a public relations consultant on retainer to the International, and UFCW representatives, who handed out notices of a press conference to be held by Anderson as soon as ours ended.

Before the press conference opened, I urged Guyette and Rogers not to take on the whole labor establishment. Let's say that the UFCW leaders are out of step, but not the whole of AFL-CIO officialdom, I said. Follow your own advice, I told Rogers: divide your opponents; don't provide the rhetoric that will cause them to unite behind Wynn.

This was the approach of our position paper, "The Controlled Retreat." It focused on the UFCW's double-dealing and attacks on P-9 and allowed officials from other unions to dissociate themselves from the situation.

But it didn't matter what I said. Guyette reported that Federation president Lane Kirkland had shown his insensitivity to workers' problems by refusing the local leader's request to address the AFL-CIO's executive council. "We feel confident that we can win this situation with the support of the labor movement that is not down here in Bal Harbour out on the golf course or in the jewelry shops," Guyette announced, indicting all conventioneers.

"A lot of workers in the labor movement would like to sit before the AFL-CIO leaders and say, 'Do you really understand what the steel workers are going through, the

auto workers, the secretaries, the hotel workers?'" he ela-
borated.

Rogers called Wynn "one of the most anti-union people
I've ever come across" and said he and other labor leaders
had become accustomed to a soft life and high pay, acting
and dressing like corporate executives. He said the Austin
workers were calling Wynn the "Mr. T of the labor movement" because, like the television personality, he wore a
number of gaudy gold chains, rings, and a flashy watch.

Next stop: their press conference. There, Anderson again
put special emphasis on the "devastating" loss of jobs and
the "anti-union" nature of P-9's activities in the midst of an
overall anti-union climate. "Clearly they've lost the strike,"
he announced. "It's a colossal failure."

Guyette stood in the first row, asking questions about Anderson's statements and pulling out documents from his
briefcase in an attempt to refute the charges. Hadn't the Ottumwa and Fremont workers circulated petitions to urge the
International to sanction extended P-9 picketing?

"You know how easily those things can be manipulated,
Jim," inserted Ken Kimbro, the most vocal of three FDL and
Hormel rank-and-file workers flown in for the occasion.
Kimbro, whose demonstrations of loyalty to UFCW officialdom would pay off in time, was a steward at the FDL
plant in Rochelle, Illinois. P-9's anti-union rhetoric, he said,
had "damned near destroyed" a union organizing campaign
at IBP in Rock Island, Illinois.

But the Kimbro-Guyette exchange was soon drowned out
by a heated shouting match between Rogers and Robert
Harbrandt, head of the Federation's Food and Allied Service
Trade Division (FAST). When Rogers insisted that Anderson
cite one case of a UFCW campaign that effectively mobilized

workers, Harbrandt, whose office had conducted a number of "coordinated campaigns" for the International, exploded. Rogers, he said, was not only showing his arrogance, but also telling untruths.

> Rogers: Are you speaking because you have great respect for what the leadership of this International union is doing, or are you speaking because they are paying a lot of money to FAST?
>
> Harbrandt: You've known me long enough to know that nobody, Bill Wynn, Lane Kirkland, George Meany, or anybody else can make me say anything other than the truth.

The exchange went on for 10 minutes while reporters scribbled notes and television cameras whirred. Finally Rogers announced that he had great respect for Harbrandt and his staff. Harbrandt took that as an apology and stomped away.

Serrin wrote in the *Times*: "People here said nothing like it had occurred at these meetings in a decade and a half, perhaps more. A retired labor leader said he had seen nothing like it in 30 years."[6]

The press was delighted. P-9 had provided them with a little titillation and something to write about that was not simply culled from official press releases. Among the labor people, genuine emotions were aroused: Many delegates had hoped to be able to ignore the whole Austin affair, and now they were being forced to consider their feelings and even to take sides.

Later that day Wynn held his own press conference. The high point came when the UFCW president announced that the many demonstrations on behalf of P-9 signified nothing. "Demonstrations are like masturbation," he announced.

"They give you a certain amount of relief, but they don't accomplish very much."[7]

Overlooking such obscene gaffes, Al Zack was pleased. According to several reporters, Zack was spreading the word that "we've turned it around." The press, he felt, was beginning to side with the UFCW against the local. Perhaps the UFCW's headquarters-bound staff never understood: They didn't simply have a press problem—they had a real problem among rank-and-file members.

Lane Kirkland, on the other hand, understood that there was a real problem and felt that perhaps something could be made of the unusual goings-on. In his letter denying Guyette access to the AFL-CIO executive council, Kirkland had also said that he would be glad to meet with Guyette to "hear your views." Later that afternoon he agreed to meet in a private session with just Guyette and Wynn.

Afterward, Guyette pooh-poohed the meeting. Kirkland, he said, listened to Wynn and said that the local should have settled on Hormel's terms. Perhaps more attuned to Kirkland's designs, Serrin saw something other than support for the International in the meeting. "I was stunned," he said, that Kirkland agreed to any meeting at all:

> But I don't think Kirkland likes Wynn, his style, or what he stands for. And I think he thought he might be able to do something. He said, "Jim, what can I do for you?" But Jim said, "We want X, Y, Z," which he saw as the same old thing. He could have said some subtle kind of negotiating thing, like "we're not trying to make war on the labor movement" or "it's unfortunate we can't get along with Mr. Wynn." He could have said, "Perhaps you could come to Minnesota and help to settle this thing." Kirkland was trying to make some kind of opening, but

[AFL-CIO Director of Information] Rex Hardesty told me later that Jim wouldn't respond to Kirkland's signals.[8]

For Kirkland, it was an opportunity to expand the authority and activity of the AFL-CIO into the collective bargaining process of one of its largest affiliates—something with which it did not ordinarily get involved—and to embarrass Wynn in the process. Earlier in the day, Kirkland had noted that such Federation involvement and "ambulance service" had been "the subject of extended discussion." Perhaps Guyette could have played on Kirkland's designs to advantage, but instead he had responded to Kirkland's mouthing of the UFCW line that the local had taken "its own independent course of action . . . breaking solidarity with the rest of the labor movement."[9]

The following day, the Federation executive council adopted a statement denouncing the "all-or-nothing stances" taken by P-9. "Today's economic and political climate makes it imperative that unions follow realistic bargaining strategies that will assure gains for workers and protect their jobs," it read. Henceforth, national union leaders—like Machinists' union president William Winpisinger, who sent out a letter scoring Rogers' "scorched earth school of labor relations"—would urge their members to toe the line.[10]

It was always extremely unlikely that P-9 could have broken the council's natural solidarity with itself. But we might have done a better job of introducing divisions into the group. Had we not come, the council would have adopted the same resolution condemning P-9. Our presence had not persuaded anyone to speak out on our behalf or generated enough discomfort about the UFCW's actions to prevent adoption. Instead, we had only found another forum to address the broad mass of working people and to lodge a protest—albeit a virtually unprecedented one—about the council's complicity with the UFCW.

■ ■ ■

Back in the Midwest, Perpich ordered the remaining 200 Guardsmen out of Austin on February 18 after two weeks of quiet, during which P-9 was concentrating on activities elsewhere. State Commissioner of Public Safety Paul Tschida said, though, that he recognized that the "cat-and-mouse" games would likely continue between the strikers and the company and local law enforcement.[11]

From now on, the governor and state officials would attempt to remain on the sidelines and out of sight. Earlier in the month of February, Perpich met once with each side of the dispute—telling the union board that it should encourage members to accept the fact-finder's report and "live to fight another day"—and made a number of phone calls to Guyette and Knowlton. He got together with various Minnesota labor leaders, including AFL-CIO head Dan Gustafson and representatives from the Teamsters, the Steelworkers, and the UAW, whom he urged to press for a settlement. He also met with Austin law enforcement chiefs to discuss the troop withdrawal. In late February, he told delegates at a Minnesota AFL-CIO legislative conference, where he defended his use of the Guard as doing "what he had to do under the Constitution," that no governor had ever spent as much time trying to resolve a labor dispute as he had in this case.

Neither P-9 nor the company was much impressed. In our interview, Nyberg told me that Perpich had never made any practical suggestions: "Mainly it was, 'Gee, I wish you could get together and get this resolved.'" Nor, according to Nyberg, did Perpich offer to personally mediate the dispute, as he may have privately claimed to some DFL legislators. P-9 executive board member Skinny Weis said there were conflicting reports about what actions Perpich took, but he added, "I can't see any way he helped us."[12]

The picket line stayed up in Fremont, ignored by the vast majority of workers who crossed and went in to work each day. "It was terrible cold," recalled Rod Huinker, who pulled several stints in Fremont.

> We had 40- to 50-below wind chills that never let up. The Nebraska Highway Patrol were very intimidating: They wouldn't let people warm up in their vehicles or take a break, and they watched everything, so we had to guard against breaking any minor law. Only a few honored the line, the rest just walked in every day. It was discouraging: They wouldn't talk to you a lot. They knew the truth, but the way the company was doing things, they were just scared of losing their jobs.[13]

Austin kept at least a dozen people in Fremont. They picketed around the clock in three-hour shifts and slept on the floor and on cots in a mobile home. From time to time, the pickets and a P-9 executive board member would hold a meeting to discuss what was happening, but these were primarily attended by the few Fremonters who were already observing the picket.

In Ottumwa, where the plant remained mostly closed, P-9 vice president Lynn Huston decided to pull the pickets after five weeks. The organizing team sent in by the International union had convinced the community and businesspeople that everyone was suffering solely because of the picket line. Huston talked with a number of the "radical crew" that supported P-9, and all agreed that it was time. "So we decided to put the burden on the UFCW, who'd told everybody straight out that if the picket line came down, they'd get everyone's job back tomorrow," Huston said.

> We pulled the picket line the next day. A number of people down there and up in Austin didn't agree, but I knew that we were going to become the villains real fast if we didn't. That morning, Louie DeFrieze said, "We don't want Lynn Huston anywhere around—I'm your leader and should be the one to lead everybody back." I said no, we oughta do it right. I put the picket line up, and I'm gonna take it down. And the man who's going to walk down there with me is the mayor, Jerry Parker.
>
> The 500 workers started down the street in mass. We had about twenty flags, and everyone was wearing Local 431 red hats and jackets. Louie tried to hold them back so he could be the leader, and they almost ran him over. When we got down to the plant and pulled the line, we found a big lock on the gate, preventing anyone from returning. So Louie went in to the office to talk to company executives.
>
> Meanwhile, with all the media gathered around I kept announcing, "You got a lockout here . . . just look at that lock." Finally, Louie came back out and said, "It's not a lockout, there's just a dispute, and there will be an arbitration." The company continued to partially operate with about 200 scabs, and the UFCW had "expedited" arbitration that took almost a year to get resolved.[14]

After the lockout, Ottumwa members filed for unemployment and, arguing that the lockout represented an unfair labor practice, set up their own pickets and engaged openly in other strike activities.

On the second day of the "mystery ride" picketing in Dubuque, only about 80 FDL workers honored P-9's picket, and the picketers returned to Austin. Merrell Evans later told me, "The first day enough stayed out to shut the plant down and keep it shut until the afternoon shift. Then the militant half saw that the other half wouldn't support them."[15]

And in Austin, Hormel executives led reporters on a tour of the reopened flagship plant, where company spokesmen said 1,045 people were working: 453 P-9 crossovers and 592 new hires.[16]

The picket line would remain in Fremont until May, and potential picketers stayed out near the western plants in Washington and California, ready to try again on command. The Fremont picket line could not be removed without jeopardizing the jobs of those who had honored it. Besides, as Rogers said, one never knew when some injury or incident in the plant might spark a walkout. But, in fact, the tactic of extending P-9 pickets had gone as far as it was going to go without International sanction.

The action shifted inexorably homeward.

Among the Austin ranks, there had always been strong sentiment that P-9 could not expect other Hormel workers to honor their pickets if the local could not keep its own Austin plant closed down. Moreover, since January, Rogers had talked in terms of mass civil disobedience to shut that plant and appeal to the broad public. He had led P-9 members in unlikely chants of "nonviolence . . . nonviolence" and spoken to them of the power of civil disobedience as demonstrated by Mohandas Gandhi and Martin Luther King. He had said repeatedly that strikers could not win a violent fight against the National Guard and that violence would turn the public against them.

At first, Rogers now says, he wanted no more than 25 or 50 people to lie down in front of the gates. These would be arrested and face jail or even heavy fines. He hoped to build on this, ultimately bringing in thousands of men, women, and children from outside Austin to block the gates a few at a time. As each group was arrested, others would replace them. And as those arrested were released, they would return to block the plant again.

Such arrests would place an enormous physical and economic burden on the local authorities who had become Hormel's first line of defense against the strikers. "I knew the company would have the money to offset the adverse publicity with public relations campaigns and to hold out against the workers," he told me some months later. "The question would become who could hold out the longest."[17]

A Twin Cities anti-war organization, Women Against Military Madness, came to Austin and described the nuts and bolts of civil disobedience before P-9 audiences. They held an hours-long training session, with role-playing in which some P-9ers acted the role of police and others the role of demonstrators. The WAMM women discussed arrest experiences they had had and got people to practice locking arms with each other and becoming dead weight so that they would have to be carried away.

Among the members, the basic idea was clear. In the words of Mike Bambrick:

> The idea was for many people to get arrested and fill up the jails, and they'd have to quit arresting us and then we'd be able to block the gates. . . . Pretty soon they'd realize that we weren't afraid to keep getting arrested. It would cost them so much money to keep arresting us that they would quit doing it, and that would allow us to keep blocking the gates. But the bit of being arrested wasn't as easy as people thought it would be.[18]

On March 10, 122 union members, spouses, and supporters were arrested after they blockaded the Hormel corporate headquarters near the plant. At least 200 men and women had gathered at the union hall and then, at 3 A.M., gone to the corporate office, where they chained and padlocked the gate. The key was given to one of their number, who drove away to deliver it to Governor Perpich along with a letter stating, "Our civil rights have been denied by you and the Hormel company long enough." Then protesters sat down in the road, locked arms, and demanded that Hormel officials meet with P-9's board. Company officials refused to meet "under these circumstances."

The local police arrested the first P-9er at 7 A.M. The police officers were immediately surrounded by protesters and forced to withdraw. When they returned, they were accompanied by police reinforcements from nearby counties. They gave repeated "final warnings" to disperse. More arrests followed: In each case, a band of six to ten police would push its way into the crowd, seize a protester, and wrestle him or her away to a police van. Demonstrators sang "We Shall Not Be Moved" and chanted, "We want a contract." Others shouted, "Scabs, get a decent job." It took the police until 1:30 in the afternoon to clear the drive.

The actions came on the day after defense lawyers filed papers calling for dismissal of the criminal syndicalism charges against Rogers, on the grounds that they involved selective prosecution, that the law was unconstitutional, and that in any case Rogers was not guilty. The new arrests took authorities all day to process and represented the biggest single-day glut of criminal defendants in Mower County history.[19]

Those arrested included a large number of strikers' wives (35 women altogether) and retirees. After being frisked and held for several hours, many, such as Barbara Collette, expected to be released. Instead, they were told that they were being jailed until their court arraignment. "There were 17 of

us in a cell made for 12. We were all together, we were singing, we were talking. Then they started throwing mattresses
and pillows at us and told us we were going to be there over-
night. Our whole cell went dead quiet." Carmine Rogers, the
wife of a retiree, convinced the authorities that she had to
return home to take some medication and to feed her dog.
She was driven home in a squad car, and two burly policemen stood over her as she dished out the dog chow.[20]

Cynthia Bellrichard was arrested around noon and, along
with about fifty others, held in a police training room for five
hours. Ultimately she and a dozen other women were taken
first to a filthy "drunk tank," then to an equally filthy Cell G,
which had six bunks. According to her later account, the
floor and unconcealed toilet were foul, and the dirty sink
was clogged. In time, they were brought eight more mattresses and "raggy blankets" and six towels. One woman
slept on the table and seven others on the floor.[21]

Serving as women's matron was the sheriff's wife, Sandy
Goodnature, who that evening stood outside Carmine
Rogers' six-person cell taunting the 13 prisoners inside. "She
opened up the little slot so we could see her eating popcorn
and said, 'Doesn't this smell good, don't you wish you had
some?' "[22]

Afterward, many of those jailed wrote accounts of their
experiences. From these narratives, it is clear that the local
authorities made no attempt to conceal their hostility toward
the protesters, treating them to conditions that Sandy Titus
said made her "want to scream and vomit at the same time."
All of the accounts take note of the squalid facilities, of un-
met requests that dirty toilets or floors be cleaned, and of
rude, "robotic" treatment by the guards.[23]

But the overcrowding was so severe—80 people were
housed in the Austin jail, which had a licensed capacity of

45—that many protesters were sent to other towns, including Preston, Owatonna, Faribault, Albert Lea, and Rochester, where the treatment was much better. "If I ever have to be put behind bars again," wrote Roger Diggins, "I'd definitely request that I be transferred to Preston."

> We had a telephone in the cell which we could use at random. . . They served us ice cream for dessert, we had no restrictions against us. . . . Our personal hygiene was well taken care of. . . . The facilities we had contained a TV room and also a reading room, every visitor could walk around to each cell and visit or play cards.[24]

Outside Austin, police were very sociable toward the protesters, whom they seemed to regard as curiosities.

The following day, many of the women and men had to appear before the judge in their underwear, as their clothes had been confiscated but the Law Enforcement Center had run out of coveralls. The majority were released without bail, after being charged with obstructing the legal process and unlawful assembly, misdemeanors carrying possible penalties of 90 days in jail and $700 fines.[25]

There were several simultaneous developments. On the day of the arraignments, Judge Stone lifted his February 14 order that allowed no more than three pickets and six protesters within sight of the plant because local authorities had failed to ask for an extension. (The original injunction limiting the number of pickets to three and prohibiting any blockage of the roads remained in force.) In Minneapolis, the local was again called before the NLRB, this time to face unfair-labor-practice charges that members had harassed and restrained replacement workers.

And during the evening that protesters were languishing in jail, the local membership began voting on a resolution that called for the executive board to settle its differences with the International and present a unified contract demand to the company. If approved by secret ballot, the motion would "release our executive board from all conditions placed on them to bargain a contract."[26]

The intent of the resolution was to allow union negotiators "leeway" to move away from previous sticking points such as the guaranteed annual wage and restoration of all jobs. Its author, Charlie Peterson, was a faithful backer of the local's campaign who had gotten the idea that the local could still resolve its differences with the UFCW, and perhaps the two could come up with a settlement slightly better than the mediators' proposal. He told reporters that the resolution was not intended as a vote of no confidence in P-9's officers, though Guyette had spoken against the proposal.

According to Margaret Winter, who was on hand for a meeting where the resolution was discussed:

> It was very heated. Peterson presented his resolution as a neutral thing. But those opposing it, like Buck Heegard, argued that there was no way that it would not be used against the local's leadership, to support the claim that Guyette was a Svengali who'd led members down the garden path. There was a lot of haggling over the precise language. And, finally, the majority were persuaded by Peterson that it wouldn't be misinterpreted, that it would be a way to get Anderson or some UFCW person there to ask some hard questions and tell him a thing or two.[27]

It also seems likely that many members reasoned that anything was worth a try. So a majority approved the resolution. The next day, March 15, UFCW president William Wynn seized upon the resolution to order an end to the strike and cut off strike benefits.

■ ■ ■

The move had been coming for some time. The "organizing team" was doing its work across the region, discouraging other Hormel workers from honoring P-9 pickets, bad-mouthing the renegade local, and spying on its activities. In late February, International officials Wynn, Hansen, Anderson, Foreman, and Dority met in Washington to consider de-sanctioning the strike; their ruminations were openly reported in the press.[28] Picking up on the cue, Nyberg had publicly urged the local to "resolve its differences with the UFCW," saying that P-9 members could be put on a preferential rehire list or perhaps get jobs at other company plants.[29]

Thus the minute the local members' peace overture arrived—with its tacit recognition of the International's strength and authority—Wynn proceeded as though it were a rank-and-file demand that he break the strike. When a reporter asked what authority the UFCW had to end the strike, Wynn replied that the members "asked me to."[30]

"Continuing the local leadership's failed strategy for one additional day, or one more month, or an additional year is not going to change the facts," the UFCW president said at a press conference where he announced his edict. The $40-a-week strike benefits would be ended, but the UFCW would instead pay $40 "post-strike benefits" to those who ended their picketing and halted an "unauthorized boycott" of Hormel products.

Wynn also said that he would personally begin negotiations with Hormel, adding that he did not believe the company's claim that it did not need additional employees. And, blaming Rogers for the "doomed" effort, he said that he had "a strong feeling that Mr. Rogers will not be retained by any other labor organization."[31]

In Minneapolis, Joe Hansen said that the UFCW hoped its directive would allow remaining strikers to return to work without the stigma of crossing a picket line, make it easier to negotiate a contract preserving some jobs, allow strikers to apply for unemployment benefits, and help keep the plant under UFCW representation.[32]

Local members in Austin were aghast. "If we're on a 'suicide mission,' they're committing murder," said one. Winkels told an afternoon press conference attended by 150 loyalists, "They've turned their backs on the membership and on unionism as a whole."[33] More than a little grumbling was aimed in the direction of Charlie Peterson.

Guyette was in New York when the announcement came. There, over a thousand people turned out on a cold and rainy night to champion the local's anti-concession stand and fill UAW District 65's two auditoriums, connected by a public address system. Hundreds more crammed the entranceway downstairs. Speakers included Teamsters such as Bill Nuchow and Dan Kane, who had previously journeyed to Austin, and TWA flight attendants, who were then waist-deep in their own strike.

Conscious of the UFCW directive, District 65's longtime president David Livingston announced, "The Hormel strikers are part of the family of labor, and we will go with them as far as is necessary." Farm Labor Organizing Committee leader Baldemar Velasquez told how his union's corporate campaign had led to a victory over Campbell Soup Co., in spite of active hostility from the AFL-CIO and the UFCW, which represented that company's production workers. Velasquez volunteered his 11,000 boycott activists to aid the Hormel boycott cause. And Jan Pierce said he wanted to thank Hormel and TWA: "They're giving us a reason to coalesce. They are revitalizing the rank and file. And they are making us a movement again."

Rogers again invoked Gandhi and King, urging people from across the country to "come to those plant gates and close them down." And Guyette told the crowd that in spite of Wynn's ruling, the fight would go on. "As far as we're concerned, nothing's changed," he said.[34]

■ ■ ■

Guyette's presence in New York and at a 400-strong San Francisco rally two days earlier was part of a coordinated effort involving many local board members and rank-and-filers. Following the February rally in Austin, spokespeople were sent out to major cities across the country with the task of building the boycott and making direct appeals for the Adopt-A-Family program. These emissaries would attend hundreds of local union meetings and large rallies to tell their story, urge backing for the boycott, pass the hat, and describe how unions and other organizations might adopt strikers.

Executive board member Skinny Weis was in charge of West Coast activities. In January he, fellow board member Jim Retterath, and several rank-and-filers went to Seattle with the intention of picketing the Renton plant. The morning they went to the plant, they found all 150 workers already inside by 6 A.M. The local UFCW business agent had anticipated their coming, and he encouraged the P-9ers to leave town. Instead, Skinny, Bud Miller, and Merle and Madeline Kruger began a tour of the area, speaking before 13 unions, including five Machinists locals at the immense Boeing works there, two central labor councils, and a gathering of 160 officers from union locals over the next two weeks.

Passing the hat at 30 meetings from San Jose to San Francisco, Weis and his colleagues collected over $1,500. The *San Francisco Chronicle* reported that "for militant unionists in San Francisco, Skinny and Bud bring memories of the general strike of 1934. The two strikers have been so popular in the Bay Area that they extended their stay by a week." IAM Lodge 1327 business agent John Moran said, "They come across like here's your Mom and Dad come to town and they need help."[35]

In time, Buck Heegard took over in the San Francisco Bay Area, and Weis went on to Los Angeles. Some months later Heegard recalled:

> I flew into San Francisco with a one-way ticket and $40. Three union people met me at the airport, took me home, and put me up. The next day I went to an AFSCME [state, county, and municipal employees] local meeting of about 40 people. After I got through, they passed the hat and it came back with $186. I thought, "I can do this."
>
> I spoke before high school students, church groups, anti-apartheid and Central America solidarity groups. I did a couple of labor television programs, four or five radio interviews, and a *Los Angeles Times* interview. I went to Watsonville [site of a bitter cannery strike] seven or eight times to walk their picket line. And every place I went they said, "You're really giving us an education."

Frequently, Heegard was barred from union gatherings after UFCW officials telephoned the sponsors. He was only allowed to speak before the Marin County Labor Council as part of a debate with a UFCW field representative. But the UFCW man's assertion that the local's leaders had led its members blindly to ruin could not hold up against the presence of the well-spoken rank-and-filer, out alone on the road. Thereafter, Heegard was sometimes barred from speaking because unions were unable to get the UFCW to send anyone to speak against him. Nevertheless, he did address both the California Federation of Teachers' statewide convention—

which endorsed a pro–P-9 resolution and passed the hat just after national president Albert Shanker spoke—and the Postal Workers' national convention, where he shared the stage with Lane Kirkland and Mine Workers president Richard Trumka. To promote speaking engagements, he even had a business card printed up that read "Buck Heegard, Local P-9 Striker" and listed a West Coast Office phone number.

Heegard and four others, including Ottumwans Frank Vit and "Bear" Martsching, also shut down an Oakland dock one day because of a "hot cargo" of Hormel products.

> We knew from the president of Longshoremen's Local 6 when a truck of Hormel products from Fremont was arriving. He told us that since machinery had been moved from Austin to Fremont, the strike situs was extended and that we had the right to put up a picket line. So that's what we did one Tuesday at 5:30 A.M. After about 15 minutes, this guy in a suit came out and ordered the truck to leave. The Teamsters, Warehousemen, Longshoremen, Machinists, none of them would cross our line. . . .
>
> At 10 o'clock, they had a hearing with an arbitrator right there. I testified about the extended strike situs. The truck driver testified that things had gotten a lot busier in Fremont since the strike. But at 1:30 the mediator ruled that we couldn't prove the goods were from an extended strike situs. So we pulled the line after calling the radio stations and holding a press conference at which we said we'd proved our point that we could stop the shipment of Hormel products any place, any time.[36]

Martsching also made a tour of labor meetings in St. Louis, Missouri, with P-9er Dan Petersen.

There were further sizable rallies in Oakland, Cleveland, and Detroit. The last of these drew around a thousand to hear

Guyette and Ottumwan Bill Cook, along with Watsonville striker Maria Rosario Morono. That rally clearly demonstrated the breadth of UAW support for P-9's strike: It was sponsored by the Autoworkers local at the historic Ford Rouge plant, attended by contingents from seven UAW locals, and addressed by elected leaders of three of the city's most important locals.

Over the next few months, P-9 speakers went to meetings of every description in Baltimore, Chicago, San Diego, San Jose, Cincinnati, Birmingham, Atlanta, and Miami and across New Jersey, Alabama, North Carolina, Texas, Utah, New Mexico, and Massachusetts.[37]

None of this would have been possible without the support groups that developed in cities from coast to coast. The Twin Cities group, of course, had been an integral part of P-9 activities since before the strike. But in California Weis and Heegard built their own support groups with the help of a few key backers who had good connections, such as the Machinists' newspaper editor Dan McCoslin.

Much of the legwork of arranging meetings in Seattle, San Francisco, and San Jose was performed by members of the Socialist Workers Party. In Los Angeles, Longshoremen's union and NRFAC leader David Arian was instrumental in helping Weis set up a support group with over forty members, just as NRFAC leaders Marsha Mickens and Bob Brown were key in establishing Detroit and Philadelphia support groups.

Heegard accepted assistance from a variety of leftists so long as all understood that he was in charge. (At one point, though, he disbanded a San Jose support group that he felt had "attracted every radical from the Bay Area," each with a separate agenda.) As a result of his attitude that "a drowning man doesn't ask who is extending him a helping hand," he was often the object of red-baiting. Generally, he tried to use humor to deflect it:

> At a Machinists meeting, this guy came up to me and said, "Buck, can I ask you a personal question? Are you a member of the Communist Party?" I told him I'd spent 35 years getting adjusted to the fact that I was the only Lutheran in a Catholic household. Now you want me to be the only Communist among a bunch of Democrats? He just turned around and walked away. I just got to the stage where I was able to deal with it. I was a little more concerned about the people who were threatening: I'd get calls telling me how this might be my last trip out there.[38]

Though red-baiting and UFCW-fomented rumors that Local P-9 was communist may have kept some supporters away, on balance the involvement of left-wing organizations had positive results for the local. For as long as it made any difference, NRFAC's "controllers" were energetic and helpful. (Later, in keeping with their desire to rise to the top of the labor movement, they cut ties with P-9 and attempted to make amends with the labor bureaucracy.) All NRFAC wanted in exchange was to grab the spotlight, occasionally shoving others aside. But no one complained much during the most crucial months.

The Socialist Workers Party was, in leftist argot, almost completely "tailist": Whatever strike tactics P-9's leaders chose, the SWP supported. A Los Angeles SWP member, for example, told The Militant that it was time to "get bolder" in strike support. But she did not mean to suggest an independent course of action. Rather, her new boldness consisted of "inviting speakers to union meetings, plant-gate collections, going to Austin to see the strike first hand, getting locals to support the boycott, and participating in the Adopt-A-Family program"—all activities encouraged by P-9.[39]

Again, all the SWP wanted was to associate its members with the militant strike, and to put some of its people into positions of responsibility in coordinating the out-of-town networking.

Those were the left groups with the most significant presence in P-9 support activities. As stated earlier, the Communist Party U.S.A. had little to do with the strike, though for many months its newspaper, the *Daily World,* took a quietly supportive position, often writing as though the strikers had the wholehearted support of the AFL-CIO. In early February 1986, though, the CP could straddle the widening chasm no longer. The *World*'s primary labor writer, Bill Dennison, cast the party's lot with the bureaucracy in an article that repeated the old charges about "breaking with the chain" while curiously endorsing a Hormel boycott at the same time. Later that month Dennison described the events of the AFL-CIO meeting in Miami, unfavorably contrasting Guyette's "outrageous charges" against the International with the polished restraint shown by the UFCW's imported rank-and-filers. It was the most favorable coverage that Lewie Anderson's press conference received.[40]

Aside from representatives of organized left organizations, two other types of supporters came to P-9's side in spite of the UFCW's denunciations and edict: union members and staff, including many who were already active in other union and international solidarity efforts; and mid-rank union officials, motivated by some combination of the old union spirit and opportunistic desire to make a show of militancy.

East Coast support activities illustrate the backing from these other quarters. In New York, left organizations' connections were relatively unimportant. The support group there was pulled together by Corporate Campaign staffer Susan Hibbard, had the blessing of Jan Pierce and a number of local and regional union officials, and was mostly composed of low-ranking but active union officers and staff people. Aside from building the rally, the group focused on handbilling for the boycott.

Hibbard was also able to get an impressive list of black elected officials—including two congressmen—ministers, civil rights leaders, and unionists to oppose the company's targeting of black consumers and add their names to *Amsterdam News* and *City Sun* advertisements endorsing the boycott. Afterward the New York City Council also passed a resolution endorsing the strike and boycott, though UFCW speakers said that it should not. And, in a surprise move, William McGowan, president of the state's largest union, the 220,000-member Civil Service Employees Association, and far from a leading light of progressive unionism, published a statement of support in that union's newspaper.[41]

In Boston, a support group was built largely around a network established to prevent the closing of the Dorchester meatpacker Colonial Provision Co. Brian Lang, chief steward at that plant, had met Guyette at a UFCW meeting in 1985 and had spent time in Austin before the strike, including attending a June P-9 rally. But most of his efforts during the winter were directed toward prodding the city of Boston to employ the right of eminent domain to thwart the closing, which was announced in mid-December, after the purchase of Colonial by Thorne Apple Valley Inc.

The Colonial workers built powerful opposition to the plant closing as a community issue in Dorchester, utilizing boycott activities and rallies. With media attention and the support of the Massachusetts AFL-CIO, they won city council backing for a plan to have the city buy the plant on the grounds that it provided needed jobs in a blighted area—an approach used earlier to prevent the closing of Morse Cutting Tool in New Bedford. Ultimately, though, Boston's corporation counsel ruled that the purchase would be illegal. As Lang recalls:

> December through March was a whirlwind of activity. We built a core group of 30 people to run the Colonial activities. The Colonial fight created tremendous respect for us from labor officials who had good intentions, people who wanted to be a part of it, who thought we would win. So we kicked off the Hormel boycott by piggy-backing it on the Colonial boycott. Our leaflets said, "Boycott Colonial and Hormel." With our credibility, we were able to open a lot of doors for P-9, especially among the Building Trades. When Colonial closed, we had a rally outside the plant where Pete Winkels and Terry Ahrens spoke. Two days later, we were able to hold a major rally for P-9 at the IBEW [electrical workers'] hall in Dorchester.[42]

Through Lang, the P-9ers won the important support of Domenic Bozzotto, president of a large Hotel and Restaurant Workers local, and Massachusetts Building Trades president Tom Evers.

This nationwide activity, and the involvement of left organizations, did not go unnoticed by the federal authorities. Lang was visited at his home by FBI agents, who asked about his trips to Austin. And a federal Freedom of Information Act request, now slowly working its way through the federal bureaucracy, has established that the FBI was involved in at least five investigations into strike activities, and that the strike was mentioned in the files of six other individuals or organizations. The Bureau has acknowledged having references in the files to Guyette, Heegard, Lang, Lenoch, Retterath, Rogers, and Weis.[43]

■ ■ ■

On March 16, local members voted to ignore the International's order and continue all strike activities. Lynn Huston announced that unionists from across the country had been telephoning all day long to say, "If P-9 is still in the fight, we're with you." Over by the plant, pickets tore the letters "UFCW" off their picket signs.

At the same local meeting, the 800 members attending (out of an estimated 900 still out on strike) also voted to sue the UFCW for "the irreparable harm" it had done to the local. Among the goals of the suit was to get an accounting of funds sent to Region 13—up to $100,000 that unions around the country said they had sent in checks that remained uncashed and unacknowledged.[44]

On March 20, the local barricaded Hormel again, this time shutting the plant down for several hours for the first time since the National Guard left. Several hundred strikers, around 50 Twin Cities supporters, miners from the Mesabi range, and meatpackers from the Albert Lea Farmstead plant gathered at the hall at 4 A.M., then used cars to blockade the plant gate. Signs at the gate read, "Go home scab, the plant is closed." And at 5 A.M., the local radio station announced that the facility was shut.

At 7 A.M. police arrived and announced that the crowd was violating the December injunction. One hundred strikers locked arms and grouped in front of the plant gate, singing

"Solidarity Forever." Across the street, a much larger crowd, including many who had been arrested on March 10, stood and taunted the cops.

As on March 10, groups of police would single out a demonstrator, who would then be pulled from the crowd and carried to a police van. In this fashion they arrested 16, including executive board members Skinny Weis and Carl Pontius, enough to fill two vans. When they brought up the third van, the crowd from across the street linked arms and blocked the path to the demonstrators. Police formed a wedge to push through the crowd, which held them off for a bit, then pulled away. By 10:30, 24 had been arrested, and the plant gate was clear.

Around noon, 100 more demonstrators briefly blocked the corporate headquarters but were pushed aside by policemen who formed a cordon to escort Hormel officials back inside.[45]

Weis and Pontius became the first executive board members to be arrested. "There was only supposed to be one of us arrested," recalled Carl Pontius, "and that was me."

There had been a hundred and something people arrested already, none of them executive board members, which didn't look good. I had no past arrests, not even a speeding ticket. So I sat down in front of the gate in the front row, the sixth one in line. Skinny was in a zone where he wasn't supposed to be arrested, but they arrested him anyway.

At the station, the deputy sheriff was talking to me, and he said, "I suppose like last time there's going to be quite lot of people arrested." I said, "Yeah, there are busloads coming in from all over the country, and it's going to go on all day long. When you carry people from the gate, more people will fill in." They were frantic: After they arrested Skinny, I could hear him telling them the same story. They shipped us right down to Preston, because they were looking for a ton of people to get arrested.[46]

It didn't happen that way, in part because once the police broke through the demonstration and opened the gate, they decided not to arrest any more demonstrators. Strikers and supporters were unable to get past police to block the gate again, and the demonstration at the corporate office proved ineffective. Although some plant gate demonstrators tried to turn over a police van while morning arrests were going on, most protesters were nonviolent. Some crossovers and corporate office workers, on the other hand, reported to work carrying weapons, and one P-9er was threatened with a shotgun.[47]

Weis and Pontius were released by 3 P.M., so they were able to travel to Chicago for a meeting with the UFCW the following day. Others were arraigned, charged with obstructing the legal process and unlawful assembly, and released on $300 bail each.

On Friday the 21st, a hundred demonstrators gathered at the north gate at 5:30 A.M. but did not attempt to block the road. They jeered at scabs entering the plant, then demonstrated at the corporate headquarters. No one was arrested.

The Chicago meeting held the same day was allegedly to determine whether the Austin local was going to comply with Wynn's directive—something it had already announced it was not going to do. For 90 minutes, the local and International officials discussed "a hundred different areas," according to Weis.

I don't know what we went down there for. I think they were trying to force us to obey the directive. We knew what was going to happen: They were going to put us into trusteeship. Anyway, instead of letting them take off on us, we took off on them—it was round robin, each one of us hitting on a different area. I had Lewie backed into a corner, and he was admitting that he had been dealing with Schaefer and talking to not only our scabs but new scabs, prior to them going in.

Then Jay Foreman said, "Lynn, are you taping this meeting?" Huston said, "Yes," and Foreman exploded. They had to find an excuse to get out of there because they were getting hammered.

The International called the meeting off because of Huston's attempt to tape the meeting with a concealed recorder. "They didn't have the common decency to notify us or to ask permission," complained Al Zack.[48]

Five days later, the UFCW announced that it would hold hearings beginning April 7 to determine if the local should be placed in trusteeship. This would mean P-9's officers would be replaced by a trustee named by the International, who would then control all local union assets, including its treasury, hall, and newspaper.[49]

VIII

"THIS IS NOT JOHANNESBURG"

Uff da!

—Norwegian expression of alarm and dismay

Demonstrations at the Austin plant gate and company headquarters escalated from late March through mid-April. On March 27, about a hundred demonstrators tried to block the headquarters entrance, but police were able to move them out of the way. There was some pushing and shoving, some banging on car tops and kicking of fenders as executives drove in. Nyberg's car received a blue "P-9" bumper sticker.

Over by the plant, the back gate of a truck loaded with pigs somehow came open, and many of the animals made a bid for life and freedom. "The pigs were falling all over the road—it was pretty wild," recalled Mike Bambrick. The reluctant crossovers wandered about for a while until the police herded them inside along with the strikebreakers.[1]

Six days later, on April 2, several hundred strikers and other demonstrators again blocked access to the plant, beginning at 6 A.M. They stopped cars with their bodies, then surrounded them and shouted, "Scabs go home!" Two "P-10ers"—including P-9 loyalist R. J. Bergstrom's brother,

Ronald—drove a car into the crowd, and an injury was narrowly avoided. Police began making arrests, saying that demonstrators were vandalizing cars.

When the arrests began, the crowd surrounded the police, chanting, "Let them go." At one point, several policemen were mashed up against the Hormel fence by the angry, jeering crowd, though little more than their pride was injured. Ultimately, 13 people were taken to jail, and the gates were opened. Later, Vice President Lynn Huston was arrested when he went to the Law Enforcement Center to inquire about the others. And police served arrest warrants on 13 more demonstrators at their homes.

Most were charged with obstructing the legal process and unlawful assembly under the terms of the injunction. Two were charged with assault after they had grappled with police. Striker Ray Goodew, arrested before and a regular on the line, was thrown to the ground, injured, and maced, though he says that he repeatedly announced that he would do whatever he was told to do. He was later charged with resisting arrest.[2]

These arrests came on the day after what was to be the final negotiating session between the P-9 board and Hormel. The meeting at St. Edward's Church in Austin lasted only 50 minutes: After announcing that chief negotiator Dave Larson was unavailable, the company's spokesmen said that they had no new proposal to make and, with their contract in place, did not know how to resolve the dispute. The union demanded that the 800 replaced strikers be reinstated, to no avail. P-9's board was also attenuated, as more conservative members Keith Judd and Kenny Hagen had resigned. A new presence on the union side of the table was Texas attorney David Twedell, whose prime goal would turn out to be persuading local members to decertify from the UFCW and start a new union under his leadership.[3]

For the union, everything rested on the boycott and continued disruptions at the Austin plant. Across the country, over fifty thousand leaflets were circulated calling on supporters to "Shut down Hormel" at a "national march and rally." Organizations were urged to "mobilize and send car caravans and busloads of supporters" to Austin for a week of activities beginning April 9.

The national call led Mower County attorney Fred Kraft to assert during a hearing on the criminal syndicalism charges that Rogers should be sent back to jail. Kraft said that Rogers was violating the conditions of his bail by organizing for the rally. The judge took Kraft's suggestion under advisement, along with the motion of defense attorneys Emily Bass and Mark Wernick that the criminal syndicalism charges be dismissed and the law struck down as unconstitutional.[4]

As a prelude to the week of demonstrations, food caravans from Wisconsin—organized by the Madison Oscar Mayer UFCW local, the Dane County Labor Council, and the Milwaukee support group—and more caravans from the Twin Cities joined up and delivered 140,000 tons of supplies on April 5. Appearing at a rally after this fourth major food delivery of the strike were three Madison executive board members, recently elected on a platform of opposition to the International's attacks on P-9, and the Dane County Labor Council president, David Newby.[5]

Four days later, "Shut Down Hormel Week" began. Hoffman and Goodnature had written to the governor that "the potential this week for a full-scale riot is the strongest it has been any time during this dispute," and they asked for either National Guard assistance or "releasing the Minnesota Highway Patrol for use in riot and crowd control." But Perpich refused their request for assistance. Public Safety Commissioner Tschida responded that they had all agreed during a February meeting that thereafter the matter would be handled by local authorities. In a "confidential" memorandum sent out on April 7 soliciting help from police agencies across the state, Hoffman and Goodnature said:

> First deployment to the scene will probably occur some-time around 0500 hrs on 041086. Officers should bring full riot gear including bullet proof vests and gas mask if you have them. . . . Due to recent experience we are strongly suggesting that you purchase a nut cup or athlet-ic cup for obvious reasons. . . . Responding officers should understand that our plea for help to every law en-forcement agency in Minnesota has been for the most part unsuccessful. We will be heavily outnumbered.

The anxious plea brought out dozens of police and sheriffs' deputies from other counties—the largest show of force since the withdrawal of the Guard.[6]

On the morning of the 9th, over a hundred demonstrators gathered across the street from the plant, their way blocked by police who were, in the words of one television account, "lined up heal to toe." Hoffman later said, "It was a nice, orderly demonstration." Crossovers went unimpeded into the plant, and there were no arrests.

The next day, the number of protesters at the plant swelled to over 350. They moved to block the drive twice, but withdrew when opposed by 60 policemen. Again, the demonstration was limited to waving picket signs and shout-ing at those who drove in.[7]

On the 11th, however, around 600 demonstrators plugged up the north gate before 5 A.M. It was still dark when I rode over there with Carole Apold, who was directed to pull her small Chevrolet into a wedge of cars at the gate, behind which the demonstrators massed. The light slowly came up on a beautiful early spring day, showing that almost all the humans in the vicinity other than demonstrators were carry-ing cameras. Hormel security men videotaped the proceed-ings from platforms raised on the back of trucks inside the gate; police did so from the nearby interstate highway over-pass; television newspeople and filmmaker Barbara Kopple's film crew stood near us.

"Who are we?" the crowd chanted: "P-9!" A single Amer-ican flag fluttered from the top of the automobile barricade. After a while, the State Patrol blocked the exit ramp leading from the interstate, and over a hundred police began gather-ing in small clumps, about a quarter of a mile away.

Around 6 A.M. the police announced over a loudspeaker: "You are violating a court order. If you do not clear the street, you will be arrested."

The crowd responded with an eerie mix of sounds, sig-naling a readiness to meet whatever the lawmen had to offer. Fists thumped on cars in time to the chant, "No surrender, no retreat"; a variety of ululations, hoots, and yells played off this rhythm section.

More time passed, and nothing happened. Somewhere the police "brain trust" were puzzling out how to proceed. Perhaps they were hoping the demonstrators would get bored and leave.

Sometime after 6 A.M., there was a customary "third and final warning." Everyone ignored it. One group of P-9ers were singing along with a tape of union songs put together by union member Larry Schmidt, folksinger Larry Long, and others.

Finally, the police began to form a cordon, lining up on both sides of the road from the car barricade to a distance of 40 feet away. Then a police van backed into the cordon. It was 6:30 when police attached a chain from the van to one car in the barricade and towed it a few feet away.

A larger police van pulled up to the end of the cordon. The crowd chanted, "No arrests, no arrests!" Then groups of five or six police made the first busts: During several charges, they grabbed individual protesters and hauled them away to the waiting van. Those arrested offered varying degrees of passive resistance. The officers had particular difficulty carrying burly Frank Vit and getting him into the vehicle. Each of the eight arrested demonstrators was frisked and handcuffed.

After a few such charges the crowd chanted, "This is not Johannesburg" and "The whole world is watching." One Austin woman screamed at the police: "This is ridiculous . . . you should be ashamed!"

Six or seven officers charged again into the crowd, and this time were met with flying coffee, dirt, rocks, a squirt of liquid, and, frighteningly, the firecracker explosion of a red smoke grenade. The police—though not the news cameramen—retreated in confusion. "Get back, get back!" shouted one panicky officer.

The harmless red haze settled slowly. Demonstrators locked arms and advanced a step or two, while police regrouped slowly at a distance. The van drove away with those who had been arrested so far.

Seven o'clock came and went. Demonstrators sang "We Shall Not be Moved" and "Solidarity Forever"; the first rank still stood with arms linked, but others milled around, smoking cigarettes and drinking coffee.

Some police donned gas masks, and all put on their riot helmets. It was as if their dress determined the surrounding circumstances: Had they put on tuxedos, they might have proclaimed the occasion a fancy dress ball; attired as they were, they announced, "We are declaring this situation a riot. Any further arrests will be felony arrests. You must leave this area immediately or we will be deploying tear gas." The demonstrators stood their ground while the peculiar announcement was reproduced in triplicate. Finally, a dozen smoking canisters were fired.

Smith & Wesson No. 2 Riot Agent CS2 smells like an incredibly pungent gunpowder. I saw some demonstrators throwing the gas canisters back toward the police as I ran to the east—a bad choice, since the wind carried the fumes right behind me. Both sides were forced to abandon the immediate area. People coughed, spat, and wiped their eyes as they ran, attempting to rid themselves of the gas's noxious effects. Eight further arrests followed. Showing up late for the action, Austin's KAAL-TV was in position to film a group of five police converging on a fleeing demonstrator, punching him, and flinging him to the ground before applying handcuffs and leading him away. Other demonstrators regrouped just to the west of the plant gate, avoiding the windblown vapor. But a rank of police pushed them back, opened the gate, and, at around 8:20 A.M., escorted the scabs in.

All parties held post-demonstration news conferences. Seizing upon the riot angle, plant manager Arnold said that Rogers and Guyette only talked about peaceful protest—"They say one thing and do another." Goodnature and Hoffman offered reporters a display of rocks and the hull of the red smokebomb. They said that some officers had been squirted with a "mace-like" substance, and that eight had been taken to the hospital (mostly, it turned out, suffering from their own tear gas) and released. They announced that 17 people had been arrested and would be charged with "felony riot"—including Ray Rogers, who had been apprehended several miles away in the K-Mart parking lot. Then the sheriff berated the UFCW: "If that International does not take over the union now, they're the most incompetent union in the entire country as far as I'm concerned. . . . It's about time they showed a little guts here."

At the union's press conference, Guyette said that the union's peaceful demonstration had been turned into a riot by police. Told that Hoffman was calling for the union's parade permit to be revoked, the P-9 president said, "This is the kind of stuff we talk about happening in Communist countries, yet we have it happening before our very eyes. . . . We don't call it Communism, we call it Hormelism."

Attorney Bass announced that the criminal syndicalism charges against Ray Rogers and Corporate Campaign had been dismissed in their entirety by Judge Bruce Stone, who had also ruled the statute unconstitutional. "Within minutes of having the first charges dismissed, the state has chosen to arrest Rogers a second time," she noted. "We have to ask the state, 'Why is it you need one, two, perhaps three shots at the apple before you can prove your case?' "[8]

To an impartial observer reviewing the slowly developing events at the plant gate, the "riot" charges would seem preposterous. Nevertheless, the *Minneapolis Star and Tribune* chimed in, proclaiming the "Outburst among worst in state labor history." (Contradicting itself, the article cited two small, recent strikes involving greater violence: In one a strikebreaker had been shot off his motorcycle, and in the other a truck had been overturned and burned.) The *St. Paul Pioneer Press and Dispatch* editorialized that the violent confrontation reaffirmed the wisdom of calling out the National Guard in January.

No one had been seriously hurt, no property had been damaged—yet seven Austin union members and nine out-of-town supporters from as far away as Boston and California were charged with felony riot, gross misdemeanor riot, unlawful assembly, and obstructing the legal process. Rogers and Guyette faced charges of aiding and abetting the felony, gross misdemeanor, unlawful assembly, and obstruction of the legal process. Lesser charges were brought against 25 other union members, including all the executive board. Rogers was placed in solitary confinement, and Guyette went into hiding.[9]

In spite of the urging of the company and the law enforcement officials, the parade permit was not withdrawn. "With all the people in town, it will be easier to keep track of them at the parade rather than cancel the permit," said a city councilman.[10]

Between 5,000 and 6,000 people from 16 states participated in the march and rally. Signs identified contingents of California chemical workers and longshoremen, Texas oil workers, Maine shipbuilders, Pennsylvania mineworkers, Minnesota machinists, Chicago clothing workers, and New York communications workers. TWA, Chicago *Tribune*, and Watsonville strikers all marched. Ottumwans in their red hats and jackets carried a banner that read "We honor picket lines." Other large banners were displayed by the Kansas City Coalition of Labor Union Women, the Twin Cities Support Committee, Communications Workers of America members from New York, and the Workers' League. And there were floats and displays: One group of workers carried a small "M. B. Thompson tar-paper shack"; another group, a coffin labeled "civil liberties."

Marchers jammed the town arena, where 30-foot banners proclaimed "Solidarity with P-9, Boycott Hormel" and "No Retreat, No Surrender." First to speak was Guyette, who emerged from hiding surrounded by a bodyguard of several brawny members; then Lynn Huston spoke. Many who followed had little claim to celebrity: They included a New

York teacher, a Baltimore steelworker, and a San Francisco letter carrier, all of whom described why they had been drawn to P-9's side. The official sponsor of the rally was NRFAC, and its officers Brown, Mickens, and Dave Foster also addressed the crowd. Surprisingly, though, perhaps the most eloquent speaker of the afternoon was the television actor David Soul, drawn to support such struggles through the activism of his brother, a Lutheran minister who was fired for his zealous involvement in Monongahela valley anti-plant-shutdown activities.

> The days when people said, "I don't know what to do, I have no voice," are over. The values that you grew up with need to be tested and need to be risked. If you don't risk them, you stand a greater chance of losing strong families, strong unions, and strong companies.[11]

Muted was Ray Rogers, who, along with the 16 others facing felony charges, spent the weekend in jail. Bostonian Brian Lang was among the first to be arrested on Friday, and Buck Heegard, among the last. According to Heegard, who had not expected to get arrested:

> It turned out to be a great experience. There were 16 in our cell, nine from out of town, including the former president of the Dallas–Ft. Worth PATCO local, who had only recently been released from federal prison, where he'd been because of their strike. We had the best union meeting ever—we spent all the next day composing a letter to be read at the rally, and everyone in Cell Block D signed it.[12]

The authorities refused to let Soul or anyone else see the prisoners. But on Sunday, as had been previously announced, the Reverend Jesse Jackson arrived. The once and future presidential candidate had contacted Jan Pierce on April 9, seeking advice about whether or not to go to Austin. As Pierce remembered:

> I got a call one morning at 6 A.M., and this gravelly voice said, "Jan, this is your long-lost brother." I said, "Where in the hell have you been?" He said, "Is that any way to talk to a minister?—this is Reverend Jackson."
>
> I didn't know him at all. But we flew to Washington together. We talked about the problems facing farmers and wage-earners. And he talked about the advisability of getting involved in Austin. In Washington, we saw [Congressman and former UFCW official] Charlie Hayes, who told him to go. Jackson also called Bill Wynn to tell him he was going.[13]

Jackson and Pierce were welcomed by 300 P-9ers at the small Austin airport. From the mayor's office, they called the sherriff, who said that no one was being allowed to visit the prisoners. Jackson got on the phone and asked if the sheriff intended to deny a minister the right to hold services for the inmates on the Sabbath. Goodnature gave in.

The prisoners were anticipating Jackson's appearance, and when the jailer announced that "someone was coming to see us," everyone got excited, according to Heegard. Disappointingly, the first visitor turned out to be a local minister. Later, Jackson came in, accompanied by Pierce, attorney Bass, a television crew, and Kopple's film crew. As Lang recalled, "He came walking in and gave us the real dope before the media got inside. He said, 'It wasn't easy getting in here, just follow my lead.' Then he switched on the Jesse Jackson you see on television."[14]

Before the cameras, Jackson told the inmates, "The fact that you have not bowed means there's new life in the labor movement." Then he got everyone to hold hands and said a prayer. Since the sheriff had refused to let Rogers come into the cell with the others, Jackson then went down and met with him separately. "It was an absurd attitude that was manifested before our eyes: a union leader in solitary confinement, and he hadn't even been charged," recalled Pierce. "It was incredible and incongruous."

Jackson and Pierce also met with Nyberg at the corporate headquarters for about an hour. According to Pierce:

> The company was saying they had an obligation to the scabs. Jackson said, "When you look into the faces of your original workers, I know you can see two or three generations of people who have worked here. I simply ask you to search your soul and determine whether you truly owe the replacements more than you owe second- and third-generation workers who have been instrumental in building this company." I felt that we may have made some progress. . . . I know that Nyberg was genuinely touched.

Nyberg denies that the conversation went like that. He says that Jackson asked about a link between Hormel and South Africa—which Nyberg said did not exist—and "said he was very interested in the jobs of those who were not working." Jackson did not offer to mediate, Nyberg asserted, but said he would do anything he could to help the company and the union. "We said that mediation wouldn't be useful—we'd gone through the mediation process and gotten exactly nowhere." And according to Nyberg, that is where things were left, though Jackson telephoned him twice over the next few weeks.[15]

Jackson had already built a record as an intermediary and fixer, having sprung an American pilot from Syrian captivity in 1984. He was also in the process of broadening his constituency from the urban poor to farmers and workers: In 1985 he had come to Minnesota to support a dairy farmer who was facing foreclosure. This record raised P-9 members' hopes, and they responded enthusiastically to his coming. Hundreds packed into the union hall, and over a thousand into the auditorium of St. Edward's Church, to hear what he had to say.

At the airport, Jackson announced, "We need corporations, corporations need workers; we need each other and must have a mutual, respectful relationship." In the later addresses, he largely continued to portray himself as a neutral party and to speak as if P-9ers had lost their way and were about to spin off into a spasm of violence: "Don't lose your head, for if you do, your body will soon follow. Maintain your eyes on the prize. When your back is against the wall, don't get trapped . . . fighting a policeman or sheriff when the issue is your job, your seniority, safety, and self-respect."

To be fair, he also said that those in jail, "are not common criminals, they must be set free." And he urged, "Don't you give up; don't you bow; you stand tall." But never did he pick up on Guyette's introductory words to suggest that there might be conditions under which he would endorse and promote the boycott of Hormel products. Given the company's targeting of black consumers, such a development could have meant a lot to the union. Instead, Jackson talked about teenage drug use and pregnancy, income statistics, the Gramm-Rudman Bill, the effect of falling oil prices on American workers, and the need for a moratorium on farm foreclosures. He also showed his discomfort at speaking before an all-white group, and uncertainty that the members accorded him full legitimacy as a leader, by regularly referring to the question of race.

"There is more than a reasonable chance we will return," Jackson said at the union hall. Before the church audience, he announced, "We're going to meet with the International.

We're going to meet with Hormel. And we're not going to stop meeting, and talking, and acting until you have your jobs, your seniority, your health care, and your self-respect." Union members went home feeling that they had won a very visible and powerful friend.

Nothing ever came of Jackson's promises, though. The Reverend spoke to Hormel CEO Knowlton several times over the next weeks and asked him to participate in a meeting with P-9 leaders. But Hormel was entrenched behind the position that the company was bound by law to keep its commitment to the replacements. "A Supreme Court opinion says that state contract law applies," Nyberg told me, "and if you lay off people you've hired as permanent, you open yourself up to monumental lawsuits. We said loud and clear from day one they would be permanent replacements."

Moreover, the Hormel strike was one of the first labor disputes in which Jackson had been involved. Over the next two years, he would appear on many other union platforms, speaking for TWA flight attendants, Cudahy and Kenosha, Wisconsin, meatpackers and autoworkers, and Jay, Maine, paperworkers. In 1988 he made a point of scheduling a presidential campaign appearance at one rank-and-file labor event every day, and in promoting a "workers' bill of rights," he became a forceful advocate of wage-earners' causes. But in April 1986 he remained tentative, talking and acting as though a bitter strike could be resolved if both sides were pressed to be reasonable. It was some time before he denounced the company and talked about boycotting Hormel products.

"He was in the process then of tying struggles together," surmised Pierce when I asked about these shortcomings. "Things are probably much clearer to him now than they were at that point." Austin helped point the way toward a constituency that would lead Jackson to good 1988 electoral showings in Iowa and Maine and a victory in the Wisconsin primary. It would prove to be just one more case of P-9 giving more to an outsider than it got back in return.[16]

■ ■ ■

"At some point and at some place," Jackson had mysteriously stated, "the union must declare its Calvary and face its crucifixion in order to realize its resurrection."[17]

The crucifixion began on Monday.

That day, the UFCW began its trusteeship hearings in a small hearing room at the Minneapolis public library. After posting $5,000 bail, Guyette was released from the Mower County Jail to attend the sessions. (The rest of those who had been jailed were released on bail or their own recognizance.) Three busloads of union members, including the rest of the local executive board, also made the trip, though fewer than fifty were able to get seats in the small room.[18] The sessions were closed to all but union members, and eight UFCW organizers were appointed sergeants-at-arms to keep an eye on those in attendance.

Hearing officer Ray Wooster, the president of a Houston UFCW local appointed to this role by the International, opened by announcing that the hearings would consider one question only: whether or not the Austin local had complied with the March UFCW directive to end the strike.

There was a broader question at issue: whether or not Local P-9 *should* be placed in trusteeship. But under Wooster's rules argument over that issue would not be allowed—even though both federal law and the UFCW constitution seem to require discussion of it. According to the federal Labor-Management Reporting and Disclosure Act, trusteeships may be established "after a fair hearing" to rectify corruption or financial malfeasance, assure the performance of collective bargaining agreements, restore democratic procedures, or otherwise carry out "the legitimate objectives of such labor organization." The UFCW constitution includes much the same language, adding, "whenever in the judgment of the International Executive Committee such action is required, it shall have the power to place such chartered body in trusteeship."

But the constitution elaborates that local officers "shall have the right to examine and cross-examine witnesses, present other evidence, and argue the case for or against trusteeship." And though there are qualifications permitting the International to disallow negotiated contracts and require mail-ballot ratification votes, for example, the constitution regularly emphasizes that the members have primary say in matters of collective bargaining.[19]

In an airing of the broader questions, the local might have discussed the entire UFCW constitution, along with such announced aims of the national organization as fighting concessions and P-9's compliance with those aims. It might have introduced testimony regarding the International's "bad faith" intention to impose a trusteeship after months of interference in the strike. In that regard, it might have examined the text of the directive, which contained a number of slanted statements about the Peterson resolution and P-9 officers' actions.

Since this hearing did not seem to meet all the legal qualifications, it was not completely clear that it would be the only hearing. Was this *the* trusteeship hearing, P-9's board members would ask? It was, Wooster said, "a fact-finding" on the one issue of whether or not P-9 and its officers had obeyed the International's directive, and the ultimate decision of trusteeship would be made by the International executive committee. Later, he said that the hearing was "like a grand jury." Would there then be another hearing, Pete Winkels asked, as described in the UFCW constitution? The hearing officer told him to stop playing games and get on with it. During a mid-afternoon Winkels cross-examination, Wooster revealed his most fervent wish: "Pete, I am trying to be patient. . . . You know, I mean, we can sit here and go on with this type of questioning through every witness; and my gosh, I don't know about anybody else, but I am going to do my best to wrap this thing up. I would like to get home."[20]

Had P-9's officers abided by Wooster's limitations, the hearings would have been short indeed. There was really no question that the local had not complied with the directive to end the strike. As of April 10, only 114 members had followed directions by sending return-to-work notices to Hormel and requesting post-strike benefits, while 48 had requested benefits without applying to Hormel, and 26 others had written to the UFCW saying that they rejected the order.[21] The members' first response to the edict had been to collect hundreds of signatures on a petition for decertification of the UFCW, ready to be filed with the NLRB in case of a blitzkrieg trusteeship announcement. They had also, as noted above, voted to continue the strike and to sue the International for the "irreparable harm" done to the local.

Thus local officers, coached by Bass and Winter at the end of each day's session, determined to use the hearings as much as possible as a discovery tool and a method of demonstrating the UFCW's subversion of the strike, laying the basis for later court actions to oppose the trusteeship. And, they must have reasoned, since this was possibly the last of the many kangaroo courtrooms the local would be hauled through, why not have a bit of fun? Whether through inexperience or failure to perceive what was going on, the Texan permitted them to get away with a lot.

Wooster continued the hearing, introducing various bits of correspondence and a set of rules describing the procedures that would be followed, including such courtroom trappings as testimony under oath, cross-examination of witnesses, and a transcript kept by a court reporter.[22] But, as the hearing officer would repeatedly state, he had no power of subpoena or any other means of forcing either side to produce witnesses or documents.

Joe Hansen, who served as prosecutor, presented the International's case. First, he called the Region 13 secretary to testify that the office had been mailed Local P-9 newspapers and leaflets showing that the strike and boycott were continuing. He entered other newspaper clippings about the strike into evidence. Then he called four members of the special organizing team to testify that they had witnessed continuing boycott and strike activities.

The first of these, Pam Nelson, testified that she had gone unidentified into the P-9 hall on April 1, where she had purchased a "Boycott Hormel" bumper sticker and coffee cup, and picked up some boycott literature. Next, International representative Tom Plumb out of Indianapolis testified that he had been assigned to the "program" since February 3. Since March 14, he said, he had observed and photographed daily picketing at the Austin plant, the mass demonstration on April 2, and an April 6 Albert Lea meeting where Guyette had promoted the boycott.

Under Winkels' questioning, Plumb admitted that he had been in Austin, working with Massachusetts union representative Bill McDonough, since March 10, well before the directive; that he had been in contact with former P-9 business agent Richard Schaefer, Guyette's original pro-concessions antagonist; and that Joe Hansen had briefed him "on the whole situation" on February 3. Wooster refused to let P-9ers ask about this briefing, though Guyette expressed concern that Plumb had been sent "to substantiate a directive that hadn't even been issued yet."

It was late afternoon before Hansen got his next witness on the stand: Tom Plumb's brother Larry. Larry Plumb produced more photographs of plant gate picketing and a report from the April 12 rally, where he said Guyette had promoted a national Hormel boycott. On cross-examination he boasted to Winkels that he had been in Austin many times since he came out to Minnesota on January 31, and that he had first been sent by Hansen to observe pickets during the first week of February. Like his brother, he said that his first assignment was to field incoming phone calls from P-9 members who had questions about returning to work at Hormel.

In response to further questions from Winkels and Guyette, and before Hansen or Wooster thought to interrupt, Larry Plumb asserted that he had become good friends with Schaefer, who, he said, had introduced him to crossovers John Morrison and John Anker. Guyette established that Plumb had never made any effort to communicate with P-9's officers, though he had spoken to at least fifty other members over the phone and in their homes. Plumb further told him that there were five other UFCW representatives working in and around Austin.

Since Larry Plumb had not talked to local officers, Guyette asked, how could he be sure that the pickets he had photographed were really P-9 members? Then, with a straight face, the P-9 president posed a preposterous question—one he would ask again and again without ever drawing a smile from a witness:

> Q: Did you observe anybody physically boycotting Hormel products on April 12?
> A: You mean not buying things?
> Q: Sure.
> A: I didn't see nobody doing that, no.

If Plumb didn't see anybody not buying, how could he be sure that P-9 was really boycotting?[23]

Tuesday morning, Hansen brought organizer Michael Corbett to the stand to testify that he had seen P-9 pickets at the Fremont plant many times since the directive ordered them to withdraw. Photographs of such pickets from April 1 were introduced as evidence. Winkels asserted that the photographs were worthless, since no faces could be recognized. Corbett said he had been sent to Fremont on February 2 to help those "that had honored the [picket] lines down there . . . get back to work." When he was given the directive on March 14, Corbett said, he was "told not to say a word" to anyone other than his co-worker, Art Smith, an organizer out of San Francisco—not even to Local 22's president Skip Niederdeppe.

In the middle of cross-examination, Wooster told Guyette to stop asking irrelevant questions or he would "pick someone else to represent the local union at this hearing," which he said was "perfectly within [his] authority."

Then it was the local's turn to present its case. But unlike the International, which simply ordered its own witnesses' appearance as part of their job responsibilities, P-9 had no ability to compel the UFCW officials it wanted to call as adverse witnesses to show up. Wooster again announced that he did not have "the authority to subpoena any witness, nor subpoena power for production of materials to be produced at this hearing for either party."

"Are we supposed to kidnap them?" asked Winkels. "Our request for a fair, honest hearing and just end to this has been denied every time." To emphasize the unfairness of the proceedings, the local officers had Wooster call for a number of witnesses they knew to be absent: William Wynn, former UFCW secretary-treasurer Anthony Lutty, Jay Foreman, Bill Olwell, Robert Niederdeppe, Al Vincent, Lewie Anderson, Louis DeFrieze, and several other union officials. In each case, after there was no response, Guyette asked Hansen to telephone the officials and ask them to come out to the hearing. Hansen said he would.

Ultimately, Guyette called Hansen, who would serve as one of the local's few witnesses. Since he remained the "prosecutor," he was allowed to raise objections to questions that he was being asked as a witness. Hansen testified that he could not say why organizers had been sent to count P-9 pickets long before the directive was issued, that he was not present when the directive was formulated, that organizers reported to him and he reported to Jay Foreman. Guyette pressed him to say whether he regarded as accurate the directive's language that "on Tuesday and Wednesday March 11th and 12th, striking members in Austin, Minnesota, voted in support of International intervention." Hansen said that it was accurate, and he objected to further questions about whether the resolution called for discontinuing the strike. Wooster upheld the objection.

Winkels asked questions about the Chicago meeting involving International and local officers that took place subsequent to the directive, but Hansen objected, and Winkels was ruled out of order. "Where would we be if the officers of this local union had stated that we would support this directive, but yet our rank and file does not support the directive, when the ultimate voice of the union is the rank and file?" Winkels asked. Hansen objected, and Wooster ruled the question irrelevant.[24]

That afternoon Winkels read aloud a telegram from P-9's members protesting against the misinterpretation of their resolution and requesting withdrawal of the directive. Again, Wooster ruled the matter irrelevant, along with ensuing questions about whether strike sanction had ever been withdrawn before. On the record, Winkels was able to establish that those union members who had not complied with the directive had been "penalized" by being cut off from "post-strike assistance," while those who had complied were still receiving such assistance. (It would later be stated that those who sent "unconditional surrender" letters to the company were receiving $50 a week, rather than the $40 they had received while on strike.)

Through the afternoon and into the next day, Guyette attempted to introduce a variety of letters, telegrams, union reports, and resolutions in which the International union outlined goals of opposing concessions and following the will of the rank and file, while misrepresenting P-9's actions and attempting to undermine the Hormel strike.

Included among these were a 1983 position paper prepared by Lewie Anderson, "Coping With Employer Demands For Mid-Term Contract Concessions"; 1984 and 1985 Packinghouse Division reports that urged stronger "chains," common contract expiration dates, and the honoring of picket lines; an October 1985 Anderson letter urging support for Morrell strikers, since "an injury to one is an injury to all"; a March 1985 letter from Wynn opposing concessionary bargaining; and Wynn's December 1985 communications regarding the International's possible sanctioning of extended P-9 pickets.

Also included were a September 1984 telegram from Niederdeppe to Schaefer, which demonstrated that P-9 had not broken from the Hormel chain, but had been "disinvited" from its meetings; subsequent letters and newsletters that promoted the interpretation that P-9 had abandoned the chain; Anderson's October 1985 "Position Paper On Local P-9/Hormel, Austin Situation," which said that the corporate campaign had failed while nearly bankrupting the local; the February 1986 *Leadership Update* that was distributed at the AFL-CIO executive council meeting and then far and wide; the series of mid-March letters and press statements surrounding the de-sanctioning of the strike; and a much-circulated statement, "Ending the Hormel Strike: The UFCW Acts to Save Jobs, Union."

Hearing officer Wooster accepted very few of these documents into evidence, ruling the vast bulk irrelevant in accordance with Hansen's regular objections. Guyette asked a lot of questions about the documents anyway, and Hansen answered a few. Among other things, the Region 13 director stated that the first time he had heard trusteeship discussed was in 1985, when "a few of your own members were requesting the International put you in trusteeship." Since this was the UFCW's regular public position—the members told us to do it—Guyette pointed to a February newspaper article as evidence that the UFCW was contemplating trusteeship weeks before the directive. In that article, Hansen was quoted as saying then that he was receiving dozens of telephone calls from P-9 members demanding International intervention.[25]

"What are the reasons for strike sanction being removed?" Guyette asked.

"You would have to ask the Executive Committee. I did not make that decision," Hansen answered.

"I would love to ask the Executive Committee, however . . . no one from the Executive Committee is here," Guyette responded.

A request for financial documents from Region 13 was refused by Hansen and ruled irrelevant by Wooster; Hansen refused to respond to any questions about donations made for P-9 through the regional office. Questions about what happened to other locals who refused to follow similar directives were objected to, and the objections were sustained. (Wooster said that if Guyette wanted to know what other locals had been trusteed, he should go to the U.S. Labor Department, which kept records of all trusteeships.)

Hansen was asked if, as he had promised, he had telephoned any of the other UFCW officers that P-9 had asked to appear. He replied that Wynn was unavailable, new secretary-treasurer Jerry Menapace "had nothing that would be relevant," and neither did the other International officers or UFCW employees called by P-9 "have anything relevant to the issue." (Later, when asked if he had tried to get people to the hearing to assist P-9, Hansen said, "I had enough to do getting my case ready without worrying about P-9's.") In turn, Guyette bitterly criticized the nature of the hearings:

I believe that this whole hearing cannot be construed as a fair hearing when, in fact, the very people who issue the directive are the very ones who have the power and the right to see who gets here and who doesn't get here and, in fact, pays their people to be here. And we have no right to get any documents nor any witnesses. And the very people who issued the directive are the ones that decide their own guilt or innocence ultimately based on who is here to testify. . . . I don't know of any court in this country that would allow such a farce.

In response, Wooster suggested that Local P-9 could enter an "offer of proof" conveying what it thought such people *would* have testified—a peculiar suggestion, since there had been no discovery process on which to base such an offer.

Hansen and Wooster also refused to allow any questions or testimony about the UFCW's policy on common expiration dates, coordinated bargaining, honoring picket lines, withdrawing strike sanction, or denying a local the right to solicit funds.

Three other witnesses appeared for P-9. Tuesday afternoon, the local called Charlie Peterson to the stand to testify as to the intent of the resolution he had introduced. And although Hansen immediately objected to his testimony and Wooster upheld the objection, Peterson nonetheless was able to enter on the record that he and other union members had not thought that they were voting for International intervention and a cutoff of strike pay.[26]

Larry Kohlman, UFCW assistant to Organizing Director Doug Dority, was in Minnesota to supervise the special organizing team. He appeared after Joe Hansen, but provided little new information. When he testified that he believed a button showing the word "Hormel" with a diagonal line drawn across it meant "not to buy Hormel products," Guyette asked him how he would interpret a button that showed the word "scab" with a line drawn through it.

"Would you take that to mean that somebody didn't want you to buy a scab?" The witness replied, "Yeah, they shouldn't buy a scab."

Later, Lynn Huston pursued the issue of interpretation, asking Kohlman if he had ever gotten a ticket for parking in a handicapped parking space. Without hesitation, Hansen objected that the question was not relevant, and Wooster unblinkingly upheld the objection.

For his fourth and final witness, Guyette called Wooster's counsel, Marvin Gettler, who had been sitting in a side room in case the hearing officer needed legal advice. Gettler testified that he had assisted Wooster in drawing up the rules that narrowly defined the issue to be heard, but he invoked attorney-client privilege to avoid saying any more about the subject.

Finally, each side made a closing argument. Hansen said:

> We have submitted evidence and testimony over the last three days showing that Local P-9 has not obeyed or complied with the March 13th directive. . . . I believe that the local has failed to show that they are, in fact, in compliance with the directive and we would argue that the hearing officer should so find based on the facts and the testimony which was submitted to him at this hearing. That's it.

For P-9, Guyette argued:

> The March 13th directive is illegitimate for the following reasons: There is no authority under the UFCW constitution for withdrawing strike sanction once sanction is granted. Under the UFCW constitution, it is the local and not the International which has authority to carry out the collective bargaining . . . it is the rank and file that has the authority to make decisions as to how to carry out the collective bargaining. All of P-9's actions have been in complete conformity with UFCW guidelines on how to fight concessions. . . . The directive is part of a bad faith campaign to break the strike, to discredit and remove the democratically elected leadership of Local P-9. . . .

I would also say that this hearing and this decision affects many, many people, and I do not believe that the scope of the hearing should have been limited by anyone, and I do not believe that this hearing can be construed as anything but unfair when you have the very people issuing the directive who are the very people who call for the hearing and, in fact, oversee the entire process.

With that, the hearing ended. Written backup statements were to be sent to Wooster within 12 days.[27]

■ ■ ■

According to schedule, the UFCW's executive committee, which consisted of Wynn, Secretary-Treasurer Menapace, and Executive Vice Presidents Foreman, Olwell, and Alan Lee, were to receive Wooster's report and make a decision about trusteeship by mid-May. The local board decided that it should strike before the inevitable axe fell by filing the lawsuit against the International. Lynn Huston announced to the press that such a suit would be filed within a week to 10 days.[28] Consulting with Guyette and the board, Bass and Winter began the legal work necessary to block trusteeship.

With events at this pass, serious debate over the Hormel strike among liberals and left intellectuals began to hit its stride.

In the *Village Voice*, labor scholar Stanley Aronowitz published a paean to the Austin strike, which he called "the most significant test of domestic Reaganism" and "a source of extraordinary excitement in a labor movement that had, until now, thrown in the towel." Aronowitz said the strike had revealed the existence of a two-dimensional labor movement:

The vertical labor movement—the international unions and the AFL-CIO—has been consistent throughout its

long march backwards into the 1920s. . . . The loyalty of
labor's leaders to themselves has been matched, however,
by a movement of local unions who, crossing the bound-
aries of industry and internationals, have come to the assistance of the strikers.[29]

Equally positive was Nicolaus Mills, whose *Nation*
article, "Why Local P-9 is going it alone," declared that "P-9
is not engaged in a romantic crusade, nor is it led by radicals
out of touch with the rank and file." Mills surveyed the local's recent history (including the "missing language" controversy), the UFCW's rationale, its attack on the local, and
the several months of strike activity. He concluded on a
hopeful note:

> there remain more than enough reasons for P-9 and the
> UFCW to make peace. . . . Most of the Hormel contracts,
> with the exception of the plants in Ottumwa and Knox-
> ville, Tennessee, come up between May and September.
> During this period Hormel will be extremely vulnerable.
> If a master agreement with a common expiration date
> could be reached, it would give everyone—rank and file
> as well as the international—enormous bargaining power
> in the future.[30]

In late February, UFCW staffer Bill Montross and I had
traded polemics in *The Guardian* and *In These Times*.
Montross charged P-9 with being a "johnny-come-lately" to
the anti-concessions struggle—behind the International—
and accused the left of having adopted a knee-jerk anti-Inter-
national reaction to the intra-union squabble. *Labor Notes*
editor Kim Moody now reprinted Montross' arguments and
ripped into them personally:

> The International's "strategy" has been a complete failure.
> Montross calls the UFCW's approach to the changes in the

meatpacking industry . . . that occurred in the 1970s a "strategy to stop concessions in the meatpacking industry." This it never was. Rather, it attempted to use a major concession as a means of stabilizing wages and, hopefully, reducing further employer demands for concessions.

Step by step, Moody traced the UFCW's muddled attempts to stabilize wages. Then he described the world view of "business unionism," in which, he said, industry wage patterns cease to be a tool for raising workers' living and working standards and become "a bureaucratic means of maintaining order in the industry even if it means depressing the living standards of the entire workforce."[31]

In the *New York Times*, Serrin quoted other labor intellectuals who were equally condemnatory of the International. Les Leopold of the Labor Institute in New York called the strike and the ground swell of support for it "an expression of protest from the bottom to do something about the weakness of the trade union movement." Cornell historian Nick Salvatore said the labor movement could not hope to regain its vigor when it refused to aid workers such as those in Austin.[32]

Running somewhat late, the liberals, social democrats, and nonaligned radicals had weighed in: Doing what they do best, they had written what they thought. Old socialist Irving Howe was said to be mightily irritated with the International, and Mills was given leave to expand upon his arguments in the pages of *Dissent* magazine.[33]

The UFCW officialdom, who imagined that they had overcome the worst damage to their reputation back in February, had almost no intellectuals of this stature in their corner. Their only apparent support of this kind came from the Communist Party. But you go with what you've got: Al Zack sent out copies of Bill Dennison's "Hormel: Unity is the only winning strategy" from the CP's theoretical journal *Political Affairs* to his press contact list. Along with a brief history of union struggles in the meatpacking industry, and a repeat of the UFCW's oft-heard charges that P-9 had "broken with the chain," Dennison launched one of the most scathing attacks anyone had made on Corporate Campaign:

> Surrounded by those who do nothing but attack the labor movement and following a strategy opposed by the rest of the union's meatpacking workers, the local has been led into a quagmire of separatism and isolation. Most recently, P-9's leadership has initiated a suit against the UFCW charging it with "irreparable harm," "maliciously hurting" their strike. . . . While obviously an effort to cover up the failure of CCI's strategy, it is hard to see it as only that. Honest differences over strategy between trade unionists are not carried this far by anyone who has workers' interests at heart.[34]

In time, such primitive distortions and slanders would be replaced by more subtle attacks, notably that of United Electrical Workers staff attorney Lance Compa. His widely circulated "Second look at the Hormel strike" (again rushed out to Zack's press list) accused the local of enterprise unionism, "where a single local works the best deal possible from local plant management." Compa faulted the local for undermining industry-wide bargaining and industrial unionism, the importance of which was in "taking labor costs out of competition so that employers cannot ratchet down contract conditions."

From such talk, one might imagine that P-9's members were advocating wage concessions to save their own skins, rather than an end to all givebacks made to profitable companies. The paper was convincing enough, or perhaps confusing enough, to lead the left-wing National Lawyers' Guild to table a pro–P-9 resolution at its summer convention. But, in the end, Compa's high-sounding categorization represented nothing more than flimsy new packaging for all of the UFCW's old arguments about P-9's breaking with the chain and going off on its own because it thought it knew better than the UFCW and its "young leader Lewie Anderson."[35]

For all the difference it made, the International had lost the war of words. Its reputation, which it was very concerned about, had taken a major hit. The only cure for such shaming would be the sweet balm of public forgetfulness. But the Austin strike had become such a sore point that, for months to come, UFCW officials continued to lecture union members and the public about what it saw as the meaning of the strike.[36]

THE CHAIN OF COMMAND

The UFCW made a mistake. . . . It should have cooperated fully with the tough men and women of Austin, and thus might have struck a spark in its whole organization.

—*Monsignor Charles Owen Rice*[1]

In late April, NLRB attorneys went before U.S. District Court Judge Edward Devitt—the judge who had enjoined P-9's First Bank activities back in September 1985—seeking federal restrictions on P-9 plant gate protests. It was the first time in a decade that the NLRB had sought such an injunction. The board said it needed a restraining order while it considered Hormel's charges that the union's mass demonstrations had violated federal labor law. According to both the board and the company, the state injunction was not enough, as it had failed to prevent "multiple acts of violence and property damage at the plant."

Citing 42 incidents in which strikers had engaged in mass picketing, rocked trucks, pounded on auto windshields, threatened or photographed crossovers, and encouraged civil disobedience, along with two cases of assault, Devitt issued a sweeping order. Union members were prohibited from threatening or harassing crossovers by any means. Mass picketing was out, as was any photographing of those who went in to work. The injunction would stay in effect until the NLRB issued its ruling. The U.S. Marshals special operations group announced that, if necessary, as many as 150 marshals augmenting 22 sworn federal deputies could be sent to Austin to enforce the order.[2]

There was very little mass activity during the days that followed. Union members were left waiting to see what would happen next, and local officers gave their attention to the many legal considerations that lay before them, including their lawsuit against the International. Yet a problem had arisen. In the words of attorney Winter, "At a board meeting where David Twedell and I were present, he had spoken in favor of the lawsuit, and I thought he was going to do the legal work on it. Instead, he left town the next day, and that was the last we saw of him for a while."[3] This left the suit in the hands of Winter and Bass. The two attorneys spent some time studying the trusteeship hearings for errors committed by the UFCW and working on a lengthy affidavit that would clarify the history of P-9's dealings with the UFCW and the Hormel chain.

On May 6 they filed suit in Washington, D.C., federal court, asking for $13 million in damages because of the parent union's "malicious, willful, and bad-faith" effort to undermine the local and to bring an end to the strike. Among P-9's charges: The UFCW had waged a publicity campaign against the local, withheld money sent to Region 13 for the strikers, lied about the contents of the agreement that allowed the 23 percent wage cut (the "missing language"), and sent spies to interfere with local activities.

Al Zack called the suit "foolishness" and a "publicity stunt." For a stunt, it brought a quick reaction: Two days later, the UFCW announced that it would trustee the local.

Zack said that Wooster's report recommending trust-eeship happened to arrive on the same day that the local fil-ed its lawsuit, and the executive committee took only a few hours to decide the issue. Unsurprisingly, Wooster had found that the local had not followed orders to end the strike, adding "Directly and indirectly the membership of this International union . . . granted the International Exec-utive Committee its own authority."

That same day, International union lawyer Harry Huge appeared in Minneapolis before Judge Edward Devitt, who he knew had ruled against the local and for Hormel on two previous occasions. There, the UFCW filed its own lawsuit against Local P-9 and asked for an injunction to enforce and validate the trusteeship.

Local union attorneys argued that Washington was the proper venue for the cases, as the key decision about trust-eeship had been made in that city at International union headquarters. Asserting, on the contrary, that the UFCW law-suit was related to the NLRB injunction, the International's lawyer said that the proper site for considering these matters was in Devitt's Minnesota courtroom.

Meanwhile, Joe Hansen, appointed trustee by the Interna-tional, announced that along with deputy trustees Ken Kimbro and Jack Smith, he expected to take over the Austin union hall and begin negotiations with Hormel soon.

In Austin, as television reporters buzzed around seeking reaction, several dozen people lined the sidewalk outside the Labor Center. Anticipating the trustees' arrival, they had chained the union hall door shut from the inside. How would they resist, the reporters wanted to know—with force? Most members were armed with nothing more than placards carrying slogans such as "What are your ties with

Hormel, Lewie?" one P-9er fulfilled the reporters' wishes by carrying a baseball bat as he silently patrolled the front entrance. Others mocked the media's ever-present desire for violence. Carole Apold wore "P-9 Riot Gear": a helmet consisting of a plastic ice-cream bucket and a cardboard shield. Meanwhile, Hormel affected distance from the controversy—Deryl Arnold said that the company now wasn't sure who it was supposed to be negotiating with.

Lawyers shuttled back and forth across the country in a flurry of activity. The Washington judge, Gerhard Gesell, first rejected Winter and Bass's request for a temporary order to restrain the trusteeship; at the same time, he scolded Huge for making a "clear end-run" to avoid his court, adding that the UFCW had "thumbed its nose" at him and "run out of town." Devitt, meanwhile, denied the UFCW's request for an injunction to enforce the trusteeship, but forbade the local to remove any documents from the union hall or any funds from bank accounts.[4]

Then Huge appeared before Gesell and moved to transfer P-9's lawsuit to Minnesota. The judge denied this motion, agreeing with P-9 that the central focus of the case was the activity of UFCW officers in Washington. Al Zack announced that the UFCW would still go ahead with its court actions in St. Paul.

Pressure was building on Gesell. On the 15th he again refused to give the local a temporary restraining order blocking trusteeship; on the 19th, Devitt again held back from issuing a UFCW-requested order to enforce the trusteeship, saying, in deference to Gesell's jurisdiction, that the Washington judge must rule first on the legality of the trusteeship. Devitt also accused both sides of "judge shopping" and said that it would be "preposterous" to permit two separate trials.

By degrees, P-9 seemed to be getting its way. But for un-known reasons, Gesell then did a complete about-face. "I don't see any substantial possibility in the papers I have presently before me that the local is going to prevail in set-ting aside the trusteeship," he announced. In his musings, he ignored arguments that the UFCW had not given the trust-eeship matter a full hearing and allowed the International broad authority to trustee a local. "What you've got is much like a divorce case," he said:

> The question of being whipsawed here is clearly some-thing the plaintiff [P-9] can avoid. Of course, it's being whipsawed. . . . But if the plaintiffs don't like being whipsawed either because they don't have as many law-yers or they don't have as much money or whatever, it is in their hands to resolve it or change it. The minute you want to go to Minnesota, I'll sign the order and you'll go. . . .
>
> You have your hearing on the 23rd. It will not last be-yond the 23rd. We will have it resolved shortly after the 23rd, and any other aspect of the plaintiff's case, if any remains, will have to go to the other jurisdiction.

First, he had seemed willing to arm-wrestle Devitt for the case; now, he seemed to want nothing to do with it. After the hearing Guyette told reporters, "I can't believe we went through all of this just to move."[5] But Gesell had suggested that unless the local came up with something new, he was going to rule against it. And in a few days time, the judge called P-9's local counsel, Ben Lamberton, and Huge to his chambers, where Gesell made his position absolutely clear.

"I got the sense that the judge didn't want to deal with the merits of the case," recalled Lamberton.

This case was, on its face, a very interesting case, yet he characterized it as a catfight. He kept on with this line, asking "Why are you bringing your dirty linen before me?" and suggesting that it was the plaintiffs' fault.

He was angry at the other side for its forum shopping, but ultimately I think he was more comfortable with them—they came across as being smooth players in the Washington power game. Peggy [Winter] and Emily [Bass], on the other hand, were outsiders who were presenting a difficult case backed by a lot of emotion and push. Whether it was a matter of the Establishment versus radicals off the street or his being just tired, I don't know, but he was uncomfortable with the whole thing.[6]

Having received several clear signals that there would be adverse results if they failed to agree to a transfer, P-9's attorneys signed the papers on the 22nd that authorized transfer of all issues to Devitt.

In the Minnesota court, the local argued again that it had not been given a full and fair hearing on trusteeship; that the trusteeship was being imposed for reasons not allowed by law; and, furthermore, that any injunction enforcing the trusteeship would violate the restriction of the 1932 Norris-LaGuardia Act.

P-9's case was, Bass argued, the mirror image of an earlier precedent-setter, *Benda v. Grand Lodge of International Association of Machinists,* though in the other case an International union had imposed a trusteeship in order to continue a strike rather than to end one. Both cases dealt with the same gut question: Who had the right to bargain for the employees involved? In both cases the NLRB had previously certified the bargaining agent to be the local, not the International. P-9 attorneys argued that if the International wished to supplant the local as agent, it must, as the court had ruled in *Benda*, petition the NLRB and follow its procedures for recertification. Any trusteeship imposed to get around those procedures would run counter to, rather than be justified by, the Landrum-Griffin provisions that allowed trusteeships in order to "restore democratic procedures" or "insure the performance of collective bargaining agreements."

Bass said, moreover, that any injunction issued by Devitt would violate the Norris-LaGuardia Act's firm prohibition on judicial strikebreaking. What were the avowed goals of the UFCW's trusteeship? Nothing less than terminating all strike and picketing activities in Austin and at other Hormel plants and ending the boycott.

In response, the UFCW's counsel justified the limitation of issues at the trusteeship hearing with the statement that in the past all the courts had required was that Internationals hold "some form of hearing." And, he said, if the local had wanted a hearing of the constitutional issues involved, it should have appealed from the hearing to those union officers empowered to consider constitutional issues—the International president and executive committee.

Huge emphasized P-9's "unauthorized strike activities"— the roving pickets and boycott—which he inaccurately suggested had taken place before the reopening of the Austin plant. He recounted the local's resistance to the trusteeship, referring to reports that said P-9 members had removed books and records from the hall and threatened trustees with violence. (Physical assaults on crossovers were also specifically mentioned, as were strikers guarding the hall with baseball bats.) Landrum-Griffin, he said, clearly permits the imposition of trusteeship upon locals that have acted to endanger the lives and livelihoods of other union members and violated the union's constitution.[7]

On June 2 Devitt ruled the trusteeship valid, ordering local officers to recognize Hansen as the trustee and to deliver to him control of all P-9 assets. He ignored the arguments raised by both sides concerning the matter of a full and fair hearing. Nor did he address P-9's assertions about the relevance of the *Benda* ruling or its Norris-LaGuardia Act arguments. Instead, Devitt's 13-page statement asserted flatly that "the basic issue here is a *contract*, not a *labor* dispute." And that contract, he said, existed between the local and the International as embodied in the UFCW constitution, which "reflects a vesting of controlling authority in the International."

An uninformed reader might mistake Devitt's remarks for a treatise on military chain of command: Ignoring the constitution's emphasis on rank-and-file validation of all decisions, the judge spoke only of its "broadly expressed grant of authority [that] may be exercised for, among other purposes, enforcing compliance with directives of the International."[8]

The ruling immediately touched off another battle over how much P-9 could salvage. Whenever confronted by a seemingly overwhelming obstacle in the past, Guyette and Rogers had asserted that they would not be stopped. Would they now?

The UFCW—which, for the moment, was doing business out of a storefront on Austin's Main Street—correctly perceived that the key to P-9's undoing lay in the trustee's taking over the union hall. But, technically, the P-9 hall was the property of an entity called the Austin Labor Center. Was that separate from P-9 or a mere alter ego? And what about the United Support Group and its Adopt-A-Family, Emergency and Hardship, and Legal Defense funds? The UFCW wished to take over each of these, destroy the strikers' organization, and make the loyalists wholly dependent upon the trustee and Hormel. It had already gotten banks to freeze P-9 accounts and the post office to hold for the trustee all mail addressed to P-9 and to the other entities. Now the court would have to decide in each case whether or not the other entities were separate or under Hansen's jurisdiction.

On June 2 the pickets at the Austin plant came down after 291 days. The next day, having already made an unconditional offer to return to work on behalf of all strikers, Hansen began talks with the company. And on June 5 the loyalists took the ultimate step to rescue their fight: With a petition carrying over 680 signatures, they filed for an NLRB union recertification vote under the name Original Local P-9.[9]

■ ■ ■

The courtroom activities had not removed all the pressure from Hormel and the UFCW. In early May, hundreds attended an Ottumwa rally in support of the fired workers. On May 17, P-9 supporters in cities across the country celebrated "National Boycott Day" with rallies and leafleting in front of major supermarkets. Texas sponsors of a heavily publicized annual spoof event, the SPAM-O-RAMA barbecue, announced the event's postponement, saying that they had instead "decided to honor the nationwide Boycott of Hormel products."

In Minnesota, support for the boycott was announced by the state's 6,000-member National Organization for Women chapter, the statewide branch of the Letter Carriers' union, and a large Graphic Communications' union local. On the first day of fishing season, P-9 bannered along Interstate highways, encouraging drivers to "Boycott Hormel—Eat Fish," and the local even raffled off an outboard motor, selecting the winner from those who sent in labels of Hormel competitors.

On May 19 the company reported a 26 percent earnings decline for its second quarter, or a drop of $1.8 million from the previous year, while sales increased by 25 percent to $442.2 million. Numerous costs related to the strike, including that of training replacement workers, along with heavy discounting of products to hold on to market share and costly sales promotions (including stepped-up advertising and baseball ticket giveaways) accounted for the discrepancy. Adding $2 million more to the company's costs was the state of Iowa's late-April ruling that the 500 fired Ottumwa workers were eligible for unemployment benefits.[10]

As for the UFCW, further troubles lay ahead. In January its leaders felt compelled to announce that the union would accept no further concessions. The International faced a year crowded with contract negotiations and a general membership restlessness that was breaking out into further open rebellions in places such as Madison, Wisconsin. In the wake of the P-9 trusteeship, meatpacker locals there and in Cudahy, Wisconsin, and Albert Lea voted to withhold their national dues. Meanwhile, the union's leadership had, by its own actions, raised serious doubts about its nerve and its integrity.

In late May the Massachusetts AFL-CIO announced that it would be awarding its annual Gompers-Murray-Meany award to Wynn. The announcement met with a chorus of complaint, and over a hundred P-9 supporters—including 40 members of the Lynn Electrical Workers' local at G.E., textile workers from New Bedford, and Boston city employees—trekked out to Cape Cod and staged a protest outside the Sheraton Hyannis Hotel as the awards dinner was in progress. Ten leaders of large unions in the area signed a letter to state federation president Arthur Osborn expressing their unhappiness. Wynn canceled his appearance, saying that his mother was ill.[11]

"The potential for support remained enormous," Rogers recalled later. In spite of the UFCW's best efforts, an embarrassingly steady stream of resolutions pledging moral and material support for P-9 emanated from the various national union conventions held during the summer. At the Hotel and Restaurant Employees' convention, Boston P-9 supporter Domenic Bozzotto was called to the podium to give an update on the Austin strike; then the union's International president pledged to raise $100,000 for the strikers on the convention floor. In spite of open hostility from International Association of Machinists president William Winpisinger, that union's Western States Conference passed a resolution of support. The nationwide Coalition of Black Trade Unionists, too, passed a resolution that openly acknowledged the need to send donations in a way that circumvented the UFCW. Other national unions that went on record for P-9, or at least against Hormel, included the National Education Association, the State, County, and Municipal Workers, the Postal Workers (who, in August, endorsed the boycott), and the Letter Carriers. Meanwhile, contributions and letters of support rolled in from unions in Britain, Canada, Mexico, Puerto Rico, and South Africa.[12]

Still, with Devitt's sweeping injunction in force and hundreds still facing trial for a variety of misdemeanors and felonies, there was little rank-and-file strike activity. Instead, local members threw themselves into a massive art project: an 80-by-16-foot mural adorning an outside wall of the Austin Labor Center. Denny Mealy and Ron Yocum, mainstays of the sign committee, had earlier painted a small mural honoring the local's officers inside the hall. At the April 12 rally, Mealy and a professional muralist, Virginian Mike Alewitz, came up with the idea of the much larger project.

"The reason for it was to maintain rank-and-file participation, which had fallen into a lull," Mealy told me later.

With the trusteeship hearings in session, the three painters, along with attorney Winter's son Alex Rottner, spent a week composing drawings that might be worked into the mural. The complex result incorporated elements of fantasy and harsh realism: A huge green serpent ran much of the length of the outside wall; at its tail-end, faceless workers marched into an industrial plant. Near the front of the building, an enormous woman meatpacker wielded an axe labeled "P-9" to chop off the serpent's head. Below her, the workers re-emerged—now with faces, having gained identity as a result of union struggle. The now-organized workers and farmers carried signs and a banner reading "All for one and one for all." Rising above the serpent were a worker holding a torch (painted just where a light bulb protruded from the wall), the face of a man behind bars, and an inscription from an old Wobbly poem: "If blood be the price of your cursed wealth, good God we have paid in full."

"We needed a basic theme for the mural," said Mealy:

Everyone felt it should somehow be that of corporations' squeezing workers and causing turmoil. We assimilated the serpent to stand for the corporations from a Russian revolutionary poster. The torch wasn't lifted from [Picasso's] "Guernica" but was Alex's idea of the guiding light of the union. And the jailed man, who people saw as a persecuted striker, was really meant to represent this business agent from a 1930s strike who was jailed for collusion between a union and a company.

Over a hundred union members worked on the project, building scaffolding, sealing the wall, and painting backgrounds and details, while a great many more looked on. The paint and brushes were donated by a St. Paul sign painters' local, and others contributed compressors, rags, and ladders. Round-the-clock security was set up to prevent vandalism.

After a discussion, the rank and file voted to dedicate the mural to jailed African National Congress leader Nelson Mandela. And on May 27 a thousand people, including Babs Duma of the ANC, turned out for the dedication.

Drawing a parallel between Mandela's persecution and that of P-9, Guyette noted that the South African could be out of prison if he would give up his fight for freedom for others, and "we could have a contract agreement if we would give away our freedom and self-respect."[13]

With the trusteeship vise closing, almost a month elapsed before the next significant mass action. During the second week in June, Guyette and Rogers announced that a tent city demonstration would take place in Austin during the week of the 22nd to the 28th. It was a carefully worded statement in which Guyette said he spoke only as an individual, "not as a representative of P-9 or its suspended leadership—the local's only legal spokesman is Joe Hansen."

> The pickets have been withdrawn, backed by the threat of many years of imprisonment. P-9 members also have been ordered by the trustee, again backed by court sanction, not to engage in a boycott. Again, I am complying under protest. Yet the boycott is being carried forward by tens of thousands who are simply exercising their First Amendment rights.

The call for the tent city was formally issued by the United Support Group. During that event, he said, union members and supporters from around the country would gather for workshops and discussions, and "spend a week discussing our common problems."[14] Because of the "unavailability" of city facilities, the gathering actually took place in a large outdoor area just north of town.

Supporters were slow to appear, but by the start of that week, a mineworker and his family, then an Indiana autoworker, a New York longshoreman, and a Colorado machinist had joined the campers at what became known as Solidarity City. Only around two hundred people turned out for a Monday evening rally at which a new local flag, emblazoned "Fighting P-9ers," was raised over the campsite. But during the week several hundred participated in demonstrations at the UFCW's Main Street office and the post office (which P-9 supporters felt was improperly diverting support group mail). And on Saturday a thousand turned out for yet another march through town and an afternoon rally at Solidarity City.

Marchers came from 20 states, including Massachusetts, Florida, New York, Texas, Missouri, North Carolina, and California. The fired Ottumwans and Fremonters were there, along with representatives from the Rainbow Coalition and the American Indian Movement.

Crystal Lee Sutton, the former Carolina textile worker on whose union exploits the movie *Norma Rae* was based, addressed the rally, as did Monsignor Charles Owen Rice, a 77-year-old priest from Pittsburgh who had attained some notoriety for his long association with labor causes. Each condemned both the company and the International. "The role of the unions at the top level is more company-oriented than worker-oriented," Sutton told the crowd. "They have become corrupted by the wealthy and are doing the bidding of the bosses." Rice, who had earlier challenged the UFCW's actions in his weekly *Catholic Bulletin* column, took note of the International's attempt to hide its repression of P-9 behind liberal posturing on other social issues. The priest instructed the strikers in a persuasive Irish brogue: "My advice to you is to hang in there. What worse can happen to you?"

And, true to form, Rogers announced, "This campaign will not de-escalate."

But it had already de-escalated. Local police were in contact with both UFCW and Hormel attorneys, and had arranged for a contingent of U.S. marshals to be in town to assist with any possible plant blockage. But there was no blockage—the only activity that remained for the local was building the boycott. And it could finally be said that the original goals were lost, since Joe Hansen was now negotiating with the company, hoping only to get terms similar to the mediators' proposal that he had tried to force members to accept back in December.[15]

■ ■ ■

Unless . . . The strikers' last hope lay in decertification of the UFCW and recertification of the independent local union, Original Local P-9.

Ironically, though, all recertification matters were put on hold by the NLRB, pending resolution of the unfair-labor-practice charge filed against Hormel for its failure to pay profit-sharing money owed the strikers. It was not even clear who would get to vote on recertification—would strikers, P-9 crossovers, and replacements all get a ballot? On July 30, the principals behind Original P-9 held a press conference in which they declared that the delay represented "a conspiracy between the Hormel company and the International union." Significantly, most of the talking was done by attorney David Twedell.

The UFCW would proclaim that the attempt to recertify under Original P-9, soon to be renamed the North American Meat Packers Union in order to avoid confusion with trusteed P-9, revealed Guyette's and Rogers' longstanding goal—the creation of a new union. For better or worse, though, neither Rogers, Guyette, nor many of the executive board members ever had much to do with the direction of NAMPU. Originally, the board members (except for Carl Pontius, who formally resigned from the UFCW to join the NAMPU board) kept their distance for legal reasons. Some, like Skinny Weis, disagreed with the tactic, feeling that everyone should stay and fight within the UFCW. In time the group of rank-and-file activists running the new union made it clear that NAMPU was their baby, not that of the board. In reality, the new union was never much more than a cats-paw of David Twedell, a former UFCW staffer who had a personal grudge against the International, which had fired him, and who was already involved in other recertification efforts in Texas.

"P-9 had a hard time reaching agreement before, due to outside interference from the UFCW," Twedell proclaimed at the press conference. "Once the UFCW is out of the picture, it's going to be Austin workers against an Austin company, and we think we can get a contract." Twedell offered the group many pat answers involving the recertification process and wrote radio spots to woo the scabs away from the UFCW, but did not get an election in Austin until April 1989, when NAMPU was soundly defeated. In the short run, NAMPU's primary achievement was to push Hormel and Hansen into speeding up their negotiations.[16]

One month to the day after Devitt's order upholding the trusteeship, the judge turned over the union hall to the UFCW, ruling that the Austin Labor Center was an alter ego of P-9. But Devitt refused to allow the UFCW to take over the United Support Group or its funds, which he found to be independent.[17]

The International had already initiated a campaign of repression in the town. In June strikers had received letters ordering compliance with Devitt's first order and threatening them with arrest and prosecution should they interfere with the trusteeship. Union officials circulated through the town photographing cars with anti-Hormel bumper stickers and telling activists that they would lose all hope of reinstatement if they continued to speak out. At least one store owner was told that *he* was violating the court order by refusing to stock Hormel products. In addition to having P-9 and support group assets frozen and their mail diverted (acts that were partly rectified by United Support Group lawyers), Hansen fired P-9's clericals, its lawyers, and Corporate Campaign. The local officers, too, were fired, Hansen asserted, as he formally challenged their right to receive the unemployment benefits that other P-9ers had begun getting after the return-to-work offer was made. And he announced that he would not call any local meetings without a petition signed by 600 local members.

With the takeover of the hall, the UFCW sent in 30 organizers to claim possession of the building and exert an intimidating physical presence in the town. Though local officers had cleaned out most of their possessions back in June, support group members had only a couple of hours to remove their belongings following the July court order. The International changed the locks and left the building vacant for a period. The effect of the takeover would be to fragment union business among four locations: the UFCW office on Main Street, a new support group office, the mostly unused P-9 hall, and NAMPU's office, the last three within a few blocks of each other on 4th Avenue.

The UFCW's organizers would remain on through the summer, policing the loyal strikers and attempting to enroll the strikebreakers into the UFCW while Hansen continued to bargain with Hormel. On July 3 Nyberg announced that the talks were proceeding smoothly, and since the two parties had resolved all other outstanding grievances (the UFCW dropped most of the over fifty grievances that had been earlier cited for arbitration), he said that the long-overdue profit-sharing money would be paid to the strikers. But since this opened the way for a recertification election, the International filed other charges against NAMPU (it alleged that the new union was harassing its organizers), delaying the election further. Meanwhile, deputy trustee Kimbro met occasionally with selected groups of "replaced workers," assuring them that Hansen would get them their jobs back as part of the settlement he was working on.[18]

The United Support Group continued its attempts to maintain the P-9 community, though it was largely unable to continue the struggle. Over 800 families still received Adopt-A-Family stipends of from $100 to $600 a month. Wednesday evening community suppers were provided for all who would come. And the group organized an August 17 strike-anniversary picnic that drew several hundred people to Todd Park.

On the occasion, Guyette declared, "This war will continue until each and every person gets their jobs back." Supporters from New York, Boston, and Phoenix pledged their continuing support. And Rogers was unflagging: "As long as you people are willing to stand up and fight, we will stand with you and fight with you with everything we have," he pledged on behalf of the Corporate Campaign staff. Like Guyette, he remained focused on holding out, raising funds to support the loyalists through door-to-door canvassing, and building the boycott.[19]

Meanwhile, Nyberg and Hansen announced that they expected to have a contract wrapped up by September 1. Hansen said that the negotiations were adversely affected by the company's implemented contract and the presence of replacement workers in the plant. His goals, he told the *New York Times*, were to win recall rights for as many strikers as possible, to dismantle the two-tier wage system, and to get common expiration dates for all Hormel contracts. To that end, Hansen opened negotiations for six other Hormel plants as well as the Austin facility.[20]

On August 27, Hansen and Hormel's Dave Larson announced that they had reached a settlement after eight days of intensive talks. But in that first announcement, after saying, "I think we've achieved our goals for Austin," Hansen admitted that no terms had yet been reached on two of his key goals: recall of strikers and common contract expiration dates.

Two days later it was clear that the contract did not provide for recall of any strikers, only phased out the two-tier schedule over four years in exchange for ending all of the old escrow payments, and provided for common expiration dates at all plants but Austin, where the contract would run for a year longer. By 1988 wages would rise to $10.70—a penny more than workers made back in 1981. The only return-to-work victory came, by coincidence, in Ottumwa, where an arbitrator ruled that the 507 who had honored the picket line must be reinstated by mid-September with full seniority. As for P-9's other issues—safety, seniority, job security, the guaranteed annual wage, past practices, some kind of expedited arbitration—there were no changes. The company language that had led members to strike in August 1985 stood.

Hansen said that all P-9 members would be eligible to vote on the contract, including 300 of the 600 replacement workers who had signed up for the union, strikers who crossed (even those who had resigned from the union in order to cross), and those who stayed out. "What we have is a hell of a victory for the union," announced a long-silent Lewie Anderson. "This is the best contract in the meatpacking industry. . . . It proves we are making up for lost ground."[21]

Two years later, Anderson was less positive. "My impression was that Joe was not supposed to bargain until we could get the rest of the [Hormel] local unions involved," he told me.

> I thought the only way to save things was to use the strength of the other locals in negotiations. But it didn't happen that way. What started out as a negotiation to preserve a bargaining unit ended up as in-depth negotiations. As a result, we incurred greater losses than we should have.[22]

■ ■ ■

The contract was ratified—according to the UFCW's count, by a vote of 1,060 to 440—in another mail ballot that was tabulated on September 12. A week earlier, the UFCW had explained the settlement during separate meetings held with those who had crossed the line and with those who stayed out. Turnout among the crossovers was light; around 500 of 800 strikers showed up for their meeting. As in 1981, all were asked to vote on the basis of a two-page summary, rather than the contract itself. As Lynn Huston recalled, "We went over the summary and people asked questions of Lewie and Hansen."

> Our guys tried to pin them down, but they've got a knack for not answering. Finally, Hansen would say, "I just don't know." People were so disenchanted that they didn't ask over and over—a lot just got upset and left.
>
> Near the end, Merrell Evans, who hadn't said anything, got up and asked Lewie, "How can you stand up

there and call yourself a union man?" Lewie directed [Larry] Kohlman to turn the mike off. Evans turned it back on, and Kohlman turned it off again. Then Guyette got up to speak and put his hand over the switch. Kohlman tried to push Guyette's hand away. That made about half the people there jump to their feet. Hansen said, "Everybody, calm down," and to Kohlman, "Get the hell away from there." Then all the UFCW organizers ran up to the front of the stage, while Lewie and Hansen ran out the back door.

That was the end of the meeting. Overall, we were given the message that the only chance we had to get our jobs back was if the agreement was ratified.[23]

Anderson predicted that Hormel would rehire "everyone who wants to go back within two years." In the cover letter sent with the mail ballot, Hansen noted, "There are approximately one thousand employees in the plant at this time but I believe as most of you, that for that plant to run most efficiently . . . hundreds of more employees will be needed." The strikers remained skeptical: "I don't like it," said 35-year veteran William Barnett, "but if it doesn't pass, then what have you got?"

Huston is certain that no member of the trusteed P-9 executive board voted for the settlement. But according to the UFCW, the vote among strikers was 55 percent against, 45 percent in favor.[24]

■ ■ ■

Those who lose must pay the penalty. What happens to those who refuse to admit they've lost—must they pay even more?

Over the summer, supporters of the local had begun raising funds for the legal defense of those charged with felony riot in April. Attorney Kenneth Tilsen accused the Austin police and the county attorney of indiscriminate arrest and lodging bogus charges.[25] An emergency appeal letter, calling for all charges to be dropped, was signed by Miles Lord, Eugene McCarthy, Pete Seeger, and writers Studs Terkel and Tillie Olsen among others.

Given the manner in which Goodnature had treated the strikers arrested in March, it was reasonable for the defendants to worry that the authorities intended to persecute them further. But by the fall it no longer mattered that much: The strike was broken, and there was little likelihood of more mass activity. Thus in September Judge James Mork terminated the prosecution of 200 people, dropping their misdemeanor charges in exchange for 8 to 20 hours of community service each and pledges not to repeat their offenses.

Since no one was required to admit guilt, only a few refused the offer in order to contest the charges. Most agreed to work in area schools, parks, or charities, though, as a matter of principle, many would do no work within Austin's city limits. "People jumped at the chance to do community service—a lot didn't want to be fined because they didn't have the money," recalled Jeannie Bambrick.[26]

It would be early December before the court ruled on the felony and gross misdemeanor charges. But at that time Judge William Johnson dismissed all felony charges for lack of evidence against the charged individuals, along with most of the associated assault and gross misdemeanor charges. All charges against Rogers and Guyette were dismissed on constitutional grounds. For what it was worth, though, the judge agreed that "a riot occurred."[27]

There remained the issue of relations between the strikers and Hormel. The activists sought to continue pressure by means of an October 11 rally and the efforts of rank-and-file boycott organizers sent out across the country. Both Hansen and Deryl Arnold sent letters to P-9ers noting that "disciplinary action up to and including discharge" could result. The UFCW also argued that boycotting would lead to fewer jobs, and thus less likelihood of anyone's being rehired. But, with three other acts, the trustee inadvertently encouraged the loyalists to keep on fighting. First, he sent letters urging them to sign cards withdrawing from the union; then, deputy trustees began sandblasting the mural, concentrating their efforts first on the word "Solidarity" and on the faces of the previously faceless workers.[28]

Finally, during November it came out that, in a formal strike settlement, Hansen had agreed to limit strikers' legal claims upon their old jobs—rather than unlimited recall rights, they would be eligible for rehire only during the next two years. The "unreinstated employees" were also required to return recall registration forms by early December. Those "terminated for misconduct"—that is, picket line activity— had no right of recall, though the UFCW filed a grievance on their behalf.[29]

"The company must have had it planned who they wanted to fire before the strike ever started," said Jim Getchell, who along with two others had been fired in the early spring for unlawful picket line activity. "We just saw a carload of scabs going into the plant and hollered at them, 'Stay out of there.' The next day I got a letter in the mail saying I'd been fired." Altogether, 16 were fired in this way.[30]

A large group of disabled workers came in for a special raw deal. "Under the workers' comp law, disabled workers have 90 days after reaching 'maximum wellness' to return to work," explained Frank Collette.

After that, they must either go back to a job that doesn't reinjure them or they receive a one-time payoff. Well, none of those out on disability at the time of the strike were recalled, so everybody got the payoff. But now, when they go to look for another job, everyone gets asked if they've ever been on disability, and they have to say, "Yes, at Hormel." They don't get hired because of a double stigma: as disabled workers and P-9 strikers.[31]

With no one back to work, the town of Austin settled into a kind of long-term, low-intensity civil war between those still out and those inside. Each side attacked the property of the other: A favorite union tactic employed weed-killer to write the word "scab" on a crossover's green lawn. The crossovers in turn defaced strikers' property.

Police reports include complaints from one crossover that poison had been dumped into his swimming pool, causing his daughter to become violently ill; from Skinny Weis and his daughter, who said that three scabs had repeatedly driven by their house cursing and ultimately threw a smoke-bomb into their yard; and from striker Dick Shatek, who said that someone had shattered a window in his house. According to Chief Hoffman's year-end summary, there were 1,047 reported incidents of vandalism during 1986, up from 560 in the previous year.[32]

Jim Getchell, whose family was solidly union, believes that three of his sister's horses were poisoned by scabs. His brother's car was "torched." He himself received letters in the mail threatening his children, and his wife got sexually threatening telephone calls. Jim Getchell, Jr., one of the leaders of the high-school-age union supporters, was jumped and beaten up by a group of crossovers, then arrested by police, who he says planted marijuana on him.[33]

Like many others, Darrell Busker's family disintegrated after the strike. His wife, who took their three kids and left him, is now "running with scabs," he says. She was once a support group member, but in the end the strike "just got to her." Busker, who now earns $5.00 an hour making archery equipment, remains extremely bitter toward the crossovers.

> It made my stomach sick to see people who were my friends going in there. My dad and I were looking at my high school yearbook this afternoon, and I could point out 15 of my classmates who were scabs. A lot of close friends who I used to play ball with, now I can't even look at them. But this town is owned by Hormel . . . it's just a one-horse town.[34]

Lynn Huston, Merrell Evans, former mayor Tom Kough (defeated in a bid for state senate), Jim Retterath, Cecil Cain, R. J. Bergstrom, and scores of others left town to find work, sometimes only to return frustrated with the alternatives. Many tried to sell their Austin houses, but were unable to find buyers. Mike and Jeannie Bambrick saw their house repossessed by the bank. They moved to Florida but returned after four months, feeling the pull of family and the small town they had always lived in. Skinny Weis, Buck Heegard, and others who had put in sufficient years retired.

A number of union sympathizers—and those who were perceived as inappropriately tolerant of the union—either lost their jobs or were forced to leave town. Catholic priest Father Charles Collins was transferred elsewhere because of his too-obvious P-9 sympathies. High school principal Kevin O'Dell was fired for renting the school gym to P-9 for a fundraiser, while history teacher Robert Richardson was forced out for wanting to talk about the strike in his classes.

Hormel shut the Ottumwa plant in the summer of 1987—it had only rehired around 250 of the 500 fired workers, and now they were displaced again. In the fall of that year, it leased the plant to Excel Corp., a low-wage subsidiary of Cargill Inc. that paid $5.50 an hour. Over twelve hundred people applied for the Excel jobs, including many who had worked for Hormel at $10.30. About a dozen of the former Hormel workers were able to take advantage of an arbitrator's ruling and "bump" into Austin plant jobs held by crossovers with lower seniority; 20 others opted to take a "one-time, lump sum settlement of all claims" that amounted to between $14,000 and $20,000.[35]

Two P-9 supporters, Ottumwa steward Dan Varner and Fremonter Bob Langemeier, were singled out for special punishment by Hormel. Varner was fired for aiding and encouraging the Austin pickets. (In our interview, Nyberg expressed particular resentment toward Varner, "the first employee we hired in Ottumwa," for speaking against the incorporation of Ottumwa seniority language in the mediators' proposed settlement for Austin.) His firing was upheld in arbitration, and the NLRB denied his "failure to represent" charges, filed against the UFCW for what he claimed was a mishandled arbitration. Langemeier was fired before any extended picketing in Fremont—he says merely for wearing a P-9 hat in the Hormel plant. But the company has refused to place Langemeier on a recall list (unlike the 23 Fremonters who were fired for honoring P-9's picket) and has appealed an NLRB order that it rehire him.[36]

Bob Johnson, the Hormel worker accused of making terroristic threats against the company in 1985, saw all charges dismissed after two weeks of trial when the county was unable to present testimony from a voice expert. Its case collapsed, but the company immediately filed a lawsuit against Johnson.[37]

Guyette pushed ahead with a "don't buy Hormel" campaign, at first quietly, then without restraint. He began traveling around the United States and England, where he got the national executive committee of the British Labor Party to endorse the boycott. Boycotting became his full-time work.

Meanwhile, he was becoming an outcast in Austin. His brother-in-law had him expelled from their small Lutheran church, which saw civil disobedience as "the devil's work," in light of Biblical injunctions to submit to authority. Since the beginning of the strike, the family had received numerous telephoned and written death threats, and these continued. One included a drawing of hanged children. The Guyettes were reduced to living off food stamps and paying the mortgage with loans from a group of Hormel retirees.[38]

And Guyette continues to be hounded by the UFCW. Soon after the trusteeship was imposed, the International began making accusations that Guyette had misused money. In July 1987 the UFCW filed suit against him and Financial Secretary Kathy Buck, charging that they had used pension funds to finance the strike. Guyette maintained that the events in question happened before the strike, when he was a newly elected local president, and that he was assured of their legality by the then-serving financial secretary and union attorneys. And he in turn asserted that UFCW Region 13 is guilty of misappropriation of donations intended for P-9—how else could the trusteed local have repaid the UFCW $1,373,000 for P-9's "strike advance," as the UFCW's 1986 labor-management reporting forms show it did?

As far as Hormel is concerned, there is some evidence that it still has private security men on Guyette's trail. He told me that while in Chicago in 1987, he was approached by a man who identified himself as an operative of California Plant Protection, the private security service hired by Hormel to maintain security during the strike. Moreover, an alleged Cudahy striker who came to Austin in 1987 and traveled with former P-9 strikers to the AFL-CIO meeting was later identified by Wyoming mineworkers as a security operative who had videotaped strikers at a Decker Coal strike.[39]

The community of strikers and supporters has been torn by division. Old dislikes, put aside for the duration of the strike, resurfaced, and new disaffections arose. After a bit, NAMPU leaders had nothing good to say about Guyette, the support group split down the middle over money problems, and the trusteed executive board members started pointing fingers at each other.

Some of this infighting may have been the result of stepped-up police infiltration of support group and "Original P-9" activities during 1987. Internal memos to Chief Hoffman reveal that one turncoat reported on the most mundane details of support group meetings, the group's successes and failures, and which persons remained active. Spying on protests against the company's 1987 "Spam's 50th Anniversary" bash, another police agent delivered a lengthy and very giddy report, which read in part:

> . . . there was one guy from Milwaukee, that came over here just to quote the P9ers. He worked in either auto or something of that sort. . . . At these things there was also a lot of different people, some really I don't know what you'd call them, talking to one guy from political rights defense fund on Socialist party stuff and Nicaragua and all this other stuff . . . and how the Hormel Company has dealings with South Africa and all kinds of gobbeldy goop. . . . I listened to quite a few of them, I really didn't understand what they were trying to say. . . .
>
> As for the painting of the Mayor's house and the digging up of the greens at the golf course, I didn't—the whole weekend I didn't hear anyone mention anything of it.

I always kinda laughed to myself when they talk to highly [sic] of the police and law enforcement that they would really be burnt bad if they knew that sitting right in front of them was a cop. . . . I thought it would be harder getting in and kinda being a supporter but I found out that there's such a weird group of people that does come and support some of these P9ers that . . . they just don't really suspect anybody.

For his part, Police Chief Hoffman began to promote himself as something of an expert on labor disputes and civil disobedience, touring the state and speaking at a variety of police institutes and seminars. According to what appear to be Hoffman's speech notes, obtained from police files, from the start of the strike his "primary objective was to keep the police image in the best possible light." This required staying in communication with all parties and remaining low-key and impartial.

But impartiality was apparently difficult to maintain. In the face of "so much civil law that we were unfamiliar with," lawyers from the International UFCW were "happy to provide me with their input," as were "the local staff of management," his notes say. While expressing a certain wariness, he suggests that he was able to reach an understanding with the company's legal staff, who "were helpful and tried to be patient and understanding." The mayor, however, was biased, interfering, and a "spy for the union."

The union, his notes say, was composed of "basically good people" plus "a few hotheads." However, Hoffman was quite concerned about the left-wing groups who were drawn to Austin by the strike, particularly the Socialist Workers Party and the "Communist Party"—by which he likely meant the Progressive Labor Party, since the CP was hostile to the strike-

rs and had no presence in town. Other memos and pho-
tocopies in the police department's files refer to the International Committee Against Racism (INCAR), a PL front group
whose members once attended a rally bearing a "Fight for
Communism" banner. The chief's anxiety about this Red
Menace led him earlier to write to the local Veterans of Foreign Wars post commander, urging "that we make a public
statement about Americanism and Communism," without
"tak[ing] sides in the labor dispute."

After April 1986 Hoffman seems to have turned solidly
against the local union's leaders. He wrote to U.S. Senator
Rudy Boschwitz, a number of federal agencies, and to President Ronald Reagan, among others, regarding his suspicions
that P-9 was skimming money off the Adopt-A-Family funds.
Boschwitz was "helpful," he notes, though the Internal Reve-
nue Service was not, since it viewed the situation as "too hot
politically."[40]

Hoffman had met regularly with Hormel security consultant Gary Baker since July 1985, but kept his distance since, as
he noted in his post-strike presentations, private security
tend to engage in "overkill" in order to "keep the employer
nervous." Now the police began accepting Baker's reports on
P-9 supporters. A June 12, 1986 report from an unidentified
officer states, "Ken Carlson and the sheriff stopped in with the
report from Baker on [Twin Cities Support Committee head]
Peter Rachleff." Elsewhere in Hoffman's files is an unsigned
report on Rachleff—probably the Baker paper—that is filled
mostly with innocuous data, noting his excellent credit rat-
ing, clear driving record, and lack of criminal record. But in
an attempt to associate Rachleff with "subversive or militant
factions," it states he is "indirectly connected" to the American Indian Movement, "which had private meetings with
Muammar Qaddafi . . . concerning militant activities in the

United States." (Rachleff says he met AIM leader Vernon Bellecourt once.) The report also alleges links between Rachleff and "4 to 5 Trotsky groups," the Honeywell Project, Women Against Military Madness, the Revolutionary Communist Party, and "Green Party terrorist groups."[41]

Investigations, surveillance, and open hostility from the authorities led to further opportunism. Striker Dale Francis had traveled all around the country speaking on the local's behalf and had written letters and articles for such diverse organs as *The Militant* and *The Bulletin*, in which he defended P-9 and NAMPU and denounced the UFCW. Many P-9ers never trusted him, knowing that he had once scabbed at IBP. In November 1986 Francis confirmed these suspicions by addressing a UFCW National Packinghouse Conference, where he told delegates, "you could almost say I was brainwashed" and "the International union was totally right from the beginning." In 1987 Francis took his story to the Austin police and the FBI, where he described Socialist Workers Party involvement in the strike and identified various strikers as likely to "involve themselves in vandalism."[42]

None of this was particularly healthy for the children of the town. P-9ers' kids could no longer hang out with management kids or scab kids. The schools, public playgrounds, and streets were areas of conflict; fist-fights and name-calling became part of the daily routine. The family doctor told Vicky Guyette that her children were too serious and needed to be able to laugh more. "Now, you tell me how to make that possible," she replied.[43]

■ ■ ■

Supporters elsewhere suffered too. In New York, Ray Rogers and Corporate Campaign were, as Wynn had foretold, blacklisted. Far from getting rich off P-9, CCI received around $111,000 for almost two years' work—not nearly enough to pay modest staff salaries. Between fees not paid and other offers that he let pass by, Rogers estimated that CCI lost about a half-million dollars. The staff was forced to move from a suite of offices into a shoebox. "What's this?" Guyette asked during one New York visit; "This is the house that Guyette built," replied Ed Allen.

From the time the strike started until spring of 1986, I believed that P-9 would reach some sort of settlement and that members would go back to their jobs in the plant. But after April, it seemed that P-9 had lost absolutely, and most staff members fell into a deep funk. Rogers, though, simply refused to disengage from the strike, to acknowledge that there had been at least a serious setback, or to leave Austin. For months after the trusteeship was imposed, he was still sending crews out to do door-to-door fundraising in order to continue the fight. Finally, though, he managed to get CCI involved in the strike of the non-AFL-CIO Independent Federation of Flight Attendants at Trans World Airlines and to disengage emotionally from P-9 without ever turning his back on the members. Less than two years later, CCI was working for the Paperworkers International Union, running a campaign against the world's largest papermaker, International Paper.

"Anyone who says that Rogers is a has-been had better look at his history and how he operates," Nyberg said to me in April of that year. "Ray Rogers and Corporate Campaign are alive and well."[44]

Jan Pierce, one of the few union figures of national stature to support P-9, also came under attack. During a Democratic Socialists of America meeting in May 1986, former UFCW vice president Jessie Prosten cursed him before an audience

of several hundred people. Pierce has been shunned and ad-
monished by CWA colleagues, spat at and physically as-
sailed by UFCW men, but he says he has never regretted his
support. "The experience helped me grow and get back to
the rank-and-file members and the sacrifices they're willing
to make. It was a source of revitalization for me."[45]

■ ■ ■

It seems safe to say that many P-9ers will never throw in the
towel. They certainly had not by February 1987, when 40 of
the "replaced workers" traveled to Bal Harbour to protest
against their treatment at the hands of the UFCW; or by
March 1987, when a boycott rally drew a thousand people to
Austin; by the July 4 weekend of that year, when they timed
another set of activities to coincide with "Spam's 50th Anniversary"; or even by March 1988, when the Twin Cities Support Committee sponsored a "jailbird party" in honor of all
who had been arrested in the P-9 cause.

"It won't be over till everyone is back to work," Nyberg
admitted to me. Yet there is not the least indication that
Hormel ever intends to rehire the strikers. It says it has no
use for them. The post-strike business press is filled with
articles saying how well Hormel is doing—how, during record years for profits, it has been moving away from meatpacking and into packaged convenience foods.

The strike cost the company plenty. When I asked,
Nyberg would not offer an estimate; *Forbes* suggested that it
cost Hormel around $2 million. But that figure seems very
low: If you consider only the company's reported loss in
earnings from the first quarter of 1986 (which Hormel said
went to train replacements, and which likely included considerable security expenses) and the unemployment paid
out to fired Ottumwa workers, costs approach $4 million.

Then you can throw in the further costs of transferring or buying out the Ottumwans and Fremonters held to have been unjustly fired, and further millions spent on stepped-up advertising and promotions.[46] And then there is the boycott.

Numerous meat-industry observers and company executives have called the boycott ineffective. But for some reason both the company and the UFCW have worked hard to stamp it out. In October 1986 they put together a joint effort aimed at vendors. Advertisements in *Vending Times* and *Automatic Merchandiser* boldly proclaimed, "Together! . . . we're proud to say that Hormel, Dinty Moore, and Mary Kitchen vending products continue to be made by union workers who earn the highest wages, receive the top benefits and enjoy the best working conditions in the industry." The advertisement was signed by Richard Knowlton and Joe Hansen.[47]

In February 1987, eight trusteed executive board members, who had sent out a mass mailing promoting the boycott, received in the mail notices of their termination and removal from the recall list. (Executive board member Floyd Lenoch took the news hard: The day after he received it, he died of a stroke.) In October 1987, the UFCW promoted an anti-boycott resolution at the state AFL-CIO convention (it was beaten back), while in 1988 several Democratic Farmer Labor Party members attempted to rid the party platform of its formal endorsement of the boycott (they were also defeated). As recently as May 1988, former striker Steve Lovrink received a letter from the company notifying him that he faced removal from the recall list because a vehicle registered in his wife's name still sported a "Boycott Hormel" bumper sticker. Dozens of such letters have been sent out since the ratification of the contract negotiated by Hansen that ruled out boycotting.

Can it be that the boycott has become permanent among many of America's pissed-off but beaten-down union men and women? "I can't boycott USX," one such person told *Labor World* editor Dick Blin, "but I sure as hell never have to buy Spam again." Perhaps such an unofficial boycott is still costing the company some undetermined number of dollars. Or perhaps Hormel is going after boycotters because CEO Dick Knowlton, winner of Carnegie-Mellon University's 1987 "outstanding crisis manager" award for his handling of the strike, just cannot regain his cool. According to the Bureau of National Affairs, he still refuses to refer to Ray Rogers by name.[48]

Meanwhile, what might serve as the UFCW's last word on the strike was spoken by its executive vice president, Jay Foreman.

The 40 P-9ers who traveled to the AFL-CIO meeting in 1987 included many of the most senior workers, who felt that the truth about the Hormel strike must be told. They found that the UFCW had told other union leaders that all the strikers were back in the Austin plant, working under an excellent contract. "Most had no idea that 25-year-plus veterans were out in the street," said one worker.

On Sunday, the opening day of the executive council meeting, the workers gathered in the lobby of the sumptuous Sheraton Hotel wearing their blue "Cram Your Spam" and "Union Solidarity" T-shirts. For the next several days they stood outside the building holding signs that spoke in no uncertain terms of the UFCW sellout. And they interrupted the UFCW men's leisure moments in restaurants, in bars, and at poolside.

Rich Waller, a 27-year Hormel veteran, approached Lane Kirkland while the AFL-CIO leader was lunching at a hotel restaurant. Kirkland told him that he would be better off speaking with Foreman, who was at a nearby table with his wife. Waller then went over to Foreman and asked him how it was that the strikebreakers got to vote on the proposed settlement with Hormel when they were not yet dues-paying members. Foreman told him that such a vote was allowed by executive privilege, something like the president of the United States could do.

Waller persisted in asking how he could get his job back. But Foreman, whose lunch was getting cold, was tired of the conversation. "What can I tell you?" he said at last. "You lost your jobs—the scabs are the new union."[49]

X

CONCLUSION

Labor leaders are more than sweethearts, they're concubines.
—*Studs Terkel*[1]

The Hormel strike left its critics and sympathizers with two fundamental questions: Could the strikers have emerged with some kind of victory if they had chosen different tactics? And did the experience offer any direction for American labor?

On the question of tactics, there is now widespread feeling among the former strikers that they should have employed violence to keep the Austin plant closed. Somewhat paradoxically, many also say that the mass displays of nonviolent civil disobedience were helpful to the cause. Most still believe that the odds against them were not so great that victory was impossible. No one I talked to says they should have thrown in the towel and conceded defeat at some point just to save their jobs.

"The strike doesn't gain when you look at a scab and say, 'Have a nice day,'" reflected Darrell Busker. "We should have broken the scabs' kneecaps the first time they tried to cross the line," said Vicky Guyette—to which a nodding Barbara Collette added, "Of course I wouldn't have wanted to be the one to do it . . ." But there's the rub: For people who made their living as killers of animals, few in Austin had the killer instinct where people were concerned.

"I believed in civil disobedience," said Rod Huinker. "We should have kept it up, we should be doing it now. People have to do it when things aren't right, when they take your rights away—it makes you visible."

"A serious mistake we made was ending the demonstrations at the bank," Skinny Weis told me. "We totally backed off when we should have gone back and gotten arrested in mass. That would have brought things to a head: The bank and the Hormel Foundation were the two power structures that controlled Hormel."[2]

Several P-9ers emphasized the importance of the 450 union crossovers to the company. "The only way to have gotten anywhere was if nobody had gone back," reflected Pete Winkels.

> Then it would have seemed that Hormel indeed meant to break the union. Instead, they were able to say, "Look, even their own people are coming back." They played on that, saying that they had one-half old scabs and half new scabs. But had no one gone back, they'd have had no choice but to bargain. A completely new work force wouldn't have been tolerated in Minnesota. They knew that, so they waited until they had enough people ready and willing to go back in before they reopened the plant.

"I really believe that if not one person had crossed, we could have won," agreed Huinker. "If no one had crossed, they would have made more compromises."[3]

For Ray Rogers, the key obstacle to winning was the active opposition of the UFCW.

The plan was to neutralize the bank, shut the company down, and, with the Adopt-A-Family money, make sure that the members didn't get starved out. Then to turn to massive civil disobedience.

But I never counted on the International fighting so hard against us. I would never have believed that they would attack us, ignore us when the National Guard came, that Kirkland and Winpisinger would get involved against us, and that they'd spend the millions that they did to defeat us. I never figured they'd do anything one way or the other.[4]

Some critics say that Rogers should have known that the International officers would intervene to protect their turf—these were "their members," the UFCW often asserted proprietorially—and what they saw as national bargaining goals. But, more importantly, critics also fault Corporate Campaign and the members for continuing to strike at all during such anti-union times.

Several journalists, including Peter Perl of the *Washington Post* and David Moberg, have suggested that when the National Guard was sent in, P-9 should have gone back to work without a contract and employed so-called in-plant tactics to bring Hormel to reason. These "in-plant" tactics, popularized in the United States by Jerry Tucker of the UAW's New Directions caucus, consist of organizing members to slow down, to "work-to-rule," to file mass grievances, and generally to make it difficult for management to realize its production goals. In Brazil, auto workers have referred to similar tactics as "building the car upside-down."[5]

But there are as many problems and uncertainties attached to this approach as to the one employed by P-9. As

Tucker himself has reminded union audiences, companies will invariably begin firing union leaders in response to in-plant slowdowns or sabotage of production goals. Employees working without a contract have no remedy for such firings, and those who remain on the job have no recourse but further escalation. In general, Tucker makes extremely modest claims for these tactics.[6]

William Serrin suggests that rather than adopting such a "wimpy" in-plant approach, P-9ers should have seized the Austin facility.[7]

P-9 members, though, say that they considered all these options and bet instead on escalating the strike with extended picketing. "A plant sitdown was rejected in favor of the roving pickets, in part because we heard that the company had armed guards in the plant," Guyette told a conference sponsored by the publication *Labor Notes* in November 1986. "But we also knew that we had to deal with [production at] the other plants."[8]

"I still don't think anything good would have come out of going back, though as it turned out, not much good came out of staying out," reflected Lynn Huston. "The executive board members might have stayed in power, and there probably would have been no trusteeship. But if we had gone back, they'd have fired all the [rank-and-file] leaders immediately. They'd have gotten the same result: Only the goddam sheep would have been left."[9]

From my point of view, P-9 bet on the best option—the fact that it failed does not mean that another option would have succeeded. The gamble that P-9ers chose had a chance not only to win their strike goals but also to point the way forward for labor. Substitution of violent plant gate confrontations, an attempted seizure of the Austin plant, or, particularly, use of in-plant tactics would have afforded less of a chance for either, for the reasons described by Guyette and Huston.

I agree with many others that the key period was in January and February 1986: The use of the National Guard against the strikers, followed by big labor's repeated denunciations of the strike, created powerful public sentiment in P-9's favor. But in addition to shutting Ottumwa, P-9 *had* to shut down the Fremont plant. Even with the 1985 acquisitions that increased Hormel's slaughtering capacity by more than two-thirds, Fremont's slaughter and production remained crucial.

A shutdown there "would have affected us severely," Nyberg said to me later. "We were able to subcontract a large amount of the company's production—in fact everything from Austin—and we could have subcontracted from that plant too, but it would have taken some scrambling."[10]

Had P-9 shut Fremont and kept more of its own members from weakening—the two *ifs* are probably inextricably joined—Hormel would have needed to find a way out. Public sentiment would have been running deeply against the company, and Hormel would have been hard pressed to replace all the Austin, Ottumwa, and Fremont workers. Had P-9 shut down FDL, Hormel would have been in serious trouble indeed.

With Fremont and the two FDL plants operating, and the intervention of the state of Minnesota on Hormel's side, the strikers had little chance to realize their goals. What's more, as Jan Pierce understood, Hormel likely had broad behind-the-scenes support, as it was "carrying the ball for Corporate America."[11]

Should P-9 have moved earlier to shut down Fremont and Ottumwa? Perhaps. But one cannot be sure that union members in these other locations would have taken P-9's extended pickets seriously before the reopening of the plant and the arrival of the National Guard in Austin.

I do not agree with Rogers about the role of the UFCW. As this account has shown, the national union mounted a concerted effort to undermine the strike from its beginning, and that hurt the strike effort. But it helped as well: Without International opposition, the Austin strikers would not have attracted anything like the support that they won.

During 1985–86, P-9 received thousands of letters of support. Some of these said little more than "Hang in there." Many union officers and individuals said that they had walked on picket lines and knew all the associated anxieties well. A lot of people admitted they didn't have much money—they were laid off, on fixed incomes, widows, children, and strikers themselves—but they wanted to send ten dollars, twenty dollars, something. Almost everyone said that no Hormel products would be allowed in their households. And a lot of people suggested that the opposition of the UFCW had further convinced them of the rightness of P-9's cause.

"I have never been much of a union person and have believed (and still do) that many union officials bleed their workers dry financially," wrote one San Diego woman. "However, I feel you are being wronged by Hormel."

A laid-off Pennsylvania steelworker wrote: "Our U.S.W.A. International has sold its members out the same way your international union has. My prayers and support are with you. . . . Your unity and stand at the local level is unionism at its best!! Go for it at all cost."

And an unemployed West Virginia worker, who said he was praying for P-9ers, wrote, "The Guard, the politicians, and the labor leaders seem to pray to another God these

days. . . . You are doing a fine job and I do not want to
see your efforts go for nothing. In all of these [sic] we are
maybe rediscovering the solidarity we should never have let
slip."

These were union people who felt that they had been let
down by labor's leaders and people who had never been in a
union, but who were moved by the UFCW's perfidy to side
with the strike. "I am very distressed at the lack of support
that you've received from the UFCW International," wrote a
Pittsburgh physical therapist. "Your determination and courage in the face of Hormel interests and the bought-off bosses
of the union . . . is an inspiration to all workers," a Washington, D.C., woman said.[12]

Had the UFCW backed the strike and called upon its in-
stitutional allies for assistance, it could have placed serious
pressure on First Bank. The UFCW and other AFL-CIO affiliates might have mounted the serious threat—perhaps the
threat of withdrawing millions of dollars from pension fund
accounts—necessary to move the bank and thus the Hormel
company. In practice, though, the UFCW has not been disposed to use this sort of weapon against corporate adver-
saries. A highly publicized joint effort with the Service Employees' union against Beverly Enterprises, for example,
employed public attacks on the quality of patient care in that
corporation's nursing homes, not pressure upon creditors or
stockholders.[13]

Moreover, had the UFCW backed the strikers, there is a
strong likelihood that things would have turned out just as
badly if not worse. To consider what the Hormel strike might
have been like with the active support and direction of the
UFCW, one only needs to take a look at the 1987–88 strike at
John Morrell & Co.

In March 1987, 750 workers at the company's plant in
Sioux City, Iowa, rejected a cut of their $9.25-per-hour wage

by $1.25, which they felt came too quickly upon the heels of an earlier round of concessions at Morrell plants across the Midwest. Beginning in May, their strike was supported by the company's 2,500 workers in Sioux Falls, South Dakota, who honored an extended picket line thrown up by the Iowans.

The sympathy strike echoed not only the activities at Hormel, but also a 1986 Sioux Falls sympathy strike in honor of strikers from Morrell's third major plant in Arkansas City, Kansas. Because of company whipsawing, by 1987 workers at the three plants earned different rates of pay ($7.25 in Kansas) and had contracts that expired at different times.

The governor sent state troopers to escort strikebreakers into the South Dakota plant on May 5. Mass picketing followed at that plant gate, supported by hundreds of members of other unions. Soon the company had a court injunction limiting the number of plant gate pickets to 25, with huge fines awaiting any violators.

A rally on May 11 drew 3,000 people to Sioux Falls, including a van of former P-9 strikers. The following week, members and supporters distributed thousands of leaflets that explained their issues across the community. The International also began a campaign to publicize the high injury rate at the company, which it said had risen 76 percent since 1981: It got the Occupational Safety and Health Administration to levy fines of $690,000 for the company's underreporting of injuries and won attention from ABC's "20–20" and the *New York Times*.

Was somebody copying P-9? Much of this activity certainly resembled that of the Austin strikers. One key aspect, though, was different: Morrell is a subsidiary of the United Brands conglomerate, and the UFCW failed to mount even a publicity effort against other parts of that entity or to attack its weaknesses.

Six months after the sympathy strike began, on November 7, the UFCW called off the Sioux Falls action. Around two thousand replacement workers were in the plant there, and the company said that it would not lay them off to call back the strikers. Sioux Falls workers expressed confusion about just what the UFCW had in mind: "It's not settled . . . we're not guaranteed our jobs back . . . we don't know what the company's going to tell us," said striker Mark Reichelt.

Lewie Anderson said that ending the strike was a tactic to increase the pressure on Morrell. The original Iowa strike, he alleged, had been an "unfair labor practice" strike, and thus Morrell would be required by law to take back all strikers, give them back pay, and keep the strikebreakers as well. Already, he said, the strike had cost Morrell $40 million.

After a management shakeup, negotiators from the company and union met in November, but by December talks had broken off without progress. Then, in March 1988, the NLRB ruled that the Iowans had not been unfair-labor-practice strikers; thus no workers were entitled to reinstatement. That same month, a federal jury sided with Morrell in a $40 million suit against the UFCW and found that the sympathy strike had violated the no-strike clause of the union contract: That jury eventually awarded Morrell $24.6 million. As of April 1989, the company had recalled only around 750 of the South Dakotans; hundreds of the Iowans, who made an unconditional return-to-work offer in February 1988, also remained out of work.[14]

Notable in all this history is the fact that the workers were willing to risk their jobs and, taking the moral high road, stand up for each other. But rather than building upon their efforts, the UFCW cut the strike off after six months in order to rely instead on power games involving the federal bureaucracy. On top of the costs of the strike, the OSHA fines and bad publicity may have encouraged a Morrell management shakeup—but they failed to usher in a team that would compromise with the union. And the NLRB seems not to have made the least concession to Anderson's "unfair-labor-practice" flight of fancy.

Morrell workers would probably have done better to extend their strike efforts to all Morrell facilities and initiate a campaign aimed at making United Brands an untouchable in the financial community and its high-profile products—such as Chiquita Bananas, Broadcast canned meats, and Vernors ginger ale—untouchables on the supermarket shelves. But the UFCW seems unwilling to carry a struggle in that direction, perhaps because they fear that they might do permanent damage to a company.

The catalogue of similar union miscues is extensive. Only a few weeks after it signed the September 1986 agreement that covered all of Hormel's plants other than Ottumwa and Knoxville, the UFCW led FDL locals in Dubuque, Iowa, and Rochelle, Illinois, out on strike—ostensibly to win the same package.

Thus the union passed up a rare opportunity to shut down all of the Hormel-FDL operation and thereby win a common rate. As noted earlier, Hormel could not have made it through P-9's strike without FDL: It had arranged to take over the low-wage packer, which had a slaughtering operation with two-thirds the capacity of Hormel's, only a few weeks before the Austin local went out. Moreover, during P-9's strike the UFCW said that the FDL workers had no choice but to perform P-9ers' struck work. Now the Hormel locals, including trusteed P-9 with its "scab" membership, had no choice but to return the favor.

Within two months, the FDL strike was defeated. Workers went back for $8.50 an hour, to be increased to just over $9.00 during the next three years. Sixty strikers were not called back, having been permanently replaced.[15]

In 1987 Patrick Cudahy Inc. demanded cuts from its $9.20 hourly rate to a rate as low as $6.50, after getting almost $4.00 in givebacks in the previous two contracts. One of the "big four" packers as recently as the 1960s, Cudahy had been reduced by the 1980s to operating only one Wisconsin plant. But its 900 workers there doubted that further cuts would make much difference to the company, and they went out on strike in January of that year.

Major demonstrations followed, featuring Jesse Jackson and hundreds of labor supporters from Milwaukee and across the Midwest. Coached by Thomas Krukowski, the attorney who had worked for Hormel, Cudahy hired 700 scabs, most of them black, to replace the predominantly white strike force. In April the NLRB found that since the company had committed unfair labor practices—namely, failure to bargain in good faith—the strike represented a lockout. Nonetheless, strikers were denied unemployment benefits. And the strike continued for a year, during which the company appealed the NLRB's decision. Finally, Cudahy filed for reorganization under Chapter 11 of the bankruptcy laws.[16]

By late 1987 Hormel was ready for further wage relief. The company announced in November that it was going to close its Austin kill and cut, as it was still unable to compete with packers such as IBP, which paid hourly wages of $6.00 to $8.00. With the Ottumwa plant closed, the newly elected scab officers of renamed Local 9 surmised that the company really needed the slaughter and that the announcement was simply a ploy intended to win further concessions.[17]

They therefore refused to negotiate a further wage cut. So, in March 1988, the company announced that it would subcontract the plant's slaughter to a newly formed Texas firm, Quality Pork Processors, which would pay around $7.00 an hour. QPP opened in June with a work force of 250 people, including about 60 former P-9ers, hired from an applicant pool of over 800. But three days later, QPP was shut down as a result of an arbitrator's ruling that Hormel could not sub-contract operations covered under Local 9's contract. Soon the company announced again that it might be forced to sell the slaughter, and QPP prepared to go out of business.[18]

In September 1988 Hormel announced that it would end hog slaughtering in Fremont by August 1989 and would lay off 324 out of 770 workers there. The closure would remove Hormel from the slaughtering business altogether. Three months later QPP was back in business in Austin, as Local 9 announced that it was close to winning a union contract there. In January the tentative contract's terms were revealed: It would pay workers $6.50 to $7.00 an hour. The announcement set off howls of protest from other UFCW locals, whose members saw their wages threatened.[19]

All such whipsawing and renegotiating of contracts de-rives from a single cause: the UFCW's failure to organize the low-wage mega-packers IBP and ConAgra. These two and the low-wage but partly organized Excel Corp. buy, slaughter, and sell nearly three-quarters of the country's grain-fattened cat-tle, and more and more they are taking over pork slaughtering as well. From time to time the UFCW has announced that it was about to plunge into an all-out effort to organize one or the other of these, but not much has happened so far.[20]

The case of IBP is ironic. As the journalist Jonathan Kwitney has shown, the Amalgamated Meat Cutters, prede-cessor to the UFCW, had that company over a barrel back in 1970. In the late 1960s, IBP, which was already the largest meat company in the world, was pioneering the approach of butchering beef at the point of slaughter using low-wage workers, rather than sending whole carcasses to the point of consumption to be cut up by high-wage supermarket butchers. But the company was having no success penetrating the country's biggest meat market, New York City: Supermarkets there refused to handle IBP's boxed beef because of the understandable opposition of their unionized butchers.

In 1969 the Amalgamated struck the company's Dakota City plant, in the first of several violent strikes. Several homes were dynamited, and there was at least one murder. By April of the following year, IBP was running $9 million in the red, and Chemical Bank, the lead bank in the company's $30 million loan line, was threatening to call in its chips. Had it done so, IBP would have "gone broke," according to its chief executive, Currier Holman.

With things at this pass, the Amalgamated might have demanded recognition of the union at all IBP facilities and wages for meatpacking plant workers that would not undercut those of supermarket butchers. Instead, according to Kwitney, the union's leverage was used to win payoffs for mobsters and mob-connected union officials such as Irving Stern, still a UFCW vice president. A year after the payoffs were made, IBP was shipping 60 carloads of boxed beef a week into New York.[21]

By the 1980s IBP had become a subsidiary of Occidental Petroleum and was even more powerful. Employees at the Dakota City plant had never won a union contract without a strike. Around eight thousand workers at 10 other plants remained unorganized, partly the result of the high employee turnover intentionally generated by the company. In mid-December 1986 the Dakota City workers were out again—locked out this time, shortly after they rejected a four-year freeze of their $8.00-an-hour wages and a $6.00 rate for new hires.

Two months earlier the UFCW had announced that it was beginning a nationwide drive to organize IBP and expected to hold elections at four or five plants by late spring or early summer. In-plant organizing, conducted by a small army of worker-organizers, would be accompanied by campaigns to build community support for the union. As at Morrell, the UFCW began to pressure OSHA over IBP's health and safety record, in time leading the agency to fine the company $2.59 million for its failure to report 1,038 injuries and another $3.1 million for willfully injuring workers. IBP's callousness became such an issue that Bruce Babbitt repeatedly denounced the company during his brief presidential bid.

After seven months the Dakota City workers went back, accepting a three-year wage freeze, topped by a 15-cent increase in the fourth year, and a $6.00 rate for new hires. IBP *did* agree to take all the strikers back, however, while keeping an equal number of replacements, whom it had hired after reopening the plant in March.

The organizing drive proved largely unsuccessful. By early 1988 the union had begun quietly closing organizing offices and pulling organizers from the nonunion plants. Still, the drive was not a total loss: In June the UFCW announced that IBP had agreed to voluntary recognition of the union at its 1,700-worker Joslin, Illinois, plant. The single organizing victory very likely represented a tradeoff; in exchange, the UFCW probably supported the settlement that reduced the huge OSHA fines to $975,000 in late 1988. The *Chicago Tribune* speculated that any union contract at Joslin would probably be patterned on what it called the "radically concessionary" Dakota City pact.

Meanwhile, the company has announced plans to build a new $40 million plant in Waterloo, Iowa, where it will employ 1,200 workers and slaughter 14,000 hogs a day. Workers there will make $6.00 an hour.[22]

■ ■ ■

What about strategic direction—did P-9 offer any lesson pointing the way ahead for labor? To discover the answer, we must first look at a frequently heard UFCW criticism of the strike.

"Local P-9 gave Hormel the opportunity to gut the whole agreement," Anderson told me. "The local rewrote the whole contract. Experienced negotiators know you should never do that—they had a big enough struggle just winning the $10.69." This was another reflection of P-9's pursuit of "total victory or total defeat."[23]

Anderson's remarks ignore the fact that it was Hormel, not the local, that sought to radically redesign the contract in 1985, just as it had in 1978. But Anderson's comments also reflect the common wisdom of American labor organizations and leaders. Set a few small goals; look for long-term, gradual, and incremental gains; postpone the big struggle till the times are more favorable.

There are several problems with this approach. If, as one celebrated recent study has argued, the United States has entered a new period of industrial relations history, such a method is increasingly unlikely to win even small goals. Thomas Kochan, Harry Katz, and Robert McKersie's *The Transformation of American Industrial Relations* describes a world in which power has shifted away from corporate industrial relations professionals—who, in the 1950s and 1960s, sought to maintain smooth, established relationships with unions—and toward human resource planners, who operate from an individualistic, nonunion framework. The "fundamental, structural change" involved means that times are unlikely to become more favorable to labor on their own, nor are American labor relations likely to revert to a New Deal system of stable and routine collective bargaining, even should there be favorable alterations in labor laws.[24]

More importantly, the piecemeal, go-slow approach will not work as the basis for a movement. If labor is to have any future, there is one question that must be faced: How to "put the movement back in the labor movement." Considered as something more than a slogan, the phrase raises a number of problems—articulated most profoundly in sociologist Robert Michels' classic study of mass organizations, *Political Parties*.

In his now familiar, dour phrases, Michels articulated the lowered political expectations of 20th-century humankind. There are "immanent oligarchical tendencies"—the antithesis of democratic movement sensibilities—existing "in every kind of human organization," he said, including organizations whose alleged aim is the overthrow of oligarchy. Michels believed that these tendencies resulted from the necessary extension of the growing and maturing organization's administrative apparatus. Along with this bureaucracy grows the increasing necessity for obedience to hierarchical rules. A "fighting organization" must have centralization to be effective. More and more, the "incompetent" rank and file assume a posture of passivity and gratitude for the efforts of their leaders. More and more, reference to ethical principles becomes "a necessary fiction."[25]

Does this suggest that, as a mature organizational form, U.S. labor organizations are incapable of again constituting a movement? What the Hormel strike emphasized was that, contrary to Michels, the ethical principles of labor are not yet a "fiction" to the rank and file. Jim Guyette and his followers built a nationwide following by admonishing the company to "do what is right" and live up to its promises.

"How can you call yourselves union men?" they asked the International representatives suspected of collusion with the bosses. As much as for $10.69, P-9ers fought for "dignity"; their Ottumwa supporters proudly carried a banner that read "We honor picket lines."

Equally important to that following was the supportive, democratic union community that P-9 members constructed—and the fact that they showed this to be a more effective "fighting organization" than the centralized national bureaucracy.

Both Nyberg and Anderson now agree that the company and the International underestimated P-9. "The way we responded to the strike indicates we didn't believe the duration would be what it turned out to be," Nyberg told me. Anderson claims to have understood that the Austin workers, who had a strong sense of having been treated unjustly, were prepared for a long struggle. But, he noted, others in the UFCW "did not understand that—with the best of intentions, it went down from Wynn to Foreman to Olwell to Hansen."[26]

During a July 1986 University of Minnesota labor relations meeting, where he made a joint presentation with Hormel vice president Dave Larson, Joe Hansen further illustrated the UFCW officers' patronizing underestimation of the members. Calling himself "one of the all-time great compromisers," Hansen ridiculed the local union's negotiations efforts and said that the UFCW allowed the strike in order to let the local "get it out of their system."[27]

Both the UFCW and Hormel underrated P-9 because neither could come to grips with the strength of the local's ethical position and communitarian practices, or with the attraction that those held for the country's rank-and-file labor community. "Wynn's problem was that he is an amoral man," reflected William Serrin. "He has no moral standing—almost no labor leaders do today. Guyette, though, was the man who couldn't be bought off, and they regarded him as a strange duck."[28]

The local members' refusal to be bought off or intimidated was not strange to the broader public, though. A Virginia man wrote, "I may well not know the whole story, but from everything I do know it seems pretty obvious that you are right. Do what is right." A UFCW member from Illinois sent the local a copy of a letter he wrote to Lane Kirkland. "Labor did not become strong by pandering to the prevailing attitude of the day," he said. "Labor grew and rose up because labor was right."[29]

Are labor's national structures past being able to resurrect an ethical standard to which unorganized American workers will respond? Have they simply grown too complex and oligarchical? Less developed organizations might have embraced the Austin workers' struggle, then harnessed their energy and ability to energize others in order, ultimately, to organize the nonunion packers, much as the youthful CIO did with the energy and talent of P-9's predecessor union, the Independent Union of All Workers.

Historically, American labor has only been able to reassert its moral vision and develop appropriate forms of organization after an organizational split has allowed the emergence of a new center of labor activity. No such split seems imminent, but as in the 1890s and the 1930s, a broad and unorganized labor force—unorganized manufacturing workers, clerical and service workers, and "knowledge workers"—awaits organization. Meanwhile, it is difficult to envision the emergence of institutions able to rouse the essential "movement" response within the present organizational framework. Rather than responding to Americans' desire for

greater democracy, labor's leadership sees greater centralization as a necessary defense in the crisis before it. Speaking
about P-9 before a group of union officers, Hansen preached,
"We can't let this happen again, local autonomy be damned."
And during the same executive council meeting where he
was dragged into the P-9 dispute, Lane Kirkland suggested a
solution for avoiding further such incidents: "We [the AFL-
CIO] must be part of the general staff at the inception, rather
than the ambulance drivers at the bitter end."[30]

If they are to attract the unorganized, new labor institutions must build upon the themes of P-9. They must be decentralized, highly democratic, responsive, and communitarian. To show their dissimilarity to the cutthroat corporate world, the next generation of labor institutions must offer
opportunity for individual achievement not gained at the expense of others, along with occasions for the exercise of self-
less mutual support. They will have to draw strength from
members' friends and relations in the towns where they re-
side, and from a range of diverse organizational allies. And
rather than depending upon bureaucratic coercion, they
must win allegiance by demonstrating that labor's traditional
principles are more than a "necessary fiction."

Some may object that without highly centralized structures, pattern bargaining, labor's primary means of raising
wages in the postwar world, would be impossible. But, as we
have seen, pattern bargaining is a shambles in the meatpacking industry. And that industry is certainly not alone: The
Big Three auto contracts, the rubber contracts, the National
Master Freight Agreement, and the Bituminous Coal Agreement have all been undermined in the last few years. In
1986, the Steelworkers declared it no longer possible to negotiate a master contract and proceeded to work out separate
deals with each of six major steelmakers. The *Wall Street*

Journal recently found that plant-level union negotiations might have a greater cumulative impact than any national negotiations.[31]

Common wage rates among those who do similar work are still desirable, of course, provided they can be won within a decentralized structure. A "Packinghouse Workers' Bill of Rights," drawn up by former P-9 strikers and other rank-and-filers in the spring of 1987, illustrates workers' desire to have it both ways. Among its 15 points, this Bill of Rights called for both "an international union made up of independent autonomous locals" and "an industry-wide master agreement."[32]

Recent developments within the Paperworkers' union (UPIU) suggest some possibilities. For several years, International Paper Company successfully worked to eliminate any pattern among the locals representing some 20,000 workers at its ninety-odd U.S. facilities. Following up on the divisions it had won, in the spring and early summer of 1987 the company began demanding the elimination of premium pay for weekend work—in effect a 7 to 12 percent wage cut—and unlimited rights to subcontract work. As contracts began to expire, 1,200 workers in Mobile, Alabama, were locked out for refusing to accept the cuts; then 2,300 workers at three other locations struck.

In response to the company's attempt to divide and conquer the various locals, the UPIU encouraged a rejection of the concessions in local voting and formation of a "pool," under whose rules any subsequent offer would be voted on simultaneously by all the locals. A simple majority of all the combined memberships would suffice to ratify a proposal.

Although individual locals surrendered their identity in this pool approach—it would be possible for several to vote as a whole to reject and yet have a contract be approved—to a considerable degree the pool became a network coordinated by the locals and not dominated by the International. Its horizontal, local-to-local contact, rather than vertical contact by way of International officials, kept the pool standing firm against concessions. National events and pool meetings were set up by the locals. And ongoing "outreach" efforts, again organized by Ray Rogers and Corporate Campaign Inc., kept strikers out on the road from coast to coast, building communications among workers at the many IP locations.

In October 1988, facing decertification elections at the struck plants and drained of resources, the International indicated that it had had enough and encouraged the striking locals to call off their strikes. Those locals did so, once the other locals in the pool indicated that they had lost any hope of winning the strike. But even given this discouraging outcome, the Paperworkers' pool structure suggests a possible model for greater local autonomy combined with coordinated bargaining.

■ ■ ■

A yearning for community and mutual, ethical support can be seen not only among labor's rank and file, but also in the wider culture. Such popular urges are expressed through philanthropic and religious activities—including such mass phenomena as charity "walkathons," philanthropic rock concerts, "Hands Across America," and even televangelism. Still on the periphery, "new age" gurus attract millions who seek the communal and individual solutions that seem to elude the society's traditional organizations.

American corporations, influenced by what they know of successful Japanese practices, are tuning in to the popular urge for decentralization and mutual support. Their emphasis on "teamwork," group problem-solving, and job enrich-

ment represents an attempt to harness such popular sentiment to the wagon of corporate productivity and profit.

These themes are present in contemporary politics as
well. Ronald Reagan's attack on the federal bureaucracy may
have contained an assault on the country's poor and minor-
ities and represented a boon for the upper classes. But at the
heart of Reaganism was an attack on the governmental structures that Americans find unresponsive and amoral.

Few of these outlets combine P-9's other ingredient, democracy. Indeed, there are few outlets for democracy in current American institutions. But the promise of American labor is that working people's organizations can offer the rare
combination of community, democracy, and "doing what is
right." Unless tomorrow's labor institutions can respond to
that promise, their future is highly uncertain.

NOTES

CHAPTER I

1. Between 1981 and 1985 meatpacking had the highest rate of job-related injuries and illnesses of any industry, according to "A beef about the meat men," *Time*, August 3, 1987; "Legacy of Pain," special edition of *The Unionist*, publication of Local P-9, Austin, Minnesota, May 1985, p. 2.

2. Interview with Darrell Busker, November 21, 1987.

3. "Effort to save pay scales in meatpacking brings Lewie Anderson many spats, not all with firms," *Wall Street Journal*, August 4, 1983.

4. *Minneapolis Star and Tribune*, December 21, 1984; *New York Times*, December 25, 1984; *Des Moines Sunday Register*, January 27, 1985; *Minneapolis Star and Tribune*, March 31, 1985; press release purportedly from UFCW Hormel and Wilson chain [later repudiated by several signatories], Albert Lea, Minnesota, March 22, 1985; *Labor World*, April 18, 1985; press release, UFCW, Washington, D.C., August 16, 1985; letter, UFCW president William Wynn to all presidents of National and International Unions Affiliated with the AFL-CIO, December 3, 1985;"Special Report: UFCW Local P-9 Strikes Hormel: The International Union's Perspective,"

UFCW Leadership Update, 8, no. 4 (February 1986); James V. Guyette, affidavit in support of Plaintiff's Motion for Preliminary Injunction, *Local P-9* v. *UFCW*, U.S. District Court, District of Columbia, May 2, 1986, pp. 25–26 and 42–43; strike settlement agreement, dated November –– 1986.

5. Telephone interview with Fred Carson, February 4, 1987.

6. Interview with Vicky Guyette, July 5, 1987.

7. Interview with Jeannie Bambrick, July 5, 1987.

8. Interview with Ray Rogers, July 12, 1987.

9. Mimi Conway, *Rise Gonna Rise: A Portrait of Southern Textile Workers* (Garden City, N.Y.: Anchor Press/Doubleday, 1979), pp. 2–11.

10. "How the textile union finally wins contracts at J. P. Stevens plants," *Wall Street Journal*, October 20, 1980; "Unions: labor's new muscle," *Newsweek*, April 3, 1978.

11. "Farm group boycotting Campbell puts focus on financial concerns," *New York Times*, November 27, 1984; press release, "FLOC signs three-way contracts with Campbell and growers," February 20, 1986.

12. Interview with Ray Rogers, June 1987; "Brown & Sharpe strikers resist givebacks as eight month walkout grows violent," *Wall Street Journal*, June 23, 1982; "Ray Rogers: an organizer beset by troubles," *New York Times*, September 19, 1982; "Paper avoids a replay of J. P. Stevens," *Business Week*, June 27, 1983.

13. Jeannie Bambrick and Vicky Guyette interviews.

14. "P-9 Fights Back," special edition of *The Unionist*, January 1985, p. 2; "Who's Behind Hormel's Cold Cuts," leaflet of Local P-9, undated; *St. Paul Pioneer Press and Dispatch*, December 6, 1985; *Rochester Post-Bulletin*, December 6, 1985.

15. "The Hormel Foundation and Austin: In Whose Best Interest?" special edition of *The Unionist*, June 1985.

16. "Hormel Safety Facts," March 1985, Austin, Minnesota, unpaginated.

17. "Legacy of Pain," p. 3.

18. Ibid., p. 2.

19. Interview with Carl Pontius, July 5, 1987.

20. *Minneapolis Star and Tribune*, April 25, 1985; *St. Paul Pioneer Press and Dispatch*, April 25, 1985.

21. Interview with Jim Guyette, May 1987; Rogers interview, July 12, 1987; Guyette affidavit, pp. 18–22; "UFCW plots major campaign against ConAgra/Armour," *UFCW Action*, January–February 1985. ConAgra itself saw the announced campaign as a nonevent. "We've been hearing about boycott activities for a year," a company spokesman said. Quoted in "Union announces boycott against Armour products," *Chicago Tribune*, December 22, 1984.

22. Press release, UFCW International Union, Washington, D.C., December 22, 1984.

23. Press release, UFCW International Union, January 8, 1985.

24. Letter, William Wynn to "All UFCW Local Unions and Intermediate Chartered Bodies in Regions 11 and 13 and All Local Unions in the United States Representing Packinghouse Workers," March 7, 1985.

25. "Anderson asks Guyette to schedule meet," *Austin Daily Herald*, March 15, 1985; press release, "from UFCW Hormel and Wilson Chain," March 22, 1985; "Local criticized over Hormel fight," *Minneapolis Star and Tribune*, March 23, 1987. Later, several of the local presidents whose names appeared on the press release said that they had no knowledge of its existence; 98 out of 130 of Beloit, Wis., Local 73-A members signed a petition rebuking their president, and a similar petition was circulated in the Albert Lea, Minn., Farmstead Foods plant. See "Lewie Visits Austin, Minn.," *Labor World*, April 18, 1985; "Harder To Fight The Boss When Union's On His Side," *The Guardian*, May 15, 1985.

26. "International Union officials turn down invitation to Austin," *Rochester Post-Bulletin*, January 15, 1985; "Anderson asks Guyette to schedule meet," *Austin Daily Herald*; "Split between International union, Hormel local widens," *Rochester Post-Bulletin*, February 21, 1985. Anderson was in regular contact with the Austin police regarding the scheduling of his trip to the town and security during it, according to Austin Police Chief Donald Hoffman, memos

of February 22 and April 12, 1985, obtained through a Minnesota Government Data Practices Act request and in author's possession.

27. "Hormel union's fund vote invalid," *Minneapolis Star and Tribune*, April 11, 1985.

28. "Lewie visits Austin, Minn.," *Labor World*; "International still won't back Austin P-9," *Rochester Post-Bulletin*, April 15, 1985; audio tape of the meeting in the author's possession.

29. "UFCW head criticizes P-9 leadership," *Austin Daily Herald*, May 15, 1985.

30. "Local P-9 at a crossroads," *Rochester Post-Bulletin*, June 1, 1985.

31. "Hormel union members back leaders," *Rochester Post-Bulletin*, June 3, 1985; "P-9 okays funding corporate campaign," *Austin Daily Herald*, June 14, 1985. On the second vote, officers would only say that the assessment was approved by 65 percent of the approximately 1,200 who voted, without giving exact numbers.

32. The contract expiration date was a matter of dispute and not resolved until July 12, 1985, by arbitrator George Fleischli. The "Supplemental Arbitration Award," in the several-part "Arbitration Between Geo. A. Hormel and Local P-9, UFCW" determined the date to be August 9.

33. "P-9 Proposals for Modification of Existing Agreements with Hormel at the Austin Plant," dated July 1, 1985.

34. Interview with Guyette, November 19, 1987.

35. "Initial Proposal for an Agreement Between Geo. A. Hormel and UFCW Local #P-9," undated.

36. "Second proposal for an Agreement Between Geo. A. Hormel and UFCW Local #P-9," stamped "Received July 31, 1985."

37. Jim Guyette, negotiation notes, dated August 3–8, 1985. Guyette made lengthy notes of each meeting, in each case noting the date and those in attendance, and frequently quoting statements of negotiators from both sides—including his own statements—almost as if he were recording secretary rather than a chief negotiator.

38. "Third Proposal for an Agreement Between Geo. A. Hormel & Co. and UFCW Local #P-9," undated.

39. Guyette negotiation notes, dated August 3–8.

40. Interview with Ron Rollins, November 20, 1987. As for P-9's "inexperience," UFCW Region 13 director Joe Hansen attended all negotiating sessions after August 4. Had there been a problem of local incompetence, the International might have taken note at that time. On the Krukowski law firm see "Strike force; lawyer takes tough stand against unions," *Milwaukee Journal*, June 17, 1986.

41. Memo of Hoffman to Kough and Alderman Dahlback, dated June 17, 1985; memo of Hoffman entitled "Recent meetings that we have been involved in regarding the Hormel–Local 9 problem," dated July 9, 1985. Both obtained through a Minnesota Government Data Practices Act request.

42. Interview with Carole Apold, April 1987.

CHAPTER II

1. Fred H. Blum, *Toward a Democratic Work Process: The Hormel–Packinghouse Workers' Experiment* (New York: Harper & Brothers, 1953), pp. 37, 54.

2. Ibid., pp. 15–34, 61–62; Larry Engelmann, "'We Were the Poor People'—The Hormel Strike of 1933," *Labor History* 15 (Fall 1974): 490–93, 508–10; George Fleischli, "Arbitration Award: Arbitration Between Geo. A. Hormel and Local P-9, UFCW," dated February 6, 1984, Madison, Wisconsin.

3. Stanley Aronowitz, "Cold cuts," *Village Voice*, April 22, 1986.

4. Blum, *Democratic Work Process*, p. 22.

5. All of this was quite a change from pre-union days, when workers were poorly paid, subject to prolonged seasonal layoffs or furloughs when new products failed to meet expectations, and callously abused by foremen who, according to one historian, "took particular delight in periodically attempting to destroy the self-respect and independence of the company's laborers." Foremen had broad powers to hire and fire and used them to "trade workers" (one

laying off a worker, another hiring him back into a different department at a lower wage), to win favors, and to bully workers into voting for company-approved political candidates. See Engelmann, "'We Were the Poor People,'" pp. 487–89.

6. Blum, *Democratic Work Process*, pp. 15–17, 22–24, 33–34, 208–9; quotation from interview with Jim Guyette, May 1987. In Blum's words, the Working Agreement meant that "workers administer a considerable section of the work process; the whole system of job assignments and transfers and the speed at which they are working is self-determined. Furthermore, they can express their dissatisfactions about anything connected with working conditions" (p. 24).

7. Blum, *Democratic Work Process*, pp. 57–60, 126.

8. Engelmann, "'We Were the Poor People,'" pp. 499–503.

9. Richard Dougherty, *In Quest of Quality: Hormel's First 75 Years* (Austin, Minn.: Geo. A. Hormel & Co., 1966), pp. 197–200, 224–39.

10. Ibid., pp. 258–92, 321–33, and passim. The "tar-paper shack" comment (not referred to by Dougherty) has entered local Austin folklore. It is said to have been overheard at the Austin country club, where Thompson was complaining about the fact that Austin workers had such nice homes. A small "M. B. Thompson tar-paper shack" mounted on a flat-bed truck was a regular feature of Local P-9's 1985–87 parades through Austin.

11. Blum, *Democratic Work Process*, pp. 9–13; Engelmann, "'We Were the Poor People,'" pp. 489–506, 508–10; Frank W. Schultz, "The History of Our Union from 1933–1949," *The Unionist*, May–June 1971; Rick Halpern and Roger Horowitz, "The Austin Orbit: Regional Union Organizing in Meat Packing, 1933–1943," manuscript; David Brody, *The Butcher Workmen: A Study of Unionization* (Cambridge: Harvard University Press, 1964), pp. 161–68, 225. Ellis was elected one of the UPWA's first two vice presidents, and Lewis Clark of Cedar Rapids became president. Two years later Clark was succeeded by Ralph Helstein, a Minneapolis lawyer who had represented Local 9 (Blum, *Democratic Work Process*, p. 17; Brody, *Butcher Workmen*, p. 226).

12. Interview with Charles Nyberg, April 21, 1988; interview with Lewie Anderson, April 5, 1988.

13. The infamous "fortress IBP" is still operating in Dakota City, Nebraska, where it was struck again in 1987; David Moberg, "The return of the Jungle," *In These Times*, July 24–August 6, 1985, pp. 12–14; "Meatpackers union is facing wage issue," *Wall Street Journal*, May 19, 1986; Roger Horowitz, "Meatpacker unionism gutted," *Against the Current*, new series, 1, no. 6 (1986): 6; "UFCW Local P-9 strikes Hormel: The International union's perspective," *UFCW Leadership Update*, February 1986; "Hormel: Trying to Trim the Industry's Fattest Wages to Keep Making Money in Meat," *Business Week*, September 10, 1984.

14. "History flavors potential Hormel strike," *St. Paul Pioneer Press and Dispatch*, August 5, 1985; "Transition Agreement Between Geo. A. Hormel & Company and Local P-9 AMC&BW, AFL-CIO"; interview with Jim Guyette, November 19, 1987.

15. The four previous unions were the Retail Clerks, the Amalgamated Meat Cutters & Butcher Workmen (the old AFL craft union), the United Packinghouse Workers of America (the old CIO union), and the Boot & Shoe Workers Union. The majority of UFCW leaders, including President William Wynn, are from the old Retail Clerks union.

16. Letter, UFCW president William Wynn to UFCW Locals, December 18, 1981; "Summary of the Main Features of the Hormel Settlement," UFCW document dated December 11, 1981.

17. Interview with Jim Apold, March 1987.

18. Guyette interview, May 1987.

19. Horowitz, "Meatpacker unionism gutted," p. 7; Memorandum of Agreement between UFCW and Geo. A. Hormel & Co., 1982–1985, with cover letter dated December 16, 1981; letter, Wynn to UFCW locals, December 18, 1981; James V. Guyette, affidavit in support of Plantiff's Motion for Preliminary Injunction, *Local P-9 v. UFCW*, U.S. District Court, District of Columbia, May 2, 1986, p. 6.

20. Guyette interview, May 1987.

21. Guyette affidavit, pp. 4–7; Guyette interview, November 18, 1987.

22. Guyette interview, November 18, 1987.

23. Geo. A. Hormel & Co., reprint of "Austin: A plant of superlatives," from *Meat Industry*, February 1983.

24. Blum, *Democratic Work Process*, p. 2; the *Meat Industry* article, written in 1983, says: "With productivity and efficiency foremost among the factors that went into the plant's design . . . the actual reduction [of labor] was over 40 percent, from close to 2000 employees down to about 1150" (Hormel reprint, p. 4). There were approximately 1,500 employees there by the time of the strike.

25. Members had agreed to an arrangement whereby the incentive pay of old-plant workers would be held in escrow by the company as a sort of loan to build the new plant. In exchange, the company agreed to pay the loan back in weekly installments added on to the base wage at the new plant, and to continue such payments even after the loan was repaid. However, the bulk of old-plant workers never made it to the new plant, and at the time of the strike only 800 of the plant's 1,500 workers were eligible for escrow payments. Guyette interview, November 19, 1987.

26. Pete Winkels, letter to the editor, *Rochester Post-Bulletin*, January 17, 1985.

27. For meeting, letter of protest, and the International's response, see Guyette affidavit, pp. 7–10.

28. Ibid., pp. 11–12.

29. "UFCW Local P-9 strikes Hormel: The international union's perspective," *UFCW Leadership Update*, February 1986.

30. Guyette affidavit, pp. 13–17. In point of fact, there were several arbitration decisions, all to clear up points obscured by the existence of so many contracts. On February 6, 1984, arbitrator George Fleischli ruled that Hormel had the right to cut wages at some point in the future if a decreasing industry pattern was established. This evil omen came prior to the July meeting at which Anderson urged P-9's leaders to guarantee support for a chain-wide strike—Guyette and other P-9ers still hoped that the 1982 reopener's "no reduction in rates" language would prevent such a reduction. In October 1984 the company cut wages to $8.25, and in

December of that year, Fleischli ruled that although the company had jumped the gun, its wage cuts could stand. Since the "no reduction in rates" language did not exist (as Guyette says he learned the night before the union's brief for the second Fleischli arbitration was filed), no argument about that language was made. A third arbitration ruling came on March 16, 1985. On that date Fleischli determined that the national pattern could be derived from wages and benefits existing at Swift & Co., Oscar Mayer, and John Morrell & Co. and thus set at $8.75, rather than the $8.25 level imposed by Hormel in October. However, his ruling on a variety of fringes and benefits meant, in effect, that Hormel had "overpaid" on those accounts. The result was an attempt by the company to reclaim on an individual basis money paid out for medical benefits in the past—a move that further inflamed P-9 passions.

31. Guyette affidavit, pp. 23–24.

32. Winkels, letter to editor; Guyette quoted in "Rogers steers Hormel campaign into final two months," *Labor World*, February 21, 1985.

CHAPTER III

1. UFCW Region Council 13 Executive Board, "Region Council 13 Resolution," August 27, 1985. This document, handed out as a press release, supported the local so long as its goals were restricted to a $10.00 per hour minimum base rate with no two-tier, a weekly guarantee of 36 hours, Monday through Friday, common expiration dates, and "fair and equitable language throughout the contract." With these limitations, the region officially sanctioned the strike and approved strike benefits "for a period of four weeks."

2. Paul Klauda, "Hormel CEO 'cares and hurts' but not giving in," *Minneapolis Star and Tribune*, May 26, 1985.

3. "Local P-9 at a crossroads," *Rochester Post-Bulletin*, June 1, 1985. The original understanding between CCI and Local P-9 covered a six-month pre-strike campaign of organizational services, re-

search, literature creation, and public relations in exchange for a fee of $160,000, with a performance bonus to be calculated on the basis of the agreed-to hourly wage at Hormel. In December 1984 Rogers told the P-9 members that they should raise a "war chest" of $340,000 (or about $200 per member) to cover those fees plus the other expenses of a six-month campaign. But Rogers has a habit of forgoing fees when the client has difficulty paying them. In this case, a couple of extra months' services were thrown in for free, taking the campaign up through August, when the strike began. In the end, CCI took in only around $111,000 for two years' work.

4. "'Proud, loud' Hormel union taking its crusade on the road," *Milwaukee Journal*, September 18, 1985.

5. See, for example, "Strike clock ticking at Hormel Co.," *St. Paul Pioneer Press and Dispatch*, August 4, 1985.

6. Interview with Lynn Huston, July 5, 1987.

7. As recalled by P-9er Glen Beckman, August 1985.

8. Interview with Merrell Evans, July 5, 1987.

9. Huston interview.

10. Interview with Ray Rogers, July 12, 1987. Police in all locations knew of P-9's coming, from the press, from P-9 itself, and from Austin's Chief Hoffman, whose files suggest that he telephoned them.

11. Remarks of Jim Guyette, Fremont, Nebraska, August 29, 1985, as recorded at the time by the author.

12. All quotations from the author's transcript of the Fremont meeting, August 29, 1985.

13. The characterization of these two work forces is based on interviews with Fremont worker Bob Langemeier, Ottumwan Larry McClurg, Lynn Huston, and Jim Guyette, July 4–5, 1987. The Fremont worker's remark is from my transcript of the Fremont meeting, August 29, 1985.

14. Langemeier interview, July 4, 1987.

15. Rogers interview, July 12, 1987.

16. Interview with Jim Guyette, July 6, 1987. Eighty P-9 members went back to Algona, Iowa, on September 5 for a more com-

plete canvassing of that community, bannering and leafleting at the Hormel and Snap-On-Tool plants and at a farm implement foreclosure sale in Britt, Iowa. As in the previous caravan, P-9ers met with day- and night-gang Hormel workers at a local park and got a grilling about past "chain" history. Then, during a roadside meeting, P-9 board member Jim Retterath received assurances of local support from Local P-31 business agent Paul Fortune. See *The Unionist*, September 13, 1985.

17. "Executive of the company is following the caravan," *Minneapolis Star and Tribune*, September 1, 1985; in contrast, Nyberg told the *Ottumwa Courier* that he was there to discuss plant operational matters and not because of the Austin strikers. *Ottumwa Courier*, August 28, 1985.

18. "Hormel official faults State Patrol for allowing picketing in Fremont," *Omaha World-Herald*, August 30, 1985.

19. "On the road with the Hormel strikers," *Minneapolis Star and Tribune*, September 1, 1985.

20. Interview with Cecil Cain, July 6, 1987.

21. "Hormel strikers receive food donations," *Rochester Post-Bulletin*, September 2, 1985.

22. "Hormel posts 83% earnings gain and predicts strong 4th quarter," *Minneapolis Star and Tribune*, August 21, 1985.

23. "Hormel puts final contract offer into effect," *Rochester Post-Bulletin*, August 29, 1985.

24. "Hormel files complaints accusing Local P-9 of secondary boycotts," *St. Paul Pioneer Press and Dispatch*, September 1, 1985.

25. Remarks in Fremont, Nebraska, August 29, 1985.

26. "Hormel opponents bring campaign north," *Duluth News-Tribune & Herald*, September 4, 1985; "Strikers 'on the road,'" *St. Paul Pioneer Press and Dispatch*, September 5, 1985.

27. "Picketing of banks hits snag," *St. Paul Pioneer Press and Dispatch*, September 10, 1985.

28. "String of rulings against P-9 goes on," *Rochester Post-Bulletin*, September 11, 1985. Winkels' words were prophetic: In 1988 the U.S. Supreme Court vindicated his position in *Edward J. DeBar-*

tolo Corp. v. *Florida Gulf Coast Building and Construction Trades Council and N.L.R.B.*, 56 USLW 4328 (April 20).

29. "Hormel workers ignore NLRB order, picket Des Moines bank," *Austin Daily Herald*, September 11, 1985.

30. "Strikers, U fans share a goal—win!" *St. Paul Pioneer Press and Dispatch*, September 13, 1985.

31. "Union to Austin strikers: Stay away," *Sioux Falls Argus Leader*, September 18, 1985.

32. Edward J. Devitt, U.S. District Court, District of Minnesota, Third Division, Memorandum of Decision, case of *Ronald M. Sharp, Regional Director of the 18th Region of the NLRB* v. *Local P-9;* "Judge orders P-9 to halt bank picketing," *Rochester Post-Bulletin*, September 23, 1985.

33. "Union hails NLRB pact as victory," *St. Paul Pioneer Press and Dispatch*, September 25, 1985; "Pact with NLRB drops charges against P-9," *Rochester Post-Bulletin*, September 25, 1985; "Hormel, P-9 settle complaint but bicker," *Minneapolis Star and Tribune*, September 25, 1985. Each of these stories portrayed the NLRB and Hormel as outflanked and somewhat in disarray, while the union and CCI were shown as happy with the outcome.

34. "Union's right to boycott upheld," *In These Times*, October 9, 1985.

35. Letter, Winkels to Minnesota AFL-CIO delegates, dated September 22, 1985.

36. Press release, "Minnesota AFL-CIO supports fair trade, South Africa divestiture, striking unions, boycotts of Union Brass and Shopko Company," Minnesota State AFL-CIO, September 27, 1985; "Hormel workers get morale boost at AFL-CIO meeting," *Rochester Post-Bulletin*, September 24, 1985.

CHAPTER IV

1. Interview with Vicky Guyette, July 5, 1987.

2. "Economic Hardships Riddle Austin," *Rochester Post-Bulletin*, October 10, 1985.

3. Interview with Jeannie Bambrick, July 5, 1987.

4. Vicky Guyette interview.

5. Ibid.

6. Jeannie Bambrick interview.

7. Rick Halpern and Roger Horowitz, "The Austin Orbit: Regional Union Organizing in Meat Packing, 1933–1943," manuscript.

8. Interview with Jake Cooper, January 10, 1988.

9. *The Unionist*, October 4, 1985.

10. Peter Rachleff, "The Hormel Strike: Turning Point for the Rank-and-File Labor Movement," *Socialist Review*, no. 89 (September–October 1986): 77; undated letter entitled "UFCW Region 13 Food Caravan" and signed by Joseph T. Hansen, UFCW Region 13 director, distributed on October 19, 1985.

11. Interview with Cecil Cain, July 6, 1987. An article appearing in *The Unionist* on October 4, 1985, reports that 49 members of communications teams had visited 38 groups in the previous weeks. Among the groups listed were the St. Paul Federation of Teachers, the American Life Insurance Company, two locals of the Brotherhood of Railway and Airline Clerks, six State, County and Municipal Employees locals, and the Jobs For Peace Coalition. The communications committee's log featured hundreds of entries showing groups visited, accompanied by comments on how well the visitors were received and the amount donated, if any.

12. Interview with Ray Rogers, July 12, 1987.

13. Interview with Cindy Rudd, July 6, 1987.

14. "Perpich pushes for Hormel talks," *St. Paul Pioneer Press and Dispatch*, October 3, 1985; "Federal mediator asks Hormel, P-9 to talk," *Austin Daily Herald*, October 4, 1985; "Hormel, union, mediator to resume talks Monday," *Rochester Post-Bulletin*, October 8, 1985.

15. "Hormel talks held in Rochester show no significant progress," *Rochester Post-Bulletin*, October 15, 1985. According to Winkels and Guyette, P-9's "floating wage" proposal would have guaranteed the company profits of $7.5 million per quarter, or $30 million a year. If Hormel made more, the excess would be distributed to the workers in the form of a raise; if less, the workers

would take a pay cut. Guyette noted that the idea was first floated to the company in 1984, having been thought up by union member Ward Halverstam, who later joined the local's anti-Guyette dissidents and crossed the picket line. Interviews conducted on November 20–22, 1987.

16. "NLRB rules Hormel workers' Wis. demonstration illegal," *Rochester Post-Bulletin,* October 17, 1985; "Secondary boycott ruling issued against meatpackers," *St. Paul Pioneer Press and Dispatch,* October 18, 1985.

17. Undated and untitled memo from Eugene Cotton of Cotton, Watt, Jones & King, distributed August 1985, Ottumwa, Iowa.

18. *The Unionist,* October 11 and 25, 1985.

19. *The Unionist,* October 25, 1985.

20. Interview with Ottumwa supporter Bill Cook, January 11, 1988; interview with Bob Langemeier, January 6, 1988.

21. Interview with Carl Pontius, July 5, 1987.

22. Interview with Jim Guyette, July 5, 1987.

23. Interview with Pete Winkels, July 5, 1987.

24. Guyette interview, July 5, 1987. According to Cook (interview, January 10, 1988), Ottumwa steward Dan Varner showed the petitions of support to Wynn at this meeting.

25. Joint statement of William H. Wynn, president of United Food & Commercial Workers International Union, and James Guyette, president of United Food and Commercial Workers Local P-9, dated November 5, 1985.

26. *Rochester Post-Bulletin,* November 6, 1985; *St. Paul Pioneer Press and Dispatch,* November 6, 1985.

27. Interview with Dan Allen, November 21, 1987; Guyette interview, July 5, 1987; "Hormel strikers plan escalation, will extend picket lines," *Labor Notes,* November 1985.

28. *The Unionist,* November 22, 1985.

29. All according to Guyette's notes of negotiation meeting, dated November 13, 1985.

30. Interview with Lewie Anderson, April 5, 1988.

31. Guyette negotiation notes, dated November 15 and 23, 1985. In "baseball-style arbitration," the arbitrator chooses either the

union's or management's position—not some point in between. Thus the two sides are encouraged to stake out reasonable positions from the outset.

32. Interview with Charles Nyberg, April 21, 1988.

33. Guyette negotiation notes, dated November 23, 1985.

34. The Wisconsin caravan also visited 165 Milwaukee union offices and leafleted workers at Smith Steel Works in Milwaukee, the Oscar Mayer plant and corporate headquarters in Madison, and the Trone company and Heileman brewery in LaCrosse. United Auto Workers Local 248 provided them with office space and a floor to sleep on. See *The Unionist*, October 25, 1985.

35. "Hormel Co. files new complaint with NLRB," *Rochester Post-Bulletin*, October 11, 1985; "NLRB rules," *Rochester Post-Bulletin*. The parties also disagreed over the meaning of the settlement, P-9 saying it dropped all charges, the NLRB and Hormel saying it prohibited any further First Bank actions. Since the national office of the NLRB never approved the settlement, Minnesota NLRB spokesmen maintained that Judge Devitt's September injunction ordering an end to all bannering remained in force. They also said that the earlier settlement would now *not* be approved.

36. Local P-9, United Food and Commercial Workers Union, Respondent, and Geo. A. Hormel & Co., Charging Party, before the National Labor Relations Board, transcript, vol. 2, dated December 4, 1985, pp. 193–94. The "publicity proviso" became part of the National Labor Relations Act as amended in 1959. Attempts to close up "loopholes" in the statutes regarding secondary boycotts led to language making it unlawful to "threaten, coerce, or restrain any person" doing business with a secondary party. But Congress allowed unions to continue publicity activities, "truthfully advising the public . . . that a product or products are produced by an employer with whom the labor organization has a primary dispute and are distributed by another employer." Charles J. Morris et al., *The Developing Labor Law* (Washington, D.C.: Bureau of National Affairs, 1983), 1: 57–58; 2: 1110.

37. Decision of Administrative Law Judge Thomas D. Johnston, Local P-9 and Geo. A. Hormel & Co., United States of America, be-

fore the National Labor Relations Board, dated February 26, 1986; affidavit of Michael Grostyan, dated August 26, 1985; affidavit of James W. Cavanaugh, dated September 4, 1985; affidavit of William L. Connelly, dated September 10, 1985.

38. NLRB transcript, vol. 2: 199–209, 213–14, 243, 249–51, 258–62, 298–312, and passim. Guyette also testified to these facts later in the hearing.

39. NLRB transcript, vol. 3 (December 5, 1985): 335–75, 385–433; vol. 2: 221–34; "P-9 unfair labor practices hearing resumes," *Rochester Post-Bulletin*, December 4, 1985; "Union subpoenas Hormel chairman to testify," *Minneapolis Star and Tribune*, December 5, 1985; "Hormel's top executive testifies at hearing," *Rochester Post-Bulletin*, December 5, 1985; "'Corporate Campaign' researcher: 1st Bank primary Hormel booster," *Rochester Post-Bulletin*, December 6, 1985; "Hormel chief testifies on First Bank ties," *St. Paul Pioneer Press and Dispatch*, December 6, 1985. From December 1984 to December 1985, the bank's holding of Hormel stock declined from 16.4 percent to 12.3 percent.

40. "Meatpackers lose judge's ruling," *Minneapolis Star and Tribune*, March 1, 1986.

41. Ken Gagala, "A Wobbly-bred campaign in Minnesota," *Labor Research Review* 7 (Fall 1985): 86–88.

42. Nyberg interview.

43. NLRB transcript, vol. 3: 417.

44. Letter, First Bank Duluth senior vice president Lyle Bourdon to Wiley Welborn, president of Bricklayers Local #3; "Corporate campaign boosts morale, but other gains slim," *Minneapolis Star and Tribune*, August 4, 1985; "Corporate campaign gets MFT support," *Austin Daily Herald*, April 21, 1985.

45. Rogers told me: "During the Stevens campaign, I couldn't move as quickly as I would have liked to. I wasn't allowed to do things as openly as we did at Hormel, such as going right after the bank. For whatever reason, at first I wasn't allowed to go after the insurance company. So I had to start picking corporations off, like Avon, Sperry, and Seaman's Bank. If it hadn't been for the union

lawyers, I'd have probably taken another route." Rogers interview, July 12, 1987. The case involving secondary boycotts is *Edward J. DeBartolo Corp.* v. *Florida Gulf Coast Building and Construction Trades Council and NLRB,* 56 *USLW* 4328, April 20, 1988.

46. Nyberg interview.

47. Ray Rogers, "How to Confront Corporations," *Business and Society Review,* Summer 1981, p. 60.

48. AFL-CIO Committee on the Evolution of Work, *The Changing Situation of Workers and Their Unions* (Washington, D.C.: AFL-CIO, 1985), p. 21.

49. Rogers interview, July 12, 1987.

CHAPTER V

1. *The Unionist,* December 20, 1985.

2. Rules and Final Agenda, National Rank-And-File Against Concessions, December 6–8, 1985; "'National Rank-and-File Against Concessions' founded at Chicago conference," *Labor Notes,* January 1986; "It's now or never in the fight against concessions," *The Guardian,* December 25, 1985; Dave Foster, "What is NRFAC," *The Unifier* (official publication of NRFAC), December 7, 1985; "P-9 members 'on top' at anti-concessions conference," *The Unionist,* December 20, 1985; Peter Rachleff, "The Hormel Strike: Turning point for the rank-and-file labor movement," *Socialist Review,* no. 89 (September–October 1986): 76.

3. Interview with Jim Guyette, July 5, 1987.

4. Interview with Peter Rachleff, January 6, 1988.

5. Interview with Jake Cooper, January 9, 1988.

6. Rachleff interview.

7. Guyette negotiation notes, dated December 12, 1985.

8. Guyette negotiation notes, dated December 13 and 14, 1985.

9. A summary of the highlights and the entire contract offer as amended by the mediators was reprinted in *The Unionist,* December 27, 1985.

10. Interview with Ron Rollins, November 20, 1987.

11. Interview with Pete Winkels, January 19, 1988.

12. Ibid.

13. Guyette interview, November 19, 1987.

14. Letter, UFCW president William H. Wynn to all Presidents of National and International Unions Affiliated with the AFL-CIO, December 3, 1985.

15. Letter, Joseph T. Hansen, UFCW Region 13 director, to members of UFCW Local P-9, December 20, 1985.

16. Ibid., p. 5.

17. "200 P-9 members block Hormel road," *Rochester Post-Bulletin*, December 19, 1985; "Protesting strikers block Hormel gate," *Minneapolis Star and Tribune*, December 20, 1985; "Hormel pickets block plant gate," *St. Paul Pioneer Press and Dispatch*, December 20, 1985.

18. "International union, meatpackers clash," *St. Paul Pioneer Press and Dispatch*, December 21, 1985.

19. "Workers urged to reject bid by Hormel," *Minneapolis Star and Tribune*, December 22, 1985; "P-9 exec board urges rejection of mediator's proposal," *Austin Daily Herald*, December 22, 1985.

20. Winkels interview, January 19, 1988.

21. "Workers urged," *Minneapolis Star and Tribune*.

22. "Hormel rejects meeting with Latimer, union," *St. Paul Pioneer Press and Dispatch*, December 31, 1985.

23. Telegram, William Wynn to executive board of UFCW Local No. 9, dated December 30, 1985.

24. Letter addressed "To Whom It May Concern," and signed Rev. James Baker, Rev. Joe Matt, Father Charles Collins, Rev. Harold Luecke, dated January 2, 1986.

25. "P-9 members reject offer by 2–1 margin," *Austin Daily Herald*, December 29, 1985; "Hormel officials meet to discuss plant reopening," *Austin Daily Herald*, January 5, 1986.

26. "Hormel officials meet," *Austin Daily Herald*.

27. "Christmas solidarity brought to striking P-9ers," *The Unionist*, December 27, 1985.

28. "Arnold: we've gone as far as we're going to," *Austin Daily Herald*, December 29, 1985.

29. "Latimer meets with strike group," *St. Paul Pioneer Press and Dispatch*, January 1, 1986.

30. Ibid.; "Sovereign offers solution to Hormel strike," *Austin Daily Herald*, January 5, 1986.

31. "Austin mayor hopes 'miracle' can avert clash," *St. Paul Pioneer Press and Dispatch*, January 10, 1986.

32. "Almanac," KTCA-TV, St. Paul, January 10, 1986.

33. "Hormel, union to reopen talks," *St. Paul Pioneer Press and Dispatch*, January 11, 1986; Guyette negotiation notes, dated January 11, 1986. In addition to Nyberg, other new faces at the meeting included the local's recently elected financial secretary, Kathy Buck, and David Twedell, an attorney from Texas. Twedell's father had been a UFCW vice president and he himself had once been a UFCW staffer. But in recent years he had declared himself at war with the International and was attempting to get locals to recertify with his paper union, known as Service Assistance for Better Employee Relationships (SABER).

34. News report, WCCO-TV, Minneapolis, January 12, 1986; *Minneapolis Star and Tribune*, January 9, 1986.

35. The year after the formation of the foundation, 1942, Jay Hormel, son of the company founder, noted: "If the Hormel Foundation stands up for the purpose of which it is intended, it will . . . vote that stock in the same interests which Father or I would have in mind; namely, the protection of the integrity of this business in behalf of the community which is dependent on it." On several occasions thereafter, foundation spokesmen traveled to Washington seeking exemption from various tax-law changes on the grounds that the foundation's controlling interest in the company was intended to ensure "the welfare of the community in which it was located." They continued to make such arguments even as the company was threatening to move its operations out of Austin. In 1980 the foundation restructured itself as a public foundation with a board of directors, a majority of whom represent eight local charities. By-law changes

eliminated any mention of the town of Austin. Directors drawn from the charities have consistently refrained from "injection of our personal philosophies on the Corporate operations," in the words of Austin United Way president William Sheehy. See "The Hormel Foundation and Austin: In Whose Best Interest?" special edition of *The Unionist,* June 1985.

36. "Lord moves into union's corner in Hormel fight," *Minneapolis Star and Tribune,* December 23, 1985.

37. "Hormel strikers rally as plant nears opening," *New York Times,* January 13, 1986; news report, KAAL-TV, Austin, January 12, 1986.

38. Interview with William Serrin, January 22, 1988; Hoffman estimate from "Police Response to Labor Disputes/Demonstrations," manuscript in files released through Minnesota Government Data Practices Act request.

39. "Few of 1,500 strikers answer Hormel's call to return to work," *New York Times,* January 14, 1986; news reports, WCCO-TV, Minneapolis, and KAAL-TV, Austin, January 14, 1986.

40. News reports, WCCO-TV, KSTP-TV, Minneapolis and KAAL-TV, Austin, January 14, 1986.

41. News report, KAAL-TV, Austin, January 14, 1986.

42. Interview with Darrell Busker, November 21, 1987.

43. Interviews with various union and support group members, April 20, 1988. In May 1986 the local was found to have violated the NLRA with "numerous acts of blocking ingress and egress and picket line violence." In his ruling, however, Administrative Law Judge Benjamin Schlesinger cited only two physical assaults: one involving a Hormel photographer, who got out of his car and may have provoked strikers, and another in which a crossover was slapped. Otherwise, the violence mainly involved damage to automobiles—smashed fenders and grills, punctured tires, busted headlights and taillights, bent antennae—verbal threats, and, remarkably enough, photographing strikebreakers as they crossed the line. See ALJ Benjamin Schlesinger, Findings of Fact and Conclusions of Law, National Labor Relations Board, Local P-9, UFCW and Geo. A. Hormel & Co., May 22, 1986, p. 9 and passim.

44. News report, KAAL-TV, Austin, January 14, 1986.

45. Ibid.; news report, KSTP-TV, Minneapolis, January 14, 1986.

46. Telegram, William Wynn to executive board of UFCW Local No. 9, dated December 30, 1985.

47. News reports, WCCO-TV, KARE-TV, KSTP-TV, Minneapolis, and KAAL-TV, Austin, January 16, 1986. KSTP emphasized that P-9 members had not seen the Wynn message until its reporters showed it to them. The news broadcast showed P-9ers reading the message for the first time while picketing.

48. News reports, KAAL-TV, Austin, January 16–17, 1986; "Hormel strikers discuss tactics," *Minneapolis Star and Tribune*, January 19, 1986.

49. News reports, WCCO-TV, KSTP-TV, Minneapolis, January 19; Rachleff, "Hormel Strike," pp. 78–79.

50. News report, KARE-TV, Minneapolis, January 20, 1986.

51. News reports, KARE-TV, Minneapolis, January 20; report of Commissioner of Public Safety Paul J. Tschida on the Hormel strike, dated January 24, 1986; letter, Donald Hoffman, Wayne Goodnature, and Tom Kough to Governor Rudy Perpich, dated January 20, 1986; telegram, Austin PD to BCA, signed by Austin Chief of Police Donald Hoffman, dated January 20, 1986; Executive Order no. 86-1, signed by Governor Perpich, dated January 23, 1986. All of these documents were obtained from Tschida's office in response to a Minnesota Government Data Practices Act request. Regarding Kough's vacillation, Perpich told Duluth *Labor World* editor Dick Blin in February: "On the one hand, he's running up here [St. Paul] telling legislators the Guard should be totally withdrawn. But down in Austin, he seems to be right there with the sheriff." Cf. *The Unionist*, February 14, 1986.

52. Interview with Lynn Huston, July 5, 1987.

53. Interview with Ray Rogers, February 17, 1988. Local members and retirees later erected a monument in memory of ABC newsmen Joe Spencer and Mark McDonough. And, astonishingly, McDonough's mother sent a highly emotional letter to Nyberg, with a copy to Guyette, denouncing Hormel and blaming the company for her son's death. "You are robbing not only your workers and the entire community around you, you have robbed my son of the plea-

sure of knowing the joy of being a father . . ." she wrote. "You are a union busting firm with no regard for the people you have put out of work. What are these people who have worked for you these many, many years supposed to do? . . . I intend to boycott your products." Letter of Delores T. McDonough to Charles Nyberg, dated February 1, 1986.

54. News reports, ABC-TV, KAAL-TV, Austin, and WCCO-TV, Minneapolis, January 21, 1986; "Hormel plant shut as troops arrive and strikers thin ranks," New York Times, January 22, 1986.

55. "Guard, police surprise strikers, switch gates"; "Worry, fear underlie an upbeat union spirit"; "Hormel plant reopens; new talks planned," all in St. Paul Pioneer Press and Dispatch, January 23, 1986; "Hormel and union are locked in battle that carries high stakes for both sides," Wall Street Journal, January 23, 1986; "Hormel reopens plant as guardsmen bar strikers," New York Times, January 23, 1986; "Hormel reopens under Guard," Newsday, January 23, 1986; news reports, KAAL-TV, Austin, January 22, 1986. The State Patrol played a limited but key role in reopening the plant. The questionable legality of its actions was underscored by a February 7 memo from Patrol Commander Richard Wilberg, who noted: "I am convinced without our presence, the strikers would have shut down traffic on the interstate. The troopers involved in the detail have done a fine job." Police Chief Hoffman later reported that the State Patrol "provided men and cars to patrol the city" and thus allowed city police to concentrate on the labor dispute.

Regarding Kough and the police, on January 29, seven "supervisory" officers of the force wrote to the Austin city administrator protesting against Kough's "self-serving," politically motivated interference with police activities, such as his demand that police begin ticketing untagged vehicles entering the Hormel plant. On the 30th, Goodnature wrote to County Attorney Kraft seeking a restraining order to block Kough's involvement in strike-related law enforcement matters, given his "direct conflict of interest." Letter, Captain Gordon L. Bjorgo et al. to City Administrator Darrel Stacy, dated January 29, 1986; letter, Goodnature to Kraft, dated January 30, 1986.

56. News reports, WCCO-TV, Minneapolis, January 21 and 24; "Hormel plant shut," "Hormel reopens plant," both in *New York Times*; "Roving pickets fail to close Hormel plants," *St. Paul Pioneer Press and Dispatch*, January 23, 1986.

57. "Hormel and union are locked in battle," *Wall Street Journal*; Knowlton later said he was misquoted, but reporter Marj Charlier stood by her quotation.

58. "Hormel plant reopens," *St. Paul Pioneer Press and Dispatch*.

CHAPTER VI

1. Letter of Richard H. Long to Local P-9, dated February 11, 1986. Though Long said that he had not made more than $10,000 in any year since he had been fired for striking four and a half years earlier, he enclosed a $100 donation to P-9.

2. Interview with William Serrin, January 22, 1988.

3. "Minn. farmers extend solidarity to meatpackers' strike," *The Militant*, January 31, 1986; "Support grows for Local P-9 fight," and "Minn. farmers' tractorcade backs Hormel strikers," ibid., February 7, 1986. In contrast to the Groundswell leaders, *AgriNews*, a publication of the *Rochester Post-Bulletin*, editorialized that poor farmers might consider getting a job at Hormel, since "one man's dispute is another man's opportunity." Quoted in "National Guard herds scabs at Hormel," *The Militant*, February 14, 1986.

4. ABC News "Nightline," January 24, 1986. Also present on the program was Secretary of Labor William Brock, who was able to sidestep a thorny question about concessions by saying, "I'm going to be pretty cautious about getting between a national union and a local on a situation like that."

5. "Fact Book on Local P-9/Hormel Austin, Mn.," prepared by Lewie G. Anderson, Director UFCW Packinghouse Division, dated January 21, 1986; in fact, Corporate Campaign deferred any attempt to collect fees once the strike began, but the cost of its services continued to be a hot topic.

6. The Guard was also used against the famous 1934 Minneapolis truckers' strike and in a 1959 strike at the Wilson & Co. meatpacking plant in Albert Lea. In the latter case, DFL governor Orville Freeman declared martial law and also ordered the plant closed. Later, Freeman's move was overturned by a federal court, and 17 days after he had closed the plant, the Guard was used to escort strikebreakers in. Freeman's declaration of martial law and closure of the plant were often declared to be the cause of his subsequent political defeat. "Hormel plant shut as troops arrive and strikers thin ranks," New York Times, January 22, 1986; "Austin city limits, strikers on Guard," In These Times, January 29–February 4, 1986; news report, KMSP-TV, Minneapolis, January 23, 1986; "Worry, fear underlie an upbeat union spirit," St. Paul Pioneer Press and Dispatch, January 23, 1986; "1959: Minn. Nat'l Guard used against meatpackers' strike," The Militant, January 31, 1986.

7. News reports, KAAL-TV, January 23–25, 1986.

8. Guyette negotiation notes, dated January 23, 1986.

9. Interview with Pete Winkels, November 21, 1987; interview with Lynn Huston, July 5, 1987.

10. Interview with Jim Getchell, July 6, 1987.

11. Interviews with Carl Pontius, Jim Guyette, and Pete Winkels, July 5–6, 1987.

12. Interviews with Ray Rogers, June 1987, January 1988.

13. Huston interview; interview with Jim Guyette, June 22, 1988; news reports, WCCO-TV, KMSP-TV, Minneapolis, and KAAL-TV, Austin; "Hormel strikers resume efforts to close plants," Minneapolis Star and Tribune, January 26, 1986.

14. News reports, CBS "Evening News," and KAAL-TV, Austin, January 27, 1986.

15. Huston interview, July 5, 1987.

16. Interview with Larry McClurg, July 5, 1987.

17. Immediately after the strike began, Nyberg announced that Fremont workers might be "permanently replaced" for such action, while Niederdeppe said that he had instructed workers to cross a P-9 picket line because "there's a contract in effect." (Niederdeppe neglected to say that the contract did not contain a no-strike clause.)

On January 15, the warnings were repeated. Niederdeppe told re-porters that until roving pickets were "sanctioned," local workers would be told to report to work "to honor that contract." *Fremont Tribune*, August 15, 1985; ibid., January 15, 1986.

18. Interviews with Bob Langemeier, July 5, 1987, and January 6, 1988.

19. Winkels interview, November 21, 1987.

20. News reports, KSTP-TV, January 28 and 29, 1986; "Troops at Hormel to be withdrawn," *New York Times*, January 29, 1986.

21. "Solidarity march draws big crowd," "Church haven for strikers," "Local 431 forms food committee," *Ottumwa Courier*, January 30, 1986; "2,000 demonstrate against Hormel firings in Iowa," *The Militant*, February 14, 1986; "Hormel may rehire some workers," *St. Paul Pioneer Press and Dispatch*, January 29, 1986. Again Hormel announced that it had set a record with yearly prof-its: $38.6 million in fiscal 1985, on revenue of $1.5 billion, com-pared with $29.5 million on revenue of $1.45 billion in the pre-vious year, according to the *New York Times*, January 29, 1986.

22. Quoted in "Union top betrays embattled local," *The Mili-tant*, February 7, 1986.

23. According to "UFCW sends staff to aid in Hormel chain grievances," *AFL-CIO News*, February 1, 1986.

24. *Trusteeship Hearing of the United Food and Commercial Workers Local P-9 Union*, conducted by Hearing Officer Ray B. Wooster, in six volumes, April 14–16, 1986. The trusteeship hear-ings are discussed at greater length in Chapter IX. Information about the "special organizing team" is limited. It was obtained dur-ing the trusteeship hearings by P-9 officers in spite of Hearing Of-ficer Wooster's attempt to limit the scope of the inquiry to the issue of whether or not P-9 had called off its strike and boycott as ordered by the UFCW.

25. "Returning P-9 workers report better treatment," *Austin Daily Herald*, January 24, 1986.

26. "Fact-finder ends talks, to make report," *Minneapolis Star and Tribune*, January 25, 1986. Suspicions about Zack's motives were also voiced by William Serrin, who asked me: "Was Al Zack

trying to make sure that the fact-finding didn't work?"

27. News report, KSTP-TV, Minneapolis, February 1, 1986.

28. News report, WCCO-TV, January 30, 1986; "Last troops are withdrawn from Hormel plant," *New York Times*, January 30, 1986; letter, Tom Kough to Perpich, dated January 28, 1986; and letter, Hoffman, Goodnature, and Kough to Perpich, dated January 30, 1986, both from Department of Public Safety records. The television report also noted that most of the governor's mail opposed his sending the Guard, and that some DFL legislators had proposed a "symbolic show of support for the strikers when the legislature reconvenes next week."

29. "Hormel strikers close plant again," *New York Times*, February 1, 1986; news report, WCCO-TV, January 31, 1986.

30. News report, KAAL-TV, Austin, January 31, 1986; "P-9 votes not to consider proposal," *Minneapolis Star and Tribune*, February 2, 1986; undated chronology of Hormel strike by Paul Tschida, from Department of Public Safety files.

31. "Last troops are withdrawn," *New York Times*.

32. Employee lists released to the North American Meat Packers Union by the Hormel company, undated.

33. Interview with Margaret Winter, June 6, 1988.

34. "Austin city limits, strikers on Guard," *In These Times*, January 29–February 4, 1986.

35. News report, WCCO-TV, Minneapolis, February 7, 1986.

36. Memo of Denise Bahl to Hoffman, dated February 1, 1986; message to Supt. J. Erskine, dated February 2, 1986; memo of Austin Police Officer "Sorlie" to all officers, dated February 2, 1986; memo of M. Haider to Hoffman, dated February 1, 1986; memo of K. Hines to "all concerned," dated February 17, 1986. All memos were obtained through Minnesota Department of Public Safety. In the "telephone tap" transcript, dated April 25, 1986, Rogers gives directions to the P-9 hall and advises the Minneapolis supporters on how much money to bring for bail. Transcript obtained through a Minnesota Government Data Practices Act request.

37. National Guard log, entitled "INTSUM," was obtained through a Minnesota Government Data Practices Act request from

files of the Minnesota Army National Guard, Office of the Adjutant General. References are to entries dated January 21 through February 18. "CPP Incident Reports" also in the Guard's files.

38. "Austin city limits, strikers on Guard," *In These Times,* January 29–February 4, 1986.

39. "P-9 votes," *Minneapolis Star and Tribune;* "National Guard returns to Hormel plant in Minnesota," *New York Times,* February 4, 1986; "Judge stays jail terms in meat packers' strike," *New York Times,* February 5, 1986; news reports, KAAL-TV, Austin, and KSTP-TV, Minneapolis, February 3, 1986. Goodnature reported that he had received a telephone warning from an anonymous crossover that "he and his friends numbering approximately 100 were going to mass up at a predetermined location and proceed to work. . . . there would be a lot of baseball bats and a lot of guns, and if confronted they were going to take care of the matter." Memo, Goodnature to Col. Kiefer and Detective Hines, dated February 5, 1986.

40. Goodnature summarized his discussion with Rogers in a memo to County Attorney Fred Kraft, noting "the stated objective of this procedure would be to shut down the Hormel Corporation and to overload our court system so that it could not handle the matter." Kraft responded that any arrangement with Rogers would represent a conspiracy to allow violation of the law. Letter, Wayne P. Goodnature and Donald Hoffman to Kraft, dated February 3, 1986; letter, Kraft to Goodnature and Hoffman, dated February 3, 1986.

41. Interview with Rod Huinker, April 19, 1988.

42. News report, KSTP-TV, Minneapolis, February 6, 1986; "Labor leader and two dozen strikers arrested at Hormel plant," *New York Times,* February 7, 1986; Minnesota statute 609.405, criminal code of 1963.

43. Melvyn Dubofsky, *We Shall Be All: A History of the IWW* (New York: Quadrangle Books, 1969), pp. 381–82.

44. Much of the historical material presented here is from Emily Bass, Linda A. Backiel, and Beth Margolis, Brief of Defendant Raymond Rogers in Support of Motion to Dismiss on Constitutional Grounds, *State of Minnesota v. Raymond Rogers Jr.,* dated March 3, 1986, pp. 1–22. See also Philip S. Foner, *History of the Labor Move-*

ment in the United States: The Industrial Workers of the World, 1905–1917 (New York: International Publishers, 1965), pp. 413–14; Larry Engelmann, "'We Were the Poor People'—The Hormel Strike of 1933," Labor History, 15 (Fall 1974): 490. According to both Foner and fellow historian William Preston, an "anti-sabotage" clause inserted into the constitution of the Socialist Party in 1912—which, in Preston's words, created an "index of permissible belief and action within the framework of discontent"—was the forerunner of "criminal syndicalism" laws. Cited in Foner, History of the Labor Movement, p. 414.

45. Interview with Ray Rogers, March 13, 1988; "Union aide says strike at Hormel could continue into the summer," New York Times, February 10, 1986.

46. News report, KAAL-TV, Austin, February 7, 1986; Rogers interview, March 13, 1988.

47. News reports, KSTP-TV, Minneapolis, January 10, 1986; KIMT-TV, Mason City, Iowa, January 11, 1986.

48. Huinker interview.

49. Ibid.

50. "Striking people in a sticky situation," In These Times, February 12–18, 1986.

51. Guyette negotiation notes, dated February 11, 1986; proposal of P-9 to Geo. A. Hormel & Co., dated February 11, 1986.

52. News report, KARE-TV, Minneapolis, January 11, 1986.

53. Interview with Lewie Anderson, April 5, 1988.

54. "Today marks pivotal point in conflict," USA Today cover story, February 11, 1986; Hormel hiring list; "A strike that failed," New York Times, February 14, 1986.

55. "Hormel strikers helped by NY labor leaders," Newsday, February 6, 1986.

56. CBS News "Sunday Morning," February 9, 1986; "Ottumwa: 3,000 march for Hormel workers," The Militant, February 21, 1986; "Unionists, farmers back fight against Hormel," The Militant, February 28, 1986; "Unionists rally in Minnesota to support Hormel meat packers' strike, Labor Notes, March 1986. In addition

to the UAW activity, the Hormel boycott also drew the support of Iowa State, County and Municipal Employees, who were successful in getting Hormel products removed from all vending machines in office building in the state capital. "Farm unity group backs Ottumwa Hormel workers," *Des Moines Register*, February 5, 1986.

57. "Rogers must agree to limit demonstrations or go to jail," *Austin Daily Herald*, February 14, 1986; "Rogers faces jail unless he OKs limits on protest," *St. Paul Pioneer Press and Dispatch*, February 15, 1986; "Judge curtails Hormel protests," *Minneapolis Star and Tribune*, February 15, 1986.

58. "Unionists rally," *Labor Notes*; "Unionists, farmers back fight against Hormel," *The Militant*; interview with Jan Pierce, March 17, 1988.

59. At the time, Rogers said that half of the 900-person FDL work force honored the picket, while Hormel claimed that only 200 of 900 workers stayed out. "Guard exit from Austin weighed," *Minneapolis Star and Tribune*, February 18, 1986.

60. News reports, KSTP-TV, Minneapolis, February 10, 1986; KAAL-TV, Austin, February 20–21, 1986; "Austin students leave school in support of union," *Minneapolis Start and Tribune*, February 22, 1986.

CHAPTER VII

1. Quoted in "Hormel dispute is taken to AFL-CIO; Firm posts higher fiscal 1st-period net," *Wall Street Journal*, February 20, 1986.

2. In 1938 the Supreme Court ruled that an employer may operate his plant during an economic strike and, at its conclusion, need not discharge those who worked during the strike in order to make room for returning strikers (*NLRB v. Mackay Radio and Telegraph Co.*, 304 US 333, 2 LRRM 610). In recent years, the courts have strengthened even further the rights of "permanent replacements" to the detriment of strikers. In 1983 the Supreme Court upheld the right of permanent replacements to pursue breach of contract and

misrepresentation suits against any employer who discharges them to make room for returning strikers (*Belknap Inc.* v. *Hale et al.*, 463 U.S. 491, 113 LRRM 3057). In 1989 the high court further limited economic strikers' reinstatement rights under the Railway Labor Act by ruling that, at the conclusion of a strike, employers are not required to lay off crossovers in order to rehire "full-term" strikers who have more seniority (*Trans World Airlines Inc.* v. *Independent Federation of Flight Attendants*, 57 USLW 4283).

3. Interview with Darrell Busker, November 21, 1987.

4. "CBS Morning News," February 19, 1986.

5. "UFCW Local P-9 strikes Hormel: The International union's perspective," *UFCW Leadership Update*, February 1986.

6. "Reporter's notebook: Images of organized labor," *New York Times*, February 21, 1986.

7. Quoted in William Serrin, "Labor as usual," *Village Voice*, February 23, 1988.

8. Interview with William Serrin, January 22, 1988.

9. Lane Kirkland, executive council news conference, "draft" transcript, February 19, 1986, p. 10.

10. "AFL-CIO blasts P-9 'all or nothing' stand," *St. Paul Pioneer Press and Dispatch*, February 21, 1986; letter, William Winpisinger, dated March 7, 1986.

11. "Perpich orders Guard to leave Hormel plant," *St. Paul Pioneer Press and Dispatch*, February 19, 1986. The total cost of the Guard presence in Austin was $1.4 million, according to "Austin students leave school in support of union," *Minneapolis Star and Tribune*, February 22, 1986.

12. "Governor urges P-9 strikers to settle," *St. Paul Pioneer Press and Dispatch*, February 1, 1986; "P-9 votes not to consider proposals," *Minneapolis Star and Tribune*, February 2, 1986; "Hormel resumes hog slaughter," *St. Paul Pioneer Press and Dispatch*, February 11, 1986; "Perpich defends troop callup to AFL-CIO," *Minneapolis Star and Tribune*, February 25, 1986; interview with Charles Nyberg, April 21, 1988; interview with John Weis, April 19, 1988.

13. Interview with Rod Huinker, April 19, 1988.

14. Interview with Lynn Huston, July 5, 1987.

15. Interview with Merrell Evans, July 5, 1987.

16. "Hormel shows off Austin plant," *Minneapolis Star and Tribune*, February 19, 1986; "Hormel strikers confronting likelihood that jobs are lost," ibid., February 23, 1986.

17. "Civil disobedience urged if Hormel hires substitutes," *Minneapolis Star and Tribune*, January 19, 1986; interviews with Ray Rogers, January 9, 1987, March 12, 1988.

18. Interview with Mike Bambrick, April 20, 1988.

19. Remarks of Barbara Collette, P-9 Jailbird Celebration, March 16, 1988; "Police arrest 100 at Hormel's main gate," *Minneapolis Star and Tribune*, March 11, 1986; "Strike supporters arraigned, released," ibid., March 12, 1986; "Minnesota: 115 arrested in protest against Hormel," *The Militant*, March 21, 1986. Union records show that the total number arrested was 122, rather than 115.

20. Collette remarks; interview with Carmine Rogers, March 18, 1988.

21. Account of Cynthia Bellrichard, dated March 16, 1986.

22. Carmine Rogers interview.

23. Account of Sandy Titus, "My night in Cell Block H," undated. Carmine Rogers has over a dozen such narratives in her possession.

24. "Strike supporters arraigned," *Minneapolis Star and Tribune*, account of Roger D. Diggins, undated.

25. Carmine Rogers interview; "Strike supporters arraigned," *Minneapolis Star and Tribune*.

26. News report, KSTP-TV, March 11, 1986; " 'P-9' rank and file vote on resolution to soften demands," *Minneapolis Star and Tribune*, March 12, 1986.

27. Interview with Margaret Winter, June 6, 1988.

28. "International may halt P-9 support," *Minneapolis Star and Tribune*, February 28, 1986.

29. News report, WCCO-TV, Minneapolis, March 14, 1986.

30. "Parent union orders local to end Hormel strike," *New York Times*, March 15, 1986.

31. News reports, WCCO-TV, KARE-TV, Minneapolis, March 14, 1986; "Parent union orders local," *New York Times*; "UFCW orders end to Austin strike," *Minneapolis Star and Tribune*, March 15, 1986. According to the *Times*, the UFCW said that it had paid over $2 million in strike benefits to the local at the time it suspended the strike.

32. "UFCW orders end," *Minneapolis Star and Tribune*.

33. "Some strikers relieved, others remain bitter," *Minneapolis Star and Tribune*, March 15, 1986.

34. "Hormel strike takes on aura of a crusade," *Newsday*, March 20, 1986; "Union splits on ending Hormel strike," ibid., March 15, 1986; news report, WCCO-TV, Minneapolis.

35. Weis interview; "Support grows in Seattle," *The Militant*, March 14, 1986; "That old time unionism," *San Francisco Chronicle*, March 5, 1986.

36. Interview with Buck Heegard, April 18, 1988.

37. "Hormel strikers win support of unions around country" and "Detroit: 500 rally for Hormel strikers," *The Militant*, March 14, 1986; "1,000 trade unionists rally in Detroit for Hormel workers," *Daily World*, March 7, 1986; "St. Louis: Hormel workers win support" and "Oakland rally backs Minn. strikers," *The Militant*, March 21, 1986; "100 rally for strikers in San Jose," ibid., April 4, 1986; "Strikers: Solidarity is vital," *El Paso, New Mexico Times*, April 7, 1986; "Hormel strikers win support from Chicago area labor unions," *The Militant*, April 11, 1986; "National solidarity with Hormel strikers," ibid., May 9, 1986; "Atlanta: Hormel strikers win support" and "Birmingham unions back Hormel fight," ibid., May 2, 1986; "Strikers make appeal to Utah miners and N.C. unionists," ibid., June 13, 1986; "Hormel meatpackers tour Texas, win support for union fight," ibid., June 27, 1986; "Minnesota march backs Hormel meatpackers," ibid., July 11, 1986.

38. Heegard interview.

39. "Socialist IAM members discuss Hormel strike support," *The Militant*, April 4, 1986.

40. "The union is at stake at Hormel," *Daily World*, February 6, 1986; "A deeper look—Calls for unity to defeat Hormel union busting," *Daily World*, February 25, 1986.

41. "I'm for the strikers," *Public Sector*, April 7, 1986.

42. Interview with Brian Lang, April 7, 1988.

43. Letter of Acting Special Agent in Charge Dan L. Anderson, July 5, 1988.

44. "P-9 members vote to defy international union," *Minneapolis Star and Tribune*, March 17, 1986; "Hormel strikers vote to continue," *New York Times*, March 17, 1986; "Workers vote to continue strike," *The Militant*, March 28, 1986.

45. "Hormel protesters arrested after blockade," *Minneapolis Star and Tribune*, March 21, 1986; "Strikers shut down plant for five hours," *The Militant*, March 28, 1986.

46. Interview with Carl Pontius, April 19, 1988.

47. "Hormel protesters arrested," *Minneapolis Star and Tribune*; Mike Bambrick interview.

48. Weis interview; "P-9, UFCW truce talks collapse," *Minneapolis Star and Tribune*, March 22, 1986.

49. "About 100 demonstrators jeer as employees arrive at Hormel's headquarters," *Minneapolis Star and Tribune*, March 27, 1986.

CHAPTER VIII

1. "About 100 demonstrators jeer as employees arrive at Hormel's headquarters," *Minneapolis Star and Tribune*, March 27, 1986; interview with Mike Bambrick, April 20, 1988.

2. "P-9 official among 14 protesters arrested outside Hormel gates," *Minneapolis Star and Tribune*, April 3, 1986; "Cops, scabs attack protest at Hormel plant," *The Militant*, April 11, 1986; Mike Bambrick interview; Austin police records of arrests, in possession of P-9er Larry Gullickson.

3. Guyette negotiation notes, dated April 1, 1986; "Hormel negotiations again break down; no new talks scheduled," *Minneapolis Star and Tribune*, April 2, 1986.

4. "Prosecutor says Rogers has violated terms of bail," *Minneapolis Star and Tribune*, April 1, 1986.

5. News report, KAAL-TV, Austin, April 5, 1986; "Hundreds turn out to greet food caravan," *The Bulletin*, April 8, 1986; "Supporters of Hormel strikers gather food for fourth caravan," *Minneapolis Star and Tribune*, April 4, 1986.

6. Letter, Hoffman and Goodnature to Perpich, April 7, 1986; letter, Tschida to Hoffman and Goodnature, April 7, 1986; Mower County police memorandum to "all agencies," signed by Goodnature and Hoffman, dated April 7, 1986.

7. News report, KAAL-TV, Austin, April 9, 1986; "Hormel protest draws law enforcement units," *Minneapolis Star and Tribune*, April 10, 1986; "350 demonstrate outside Hormel plant's gates," ibid., April 11, 1986.

8. News reports, KAAL-TV, Austin, and KSTP-TV, Minneapolis, April 11, 1986; videotape of the day's events taken by union member Mert DeBoer.

9. "Outburst among worst in state labor history," *Minneapolis Star and Tribune*, April 12, 1986; "Violence in Austin confirms worst fears," *St. Paul Pioneer Press and Dispatch*, April 12, 1986; Austin police records.

10. "Tear gas halts Hormel protests," *St. Paul Pioneer Press and Dispatch*, April 12, 1986.

11. DeBoer videotape, taken April 11; "4,000 protesters march peacefully in Austin," *St. Paul Pioneer Press and Dispatch*, April 13, 1986; "Thousands back striking meatpackers," *The Militant*, April 25, 1986.

12. Interview with Buck Heegard, April 18, 1988.

13. Interview with Jan Pierce, March 17, 1988.

14. Heegard interview; interview with Brian Lang, April 7, 1988.

15. Pierce interview; interview with Charles Nyberg, April 21, 1988.

16. News reports, WCCO-TV, Minneapolis, April 14, 1986; Nyberg interview; DeBoer videotape, taken on April 13, 1986; "Jackson brings hope to Austin strikers," *St. Paul Pioneer Press and Dispatch*, April 14, 1986; Pierce interview; for contrast, see "On the line with Jesse," *The Guardian*, February 17, 1988, and "On the road with Jackson in Iowa," *In These Times*, January 20–26, 1988.

17. "Jackson brings hope," *St. Paul Pioneer Press and Dispatch*.

18. News report, KMSP-TV, Minneapolis, April 14, 1986; "Hearing here on control of P-9 sparks union friction," *Minneapolis Star and Tribune*, April 15, 1986; Austin police records.

19. 29 USC 462, 464; UFCW International Constitution, Article 9, section (H)1, section (H)2(c), Article 23, and passim.

20. *Trusteeship hearing of the United Food and Commercial Workers Local P-9 Union*, conducted by Hearing Officer Ray B. Wooster, in 6 volumes, April 14–16, 1986; vol. 2 (April 14): 6–7, 38–39, 122; vol. 3 (April 15): 253–57.

21. "350 demonstrate outside Hormel plant's gates," *Minneapolis Star and Tribune*.

22. *Trusteeship hearing*, vol. 1 (April 14): 9–22.

23. Ibid., vol. 2: 16–177.

24. Ibid., vol. 3: 211–96.

25. Ibid., vol. 4 (April 15): 304–24, 348–414; vol. 5 (April 16): 430–47, 491–514; vol. 6 (April 16): 521–57.

26. Ibid., vol. 4: 418–24.

27. Ibid., vol. 6: 605–65.

28. "P-9 hearing ends amid accusations, threat of suit," *Minneapolis Star and Tribune*, April 17, 1988.

29. Stanley Aronowitz, "Cold cuts," *Village Voice*, April 22, 1986.

30. Nicolaus Mills, "Why Local P-9 is going it alone," *The Nation*, April 26, 1986.

31. Bill Montross, "Dissidence isn't always progressive," *The Guardian*, February 19, 1986; Kim Moody, "Strike highlights two conceptions of unionism," *Labor Notes*, April 1986.

32. "The Hormel strike: a union divided," *New York Times*, April 21, 1986.

33. Nicolaus Mills, "P-9 fights the odds," *Dissent*, Summer 1986.

34. Bill Dennison, "Hormel: Unity is the only winning strategy," *Political Affairs*, April 1986.

35. Lance Compa, "A second look at the Hormel strike," manuscript.

36. The union's November 1986 National Packinghouse Strategy and Policy Conference featured anti-P-9 presentations by Local 7R staffer Mark Belkin, Anderson, and Dale Francis, a former P-9 striker who switched sides. Delegates passed a resolution condemning the "anti-union activity of the former P-9 officers, Ray Rogers, and David Twedell." Anderson also described the "hard lessons of Hormel" for the readers of *Meat & Poultry*, February 1987.

CHAPTER IX

1. "Austin struggle tests workers' endurance," *Catholic Bulletin*, March 23, 1986.

2. Edward J. Devitt, Findings of Fact and Conclusions of Law, *Ronald M. Sharp* v. *Local P-9, UFCW*, dated April 23, 1986; "Local P-9 assails labor panel action," *St. Paul Pioneer Press and Dispatch*, April 24, 1986; "150 federal marshals set if needed at Hormel site," *St. Paul Pioneer Press and Dispatch*, May 3, 1986.

3. Interview with Margaret Winter, June 6, 1988.

4. Interview with Emily Bass, June 19, 1988; "Local at Hormel sues parent union," *New York Times*, May 7, 1986; "UFCW tells P-9 it will take over," *Minneapolis Star and Tribune*, May 9, 1986; hearing officer's report in the matter of Local P-9, UFCW, Austin, Minnesota, undated; "UFCW says it's in charge of P-9, but questions linger," *Minneapolis Star and Tribune*, May 10, 1986; "Austin

strikers lose two battles over P-9 control," *St. Paul Pioneer Press and Dispatch*, May 10, 1986; news reports, KAAL-TV, Austin, and WCCO-TV, Minneapolis, May 7–10, 1986.

5. News reports, WCCO-TV, Minneapolis, May 12–20, 1986; "Ruling puts P-9 fight for control on hold," *Minneapolis Star and Tribune*, May 20, 1986; transcript of proceedings before Judge Gerhard Gesell, U.S. District Court, May 15, 1986.

6. Interview with Ben Lamberton, July 19, 1988.

7. These arguments were made before Devitt and repeated in Bass, Brief for Appellants, and Harry Huge, Gary K. Harris, and James E. Pfander, Brief for Appellees, *Joseph T. Hansen et al. v. James V. Guyette et al. / Local P-9, UFCW, et al. v. William H. Wynn et al.*, appeal from the U.S. District Court for the District of Minnesota to the U.S. Court of Appeals for the Eighth Circuit.

8. Memorandum and order, findings of fact, conclusions of law, and order, *Joseph T. Hansen et al. v. James v. Guyette et al./ Local P-9 v. William H. Wynn et al.*, dated June 2, 1986.

9. "UFCW rents an office in Austin," *Minneapolis Star and Tribune*, May 16, 1986; "P-9 officials remove pickets at Hormel," *St. Paul Pioneer Press and Dispatch*, June 5, 1986; "P-9 members seek a new union," *Minneapolis Star and Tribune*, June 7, 1986.

10. "Iowa rally backs fired Hormel workers," *The Militant*, May 23, 1986; "Hormel to appeal jobless pay ruling," *Minneapolis Star and Tribune*, May 4, 1986; SPAM-O-RAMA press release, dated May 13, 1986; "UFCW rents an office," *Minneapolis Star and Tribune*; "Hormel net fell 26% in its second period; strike at plant cited," *Wall Street Journal*, May 20, 1986; "Twins caught in the middle of P-9, Hormel fight," *Minneapolis Star and Tribune*, May 25, 1986.

11. "Meatpackers union is facing wage issue," *Wall Street Journal*, May 19, 1986; "Hormel workers win round against union top attacks," *The Militant*, May 30, 1986; "Wynn award picketed," *The Bulletin*, May 30, 1986; "Protest at award for Wynn," *Labor Page*, May 1986; interview with Brian Lang, April 7, 1988.

12. Interview with Ray Rogers, March 12, 1988; "800 rally for P-9," *Austin Daily Herald*, June 29, 1986; "Black unionists back

Hormel strikers," *The Militant,* June 6, 1988; "New union organizing drive at Austin Hormel plant," *The Militant,* July 18, 1986; "Minnesota meatpackers win new support," *The Militant,* August 8, 1986; "Hormel workers continue the struggle," *The Militant,* August 20, 1986.

13. Interview with Denny Mealy, July 6, 1987; "Mural commemorates P-9 fight with Hormel," *Rochester Post-Bulletin,* May 28, 1986; "Austin mural done in same spirit of lost WPA projects," *Union Advocate,* June 30, 1986; "Hormel strikers dedicate mural to Nelson Mandela," *The Militant,* June 20, 1986.

14. "Statement of Jim Guyette," reprinted in *The Militant,* June 20, 1986.

15. News reports, KAAL-TV, Austin, and KARE-TV, WCCO-TV, Minneapolis, June 28, 1986; "1,000 march in support of meatpackers," *St. Paul Pioneer Press and Dispatch,* June 29, 1986; "Austin struggle tests workers' endurance," *Catholic Bulletin;* "Labor-backing priest urges P-9ers to persist," *Rochester Post-Bulletin,* June 28, 1986; unsigned "Notes to the Chief [Hoffman]," dated June 12, 1986, and memo of Sergeant Simonson to Captain Steininger, dated June 24, 1986, both from Austin police files.

16. News reports, KAAL-TV, Austin, and WCCO-TV, Minneapolis, June 30, 1986.

17. "Court splits union site, strike funds," *St. Paul Pioneer Press and Dispatch,* July 3, 1986.

18. News report, KAAL-TV, Austin, July 3, 1986; "Division among ex-P-9ers continues," *Rochester Post-Bulletin,* August 16, 1986; United Support Group, *Support Report,* August 15, 1986.

19. "Picnic marks Austin strike anniversary," *Rochester Post-Bulletin,* August 18, 1986.

20. "Anniversary brings talk of settlement by Sept. 1," *St. Paul Pioneer Press and Dispatch,* August 17, 1986; "Negotiators hopeful about effort to halt long Hormel strike," *New York Times,* August 26, 1986.

21. "Hormel strike settlement eases tension in many Austin faces," "Hormel ordered to rehire 507 Iowa employees," and "New

Hormel contract has no provision for recalling strikers," *Minneapolis Star and Tribune*, August 29, 1986; "Summary of Hormel contract proposal, UFCW Local P9, Austin, Minnesota," dated September 5, 1986.

22. Interview with Lewie Anderson, April 5, 1988.

23. "Hormel strike to end," *Newsday*, September 13, 1986; interview with Lynn Huston, July 17, 1988.

24. "Hormel contract draws mixed reviews from P-9," *Minneapolis Star and Tribune*, September 5, 1986; letter of Joe Hansen, sent with mail ballots, dated September 5, 1986; "Packers ratify Hormel contract," *Minneapolis Star and Tribune*, September 13, 1986; "P-9 uncovers labor's split personality," *The Guardian*, October 1, 1986.

25. "P-9 lawyer calls prosecution of 17 strikers unconstitutional," *Minneapolis Star and Tribune*, July 11, 1986.

26. Interview with Jeannie Bambrick, April 20, 1988.

27. Memorandum and order of Judge William A. Johnson, Third Judicial District of the State of Minnesota, dated November 26, 1986.

28. The sandblasting was temporarily halted, first by a demonstration by P-9ers, then by a court order obtained by NAMPU and the artists. "Meatpackers seek order to halt mural 'blasting,'" *Austin Daily Herald*, October 9, 1986; "Judge halts sandblasting of meat-packers' mural," *The Militant*, November 28, 1986.

29. Letter of Joseph Hansen, dated September 25, 1986; strike settlement agreement, dated November—1986. The key case defining the rights of strikers to reinstatement is *Laidlaw Corp.*, 171 NLRB 1366, 68 LRRM 1252 (1968). In response to a suit by 13 former P-9ers, the company and UFCW announced in February 1988 that recall rights would be extended indefinitely.

30. Interview with Jim Getchell, April 19, 1988.

31. Interview with Frank Collette, April 20, 1988.

32. Police report of Officer M. Holten regarding victim Tom Clemens, dated May 8, 1987; police report of Officers Royce and Erickson regarding victim John Weis, dated July 5, 1987; police re-

port of Officer D. Simonson regarding victim Richard Shatek, dated July 23, 1988; memo of Hoffman to news media, dated January 6, 1987, all obtained through the Minnesota Government Data Practices Act.

33. Interview with Jim Getchell, July 6, 1987.

34. Interview with Darrell Busker, November 21, 1987.

35. "School official says firing is linked to Hormel strike," *Minneapolis Star and Tribune*, April 2, 1986; "Price paid to settle Austin's Hormel strike carries a ration of anger," ibid., January 13, 1987; "Hormel intends to close plant in Ottumwa, Iowa," *Wall Street Journal*, February 24, 1987; "Over 1,200 apply for Excel jobs," *Ottumwa Courier*, September 3, 1987; "Hormel: Ottumwans must choose between buyoff and bumping," *Ottumwa Courier*, February 4, 1988.

36. "Former steward loses appeal against Local 431," *Ottumwa Courier*, August 27, 1987; interview with Charles Nyberg, April 21, 1988; "Hormel rehires some fired workers," *The Bulletin*, August 18, 1987.

37. "P-9 worker upset over dismissal of charges," *Minneapolis Star and Tribune*, September 23, 1987; "Hormel plans civil suit against Robert Johnson," *Rochester Post-Bulletin*, October 14, 1987; dismissal of complaint, *State of Minnesota v. Robert Allan Johnson*, dated September 21, 1987.

38. Police report of Officer Wesely regarding written and telephoned death threats, dated August 4, 1985; police report of Officer Earl regarding letter sent to Raymond Arens that threatened both Guyette's and Winkels' children, dated March 21, 1986.

39. "Trustee: money to aid P-9 strikers is unaccounted for," *Minneapolis Star and Tribune*, August 28, 1986; "UFCW sues former P-9 officers for alleged pension fund misuse," *BNA Labor Relations Week*, July 8, 1987; UFCW LM-2 form for the year ending April 30, 1986; interviews with Jim Guyette, November 19, 1987, and June 10, 1988. An internal Austin police memo reports that "a private concern" has "an informant who is not in town but is travelling and in constant contact with Guyette, Shatek, etc." This infor-

mant is probably the "Cudahy striker." Memo of Captain Bjorgo to Chief Hoffman, dated June 29, 1987 obtained through the Minnesota Government Data Practices Act.

40. Memos of Captain Bjorgo to Chief Hoffman, dated June 29, July 1, and July 2, 1987; "report from [name blacked out] on his activities the weekend of the 4th of July," undated; "Police Response to Labor Disputes/Demonstrations," outline and notes; police report of officers Bartlett, Everhart, Bednar, Carpenter, and Stiehm, dated February 2, 1986, with attached INCAR and Progressive Labor Party leaflets and photo; letter of Hoffman to Commander Robert Minto, VFW Post 1216, dated April 18, 1986; memo "To Investigating Agencies" from Hoffman, regarding P-9 funds, undated; letter from U.S. Senator Rudy Boschwitz to Hoffman re "possible illegal use and disbursement of funds by the Local P-9 union," dated April 2, 1986; all obtained through Minnesota Government Data Practices Act request.

41. Hoffman, "Police Response to Labor Disputes/Demonstrations"; unsigned "Notes to the Chief," dated June 10, 1986; unsigned and undated report on Peter Rachleff in Hoffman's files. Obtained through Minnesota Government Data Practices Act request.

42. Dale Francis, "A national strike of the meatpacking industry would show these companies they can't push us around anymore," *The Bulletin,* January 17, 1986; Dale Francis, letter on NAMPU, *The Militant,* August 8, 1986; Federal Bureau of Investigation report of Special Agent Donald D. Carlson, dated February 13, 1987, in Austin police files, obtained through Minnesota Government Data Practices Act request.

43. Interview with Vicky Guyette, July 5, 1987.

44. Nyberg interview.

45. Interview with Jan Pierce, March 17, 1988.

46. Nyberg interview; "And this little pig processor does nicely," *Forbes,* February 23, 1987. During 1987 the company earned $45.9 million, or a 17.6 percent improvement over the previous year, acquired Jenny-O Foods Inc., and extended its marketing agreement with FDL, according to "Knowlton calls 1987 best year in history of

Geo. A. Hormel Co.," *Austin Daily Herald,* January 20, 1988. A record $80 million was set aside for advertising in 1988, according to "Hormel sees its future in a microwave oven," *Business Week,* February 22, 1988.

47. Letter, Richard Knowlton to Hormel Vending Customers, dated October 1, 1986, with sample advertisement attached.

48. "Minnesota AFL-CIO urges Hormel to rehire former strikers," *Support Report,* October 16, 1987; "DFL reaffirms commitment to boycott Hormel products," ibid., April 4, 1988; "The Hormel experience," *BNA Labor Relations Week,* July 20, 1988.

49. Interview with Rich Waller, March 1987.

CHAPTER X

1. Quoted in *The Guardian,* labor supplement, Fall 1986.

2. Interview with Darrell Busker, November 21, 1987; interview with Vicky Guyette, November 21, 1987; interview with Rod Huinker, November 19, 1987; interview with John Weis, November 19, 1987.

3. Interview with Pete Winkels, November 20, 1987; Huinker interview, November 19, 1987.

4. Interview with Ray Rogers, July 12, 1987.

5. "Unions have no business on the picket line today," *Washington Post National Weekly Edition,* March 3, 1986; "Hormel settlement leaves unionists bitterly divided," *In These Times,* September 24–30, 1986. Some in-plant tactics are described in the AFL-CIO Industrial Union Department's 1986 pamphlet, *The Inside Game: Winning with Workplace Strategies.*

6. Remarks of Jerry Tucker, Labor Solidarity Network of Greater New York weekend conference, April 4, 1987.

7. Interview with William Serrin, January 22, 1988.

8. Guyette, address at *Labor Notes'* "New Directions" conference, November 15, 1986.

9. Interview with Lynn Huston, July 5, 1987.

10. Interview with Charles Nyberg, April 21, 1988. In 1984 Hormel had bought Dold Foods of Wichita, thus providing itself with a new and modern plant that allowed significant expansion of smoked meats production; the July 1985 marketing agreement with FDL Foods gave Hormel Dubuque and Rochelle facilities that Nyberg said "were already slaughtering more hogs than we were." See "Hormel signs marketing pact that may insulate it from strike," *Minneapolis Star and Tribune*, July 27, 1985.

11. Interview with Jan Pierce, March 17, 1988.

12. Letters, Dorothy Long Burgess, dated January 31, 1986; James Wiley, dated January 22, 1986; Bob Rossi, dated January 28, 1986; Franklyn Smith, dated February 22, 1986; Lavonne Lela, dated February 16, 1986.

13. Charles R. Perry, *Union Corporate Campaigns* (Philadelphia: Wharton School, 1987), pp. 135–44 and passim.

14. "Meatpackers battle over pay and prices," *Milwaukee Journal*, October 4, 1987; "South Dakota meatpackers honor picket line of Iowa Morrell workers," *Labor Notes*, June 1987; "The most dangerous job in America," ABC News "20–20," November 6, 1987; "Misery on the meatpacking line," *New York Times*, June 14, 1987; "Morrell union members confused over action," *Austin Daily Herald*, November 5, 1987; "UFCW ends six-month sympathy strike at Morrell plant in South Dakota," *Labor Notes*, December 1987; "Striking Morrell workers offer to return to work," *Ottumwa Courier*, February 8, 1988; "Union will appeal verdict siding with John Morrell," *Rochester Post-Bulletin*, March 11, 1988; "Oscar Mayer Meatpackers in Texas reject 'compressed work week,'" *Labor Notes*, April 1988; "Meatpacker awarded $24.6 million over strikes," *New York Times*, November 13, 1988; interview with Linda King of Sioux Falls UFCW Local 304A, April 6, 1989. It should be noted that the Sioux Falls members did not hold Anderson responsible for this debacle, continuing to view him as a militant. "Lewie's philosophy matches ours perfectly," local president James Lyons told the *New York Times* in the wake of Anderson's January

1989 firing by Wynn. Quoted in "A union split over givebacks," *New York Times*, January 29, 1989.

15. "FDL Foods/UFCW pacts," *BNA Labor Relations Reporter*, November 17, 1986.

16. "Milwaukee labor marches for Cudahy strikers," *Labor Notes*, May 1987; "Patrick Cudahy's union-bashing a year after the strike," *Labor World*, January 21, 1988.

17. "Hormel plans to halt Austin hog slaughtering," *Minneapolis Star and Tribune*, November 7, 1987. The UFCW ended the Austin trusteeship on July 16, 1987, one day after the election of new officers.

18. "Dallas firm inks letter of intent to [sic] slaughtering operation here," *Austin Daily Herald*, March 4, 1988; "Nearly 400 apply for jobs on hog-kill line," *Rochester Post-Bulletin*, May 3, 1988; "Slaughter plant could be sold," *Rochester Post-Bulletin*, June 14, 1988.

19. "Hormel to lay off 324 in Nebraska in '89, stop hog-slaughtering," *Minneapolis Star and Tribune*, September 1, 1988; "Agreement near to reopen Hormel hog-killing plant," ibid., December 9, 1988; "Proposed Quality Pork slaughter rates worry UFCW leader at Farmstead plant," *BNA Labor Relations Week*, February 1, 1989.

20. "A meatpacker cartel up ahead?" *New York Times*, May 29, 1988.

21. Jonathan Kwitney, *Vicious Circles: The Mafia in the Marketplace* (New York: W. W. Norton, 1979), pp. 251–313 and passim. In time, several meat buyers and mobsters, along with Stern, Nicholas Abondolo, and Moe Fliss, all of the union, were indicted. The union men bargained away a charge of conspiracy to travel interstate to commit racketeering, pleaded guilty to tax evasion, and were sentenced to prison.

22. "Signs of violence arise in meat plant's lockout," *New York Times*, January 18, 1987; *John Herling's Labor Letter*, October 11, 1986; "Union aims to take on IBP with nationwide campaign," *Des Moines Sunday Register*, January 25, 1987; "Union: Iowa Beef falsi-

fies OSHA reports," *Rochester Post-Bulletin*, January 23, 1987; "Unions cite hazards in packing houses," *Milwaukee Journal*, October 5, 1987; "UFCW presses for crackdown on crippling meat plant injuries," *AFL-CIO News*, May 14, 1988; "IBP contract settled with concessions by both company, meatpackers union," *Wall Street Journal*, July 28, 1987; "IBP bristles after attack by Babbitt," *Ottumwa Courier*, January 13, 1988; "Questions raised over meatpacker's unionization," *Chicago Tribune*, June 26, 1988; "New IBP plant may force out other meatpackers," *Ottumwa Courier*, March 30, 1988; "IBP to pay $975,000 to settle charges on safety, sources say," *Wall Street Journal*, November 23, 1988.

23. Interview with Lewie Anderson, April 5, 1988; the "total victory or total defeat" phrase was used frequently by UFCW spokesmen. See, for example, "UFCW Local P-9 strikes Hormel: The International union's perspective," *UFCW Leadership Update*, February 1986.

24. Thomas A. Kochan, Harry C. Katz, and Robert B. McKersie, *The Transformation of American Industrial Relations* (New York: Basic Books, 1986), pp. 21–108, 110, and passim. The authors suggest four plausible scenarios for the future, the most likely short-term trend being a continuation of current trends in which "union-management relations will become more adversarial, managerial opposition will intensify, and management will speed the pace of outsourcing and technological change in order to further reduce vulnerability to unionization." The AFL-CIO's long-dreamed-of reform of labor laws to allow fairer representation elections would not "make any significant difference in the unionization rate of large firms or in the quality of the union-management relationship in existing bargaining units," they say (p. 252).

25. Robert Michels, *Political Parties* (Magnolia, Mass.: Peter Smith, 1960), pp. 50–52, 78–111, and passim.

26. Nyberg interview; Anderson interview.

27. "Officials charge P-9 didn't want settlement," *Minnesota Daily*, July 18, 1986.

28. Interview with William Serrin, January 22, 1988.

29. Letters, Nicholas Szast, dated January 23, 1986; Gerard Nickels, dated February 20, 1986.

30. "Legacy of Hormel strike," *BNA Labor Relations Reporter*, November 24, 1986; "Big labor tries to end its nightmare," *New York Times*, May 4, 1986.

31. "Going local: plant-level talks rise quickly in importance; big issue: work rules," *Wall Street Journal*, March 16, 1987.

32. "Meatpackers gather to develop strategies to protect jobs, rights," *BNA Labor Relations Week*, May 6, 1987.

INDEX

Wynn, William (*cont.*):
of support for Local P-9 and extended picketing, 96–98

Yocum, Ron, 256
Youngdahl, Jim, 80, 102

Zack, Allen, 97, 190, 214, 243; on

Arnold Zack, 152; on Hormel's treatment of crossovers, 152; on Local P-9's lawsuit against the International, 247, 249; prepares "Special Report" on Local P-9, 185–86
Zack, Arnold: on Allen Zack, 152; as fact-finder, 139, 143, 146, 158

DATE DUE